Civil War Scoundrels and
the Texas Cotton Trade

ALSO BY WALTER E. WILSON
AND FROM MCFARLAND

The Bulloch Belles: Three First Ladies, a Spy, a President's Mother and Other Women of a 19th Century Georgia Family (2015)

James D. Bulloch: Secret Agent and Mastermind of the Confederate Navy (2012)

Civil War Scoundrels
~ *and the* ~
# Texas Cotton Trade

WALTER E. WILSON

McFarland & Company, Inc., Publishers
Jefferson, North Carolina

ISBN (print) 978-1-4766-8127-6
ISBN (ebook) 978-1-4766-4038-9

Library of Congress and British Library
cataloguing data are available

Library of Congress Control Number 2020023462

© 2020 Walter E. Wilson. All rights reserved

No part of this book may be reproduced or transmitted in any form or by any means, electronic or mechanical, including photocopying or recording, or by any information storage and retrieval system, without permission in writing from the publisher.

Front cover images: *insets* Major Charles Arden Russell, Confederate States Army, date unknown (courtesy Carolina L. Lawson); Harris Hoyt, original portrait in pencil by Myna Ellison (author's collection); Bagdad, Mexico, and the Rio Grande anchorage, gateway for the Texas cotton trade, a collage by Myrna Ellison (author's collection)

Printed in the United States of America

*McFarland & Company, Inc., Publishers
Box 611, Jefferson, North Carolina 28640
www.mcfarlandpub.com*

To Mom, who always knew a scoundrel
when she saw one.

And to Dad, who taught me that I did not
want to chop cotton for a living.

Table of Contents

Preface   1

1—The Texas Cotton Trade   7
2—Civil War Blockade Running: Setting Up the Scheme   21
3—Winning the White House: Telling a Texas Tall Tale   31
4—The Texas Adventure Fleet: A Sinking Start   44
5—Hot, Dirty, and Full of Fleas: At the Rio Grande   66
6—Double Dealing Cotton in Texas   79
7—Escape from Texas   97
8—Deceived and Swindled from New York to Matamoros   113
9—Aiding the Enemy without Conviction   125
10—Post-War Scoundrels Reconstructed and Resurrected   133
11—Conclusion   147

Appendix 1—Scoundrels and a Few Others   149
Appendix 2—Sails, Steamers, and the Texas Cotton Trade   167
Chapter Notes   179
Bibliography   203
Index   209

Preface

Who was Mr. Maloney? That was the question that started me on the path toward writing this book. I knew that he was a merchant in Matamoros, Mexico, during the American Civil War. He also was one of the influential participants in a strategy meeting that Confederate Colonel John "Rip" (Rest in Peace) Ford convened at Brownsville, Texas, in March of 1862. This "junto" was in response to the appearance of a warship from the U.S. blockading fleet at the mouth of the Rio Grande. Maloney was among a small group of men that included Mifflin Kenedy, Charles Stillman, José San Román, the British Consul, a Texas judge, and a handful of other prominent men. The gathering is well-documented and many authors (with varying degrees of accuracy), have reported both the meeting and the attendance of a "Mr. Malony." Perhaps my question was one that other historians had never asked. If they did, they either were unable to find an answer or they chose not to share their discovery.[1]

Contemporary Civil War records readily identify Maloney as a well-regarded British merchant living and operating out of the Rio Grande. He played host to Lieutenant Colonel Arthur Fremantle during that British Army officer's brief stay at Matamoros in March of 1863. Colonel Fremantle was a keen diarist who published his observations regarding the American Civil War. During his three month sojourn in the United States, he traveled from Texas to Gettysburg. There are few details about Mr. Maloney in either Fremantle's diary, the letters of Charles Stillman, Colonel Ford's memoirs, or the official Army and Navy war records. I was looking for more information about him. I wanted to know why Rip Ford had invited Maloney into his trusted circle of diplomats, judges, steamboat owners, and businessmen.

The attempt to answer that question led me to an unlikely U.S. Congressional Report. That report describes military court martial proceedings that took place at New York City in 1865. The government had brought charges against a civilian swindler named Harris Hoyt. In Mr.

Hoyt's testimony, he identified a "Mr. Maloney" as the principal partner of a steamboat and mercantile business that was operating out of Matamoros, Mexico. The primary purpose of Colonel Ford's meeting with Maloney and the other men was to consider strategies for keeping the U.S. Navy from stopping trade on the Rio Grande and seizing their Confederate-owned and flagged steamboats. With Hoyt's brief statement, the reason for Mr. Maloney's presence at the meeting suddenly became obvious.

This revelation also added clarity to other contemporary correspondence about Mr. Maloney. Letters from Confederate Major Charles Russell and others written to José San Román and Charles Stillman all have hints of Maloney's association with a firm named Hale and Company. That relationship was now defined. Hoyt's testimony allowed me to confirm that it was the death of a Mr. Maloney and not a "Mr. Malone" that disrupted the Rio Grande business of Hale and Company in the early months of 1864. I found Mr. Maloney's given name in an 1859 newspaper article reporting his arrival at New Orleans from the Rio Grande with his partner James Hale. These sources show that John P. Maloney was the principal partner of a steamboat and mercantile business named Hale & Co. at Matamoros, Mexico.[2]

After extracting the nuggets about Mr. Maloney, I decided to dig into the fascinating character of the swindler named Harris Hoyt. The story of Mr. Hoyt and his connection with the Civil War cotton trade in Texas is an intriguing one. Several authors have addressed Hoyt's schemes, but their work focuses on the romantic entanglements of a notorious nineteenth century power couple, William Sprague and Kate Chase. Sprague was a multi-millionaire business magnate, governor, senator, and war-hero colonel from Rhode Island. Kate was the vivacious daughter of the Secretary of the Treasury and Chief Justice of the Supreme Court, Salmon P. Chase. She was also the chief promoter her father's presidential aspirations.

Much of the testimony and documentation from Harris Hoyt's court martial is contradictory, confusing, and sometimes deliberately misleading. Sorting out these conflicting stories soon led me to other scoundrels who were connected in some way with Hoyt's Texas Adventure and the Texas cotton trade. I must admit that writing about scoundrels has been fun. Many of their cons were so cleverly conceived that I found myself almost rooting for them to succeed. The Civil War had created conditions that charlatans like Hoyt and his counterparts were eager to exploit. Some succeeded, but most failed. For those who achieved success, it was usually fleeting. Like the characters in a Charles Dickens novel, it was the scoundrels who had a change of heart that were able to overcome their past and live happy and prosperous lives after the war.

While I did not feel much kinship with the many schemers who manipulated the Civil War cotton trade, the same could not be said for the places in Texas where they operated. As a result of family connections and my own 31 years of service in the U.S. Navy, I have been privileged to have lived in, or have spent significant time at or on, most of the coastal locations and bodies of water that I write about. Despite this affinity, I could not have started this work without the encouragement and support of numerous important people.

My Dad, Charlie, was born in the lower Rio Grande Valley city of Edinburg, but grew up in Collin County north of Dallas. He left his family's North Texas dairy farm and part-time work chopping cotton, for a career in the U.S. Coast Guard. Over a span of 26 years, he served on cutters, buoy tenders, and Coast Guard stations that took him, up and down the coast of Texas and beyond. He sometimes was able to let me to tag along even when he went to sea. He had assignments and travels to other places that also connect me to this story on a personal level, i.e., New Orleans, Baltimore, Washington, D.C., Boston, and Bermuda.

My saintly Mother grew up and went to school in Seadrift, Port O'Connor, and Port Lavaca, Texas. As a young woman, she was eager get away from the confines of these small Texas coastal towns situated on San Antonio and Matagorda Bays. But by the time that my four siblings and I, plus practically every other kid in our neighborhood, knew her as "Mom," she could not wait to get back home at every opportunity. My family was, and remains, salt-of-the-earth sailors, shrimpers, fishermen, farmers, and ranchers who have a deep connection to Texas, its land, and its coastal waters.

My high school sweetheart and wife of almost fifty years, Sharon McKusker Wilson, and her family are from the banks of Sabine Lake in far Southeast Texas. As usual, Sharon provided me companionship, encouragement, another set of eyes, and a sounding board as I traveled, researched, and crafted the text. But there were others....

I will be forever grateful to Dr. Gary McKay, my coauthor for our McFarland biography of James D. Bulloch. Gary inspired me to start putting words to paper. My friend and former Navy shipmate Hal Hardaway is well known for hosting the best garage parties in Old Town Alexandria, Virginia and is a fine historical enthusiast in his own right. While we were both living in London, Hal encouraged me to accompany him on his many jaunts to explore England's maritime treasures. Those treasures include the people who were helpful fonts of information about Great Britain's maritime heritage and her role in the American Civil War. Most notable are Roy Rawlinson, Bob Thorp, Richard Harris, Ian Dewar, and the now-departed, and greatly missed Bob Jones and Roger Ellis.

Authors Karen Fort and Tom Fort (Senior Historian at the Museum of South Texas History in Edinburg, Texas), whose works are cited multiple times in the text, generously provided a much-appreciated, critical review of an early text. Author and Professor Dr. Brittany Wilson of Duke University was also generous with her time in providing insightful feedback on a later version.

Another prominent author, editor, and historian, Milo Kearney, Professor Emeritus with The University of Texas, Rio Grande Valley, encouraged me to contribute to his long-running series of studies in Lower Rio Grande Valley history. The articles published in that series helped me bring focus to what had been a broad range of research about Civil War maritime activity in Texas. His university is also the sponsor of the Rio Grande Valley Civil War Trail project through its CHAPS Program (Community Historical Archaeology Project with Schools). This initiative breathes life into an important chapter of our shared history. Other helpful South Texas resources are the Texas Maritime Museum in Rockport, Texas, and the Brownsville Historical Association that preserves and maintains archival resources and historical sites including the home of Charles Stillman.

J. Barto Arnold, Director of Texas Operations at the Institute of Nautical Archaeology, was generous with his time, research, and advice that led me to explore the rich admiralty case files within the National Archives. Archivist Barbara Rust and her team at the National Archives and Records Administration, Southwest Region in Fort Worth, obligingly ferreted out all of their many records pertaining to Civil War blockade running.

Barbara McPherson and the volunteer staff at the San Antonio Genealogical and Historical Society Library allowed me quick access to a rare volume, and saved me considerable time and expense in the process. Casey Greene and Sean McConnell of Lauren Martino's Special Collection's team at the Rosenberg Library in Galveston were especially helpful in sharing their documentary and photographic treasures.

Lisa Neely, author and archivist for the King Ranch Museum in Kingsville, Texas, guided me through their unique archives that provide insight into the Civil War activities of Richard King and Mifflin Kenedy. Lisa introduced me to Lori K. Atkins, the University Archivist at the James C. Jernigan Library on the campus of Texas A&M University–Kingsville. Lori welcomed me to another fine, and recently made public, collection of

M. Kenedy & Co. Civil War records. Lisa also connected me with the accomplished author Stephen G. Michaud. I was able to work with Stephen as he researched his biography of Charles Stillman. He, in turn, helped me access and transcribe some of the wonderful letters in Harvard University's Charles Stillman papers at the Houghton Library in Cambridge, Massachusetts.

The University of Texas at Austin's Dolph Briscoe Center for American History is a national treasure. Its collection of unique Civil War era letters and documents proved to be indispensable in my research, particularly the relatively unknown papers of José San Román. Equally helpful but less well known are Roland Stansbury and his team at the Young-Sanders Center in Franklin, Louisiana. Not only do they have a rich repository of Civil War history, but I am honored to claim them as friends. Their collection of Confederate Vessel Papers and digitized Louisiana Ship Registers are readily availability and provide unique insights into the operations and characteristics of the many vessels that sailed the waters of the Western Gulf of Mexico. Together with the San Román Papers, it was the Young-Sanders Center resources that allowed me to make the connection between the schooner *Rob Roy* and its earlier incarnation as the *Francis Marguez, Jr.* Thanks to the diligence of Dr. Germain J. Bienvenu, a manifest (cargo list) for the "*F Marquez*" discovered in the Louisiana State University Libraries Special Collections was icing on the cake.

Roland Stansbury also helped me track down a forgotten portrait of Brigadier General and former Governor of Louisiana, Paul O. Hébert. This elusive image had been painted by Hébert's scoundrel of a quartermaster in Texas, Major Theodore Sydney Moïse. Following helpful leads from Rebecca Smith with the Historic New Orleans Collection and Bill Stafford with the Louisiana State Archives, I found it safely preserved at the Louisiana State Museum. Thanks to the proactive assistance of museum registrars Tom Strider and Kira Kikla, they not only confirmed the painting's existence, but provided helpful background about its history, and agreed to create and share this never-before published image.

Similarly, the descendants of Major Charles Arden Russell collectively helped point me toward unique family history resources. I owe a special debt of gratitude to Carolina Lawson who shared her never-published, tintype image of Major Russell, her great-great-great grandfather. Author and Colt weapons authority Robert Swartz of the San Antonio Breakfast Club also shared images and information about Colt revolvers that were associated with Texas. Finally, the creative and talented Myrna Ellison patiently worked with me to create a portrait of Harris Hoyt that not only reflects his appearance but his devious character as well. She also developed a collage of Bagdad, Mexico, and the Rio Grande anchorage that captures the chaotic situation brought on by the Texas cotton trade and the American Civil War.

Despite the best efforts of those mentioned above, there are, no doubt, imperfections within the following text. The responsibility for any errors or omissions lies solely with yours truly, the author.

1

The Texas Cotton Trade

The Texas cotton trade was a uniquely distinct aspect of a larger military, economic, and social struggle that ignited the passions of the nation. The competing armies, navies, and even the rioting draftees of the American Civil War gave expression to those emotions. They set literal and figurative fires that left cities, farms, fields, and families in ruin. On its battlefields, the war snuffed out the lives of between 620,000 and 750,000 young American men due to combat and disease. With a national population of only 31 million in 1860, the equivalent carnage in the twenty-first century would be almost 7.5 million lives. This long, bloody war was fought between 1861 and 1865 and it touched almost every mid-nineteenth century American in a very personal way.[1]

The individual soldier or sailor who marched or sailed into combat for the first time never knew how he would respond. He had to experience the first concussive burst of cannon fire or the terrible "zzzip" of a .69 caliber Minié ball as it scorched a deadly path from the enemy's rifle. At that moment, these inherently impersonal ballistic events quickly became incredibly personal. Each cannon ball and every bullet seemed to be aimed directly at him. The sensation that swept over him was singular and it was visceral: fear. No amount of preparation or rational thought could foretell his next reaction. Would he charge forward toward the enemy, or would he run away? The natural impulse was to put as much distance as possible between himself and such horrific sights and sounds. But the answer to those questions would only come when he encountered them. Most men did not run away. Individual loyalty to fellow comrades-in-arms usually overcame the terror. The typical soldier and sailor, Blue and Gray, stood and fought until they could fight no more.

But there was another type of wartime moral dilemma. The civilian entrepreneurs, government officials, and military logisticians who worked behind the battle lines confronted a far less life-threatening, but equally compelling emotion. The overwhelming sensation that they experienced

Civil War-era lead Minié balls and lead artillery canister ball found near Matagorda Bay, Texas (image and artifacts from the author's collection, a gift from his cousin, Delmer Scott).

was greed. The chaos of the American Civil War offered many tempting prospects for men to embrace their less noble instincts. Opportunities abounded for clever risk-takers. Less than a generation earlier, the mesmerizing allure of the California gold fields had spawned a similar collection of opportunists. Much like their Forty-Niner predecessors, Civil War swindlers looked to garner quick and easy profits with little regard for truth or consequences. Their only loyalty was to themselves, and perhaps, their immediate family.

Like the California gold rush of the previous decade, the Civil War generated a great demand for certain necessary commodities. In response, almost everyone who had a connection to those vital materials went to great lengths to obtain and profit by them. Armies needed guns, navies needed ships, and at this time in world history, the textile mills of the United Kingdom and the United States demanded cotton. These mills were national economic engines. They employed thousands of workers who worked long hours to spin the raw fibers into thread and fabric. The mills sold the finished materials to clothe their citizens and for export around the world. The desire for cotton in the United Kingdom and the New England states was almost as great as the South's need to sell it.

The Yankee and Rebel merchants who bought, sold, and transported these commodities fixed their moral compasses on the magnetic attraction of fantastic profits in the cotton trade. These entrepreneurs rationalized all other decisions to justify their actions accordingly. Consequently, the Civil War cotton trade became synonymous with deceit, swindling, fraud, corruption, and theft. The universally pejorative term "speculator" encompassed all of these villainous practices and came to be applied to anyone who was associated with trading in cotton.[2]

Institutionalized cotton speculation came into being soon after hostilities began on April 12, 1861, with the bombardment of Fort Sumter in Charleston Harbor. In addition to the requirement to formulate critical military and political strategies, that event forced both sides to make important economic decisions. How would they regulate trade with the enemy? Although the Confederate States government never enacted an outright ban, it attempted to control the export of cotton, tobacco, and sugar to the North. This prohibition, however, proved to be unenforceable. The South needed the money for survival and it little mattered who bought its cash crops.[3]

The Union faced a similar conundrum. Two thirds of the nation's exports in 1860 had been Southern cotton. The mills of the North depended upon this cotton as well. Yet, by purchasing Rebel cotton, Northern business interests were helping arm, feed, and clothe the "insurrectionary states." Lincoln's two naval blockade proclamations that he issued in April and May of 1861 were aimed at shutting off the South's ability to continue trading with foreign countries. It did not address American domestic trade across state lines. In July of 1861, the U.S. Congress corrected this omission by passing an act prohibiting "commercial intercourse" with the South. The law permitted a few carefully defined exceptions that Treasury Secretary Salmon P. Chase loosely managed through his regional agents. It was a lucrative loophole that invited favoritism, bribery, and demoralizing corruption.[4]

Speculators and certain government officials exploited Secretary Chase's profiteering Treasury agents and used trade permits to their political and financial advantage. These unscrupulous men had widespread opportunities for trading with the enemy, particularly in areas that were adjacent the battle lines. They knew that one of the missions for advancing Union soldiers was to seek out and capture abandoned Confederate cotton. The proximity of this cotton to the battle front encouraged parasitic speculators to attach themselves to the Union armies. They could acquire the cotton at bargain rates and ship it to markets in the North. Most Union generals disliked having to deal with such men, but some of the Army officers yielded to the temptation and took advantage of the opportunity to turn a personal profit. This unsavory practice was present, but not as widespread in Texas. Union speculators attached to the Army in Texas were hampered by the state's lack of transportation connectivity to markets in the East and the limited success of the Union Army in that theater of operations.[5]

There were other, more impatient, American citizens who played the dangerous game of buying and selling goods behind enemy lines, including within the Lone Star State. These risk-takers had to walk a fine line between trade and treason. The speculators who operated within the rebellious states usually had sufficient personal wealth, military authority, or political influence to prevent the exposure of their corrupt practices. In combination, these attributes allowed such men to manipulate trade restrictions and Union soldiers for personal gain. The political generals of the Union Army had all three attributes in abundance. Major Generals Ben Butler and Nathaniel Banks were particularly adept at this practice while they were in Louisiana.[6]

Invading armies, combined with the naval blockade, had completely disrupted the South's normal international trade routes. This disruption inadvertently created additional opportunities for speculators. Southern merchants who depended upon trade with the North or other foreign countries had to improvise new transportation means and modes over unfamiliar routes. They found themselves having to entrust large amounts of their cash, trade goods, and expensive vessels with relative strangers. These circuitous paths and untested partners required cotton to pass through the clutches of many grasping hands before it made its way from the plantation to the weaving mill.

The shipping difficulties and high demand for cotton created opportunities for enormous profit, not so much for the planters or mill owners, but for everybody else in between. From the beginning of the war to as late as 1864, cotton could be purchased for as little as six cents a pound in Texas and sold for $1.35 or more in New York or Liverpool. There were, however, many obstacles to overcome. Before the cotton ever reached these markets, sellers, shippers, and buyers had to learn and apply new tricks of the trade. Business managers had to improvise new ways of acquiring and delivering the precious commodity without getting arrested or killed in the process.[7]

The cotton trade, and particularly the Texas cotton trade, was a natural environment for swindlers to thrive. Although the character traits of the individual scoundrels within the Texas cotton trade were not unique, their opportunities were. The export of cotton was a challenging prospect for all of the Southern ports during the Civil War, but none more so than those in Texas. Sometimes called the "dark corner of the Confederacy," Texas was an outlier from the wartime cotton trading norms compared to the other Southern states. It was the last state to be blockaded when the USS *South Carolina* arrived at the main pass into Galveston Bay on July 2, 1861. That month, the *South Carolina*'s commanding officer, James Alden,

1. The Texas Cotton Trade 11

confidently declared that he would soon "most effectually close up every hole and corner along that line of coast."[8]

To fulfill this prophecy, Captain Alden said that all he needed was two or three captured schooners that he would convert into gunboats, plus two officers, twenty-five sailors, and one efficient steam gunboat. It was a bold statement, since the Texas coast stretched over 360 miles from Louisiana to Mexico. But for a brief period of time, Alden was correct. The mere presence of his warship completely stymied regular commercial traffic along the northern portion of the Texas coast.[9]

Another factor in Texas' isolation compared to the other Confederate states was its dependence upon maritime lines of communication for interstate and international commerce. Except for the Red River and Rio Grande on its borders, all of its navigable rivers flowed entirely within the state. The dependence upon these internal waterways was particularly true for bulk commodities like cotton. The scant transportation infrastructure that did exist within the state was focused on getting cotton downriver for transport on shallow-draft steamers. After exchanging their cargoes onto larger, sea-going vessels, the river steamers would return from the coast with finished goods. They would then transfer the freight to waiting carts

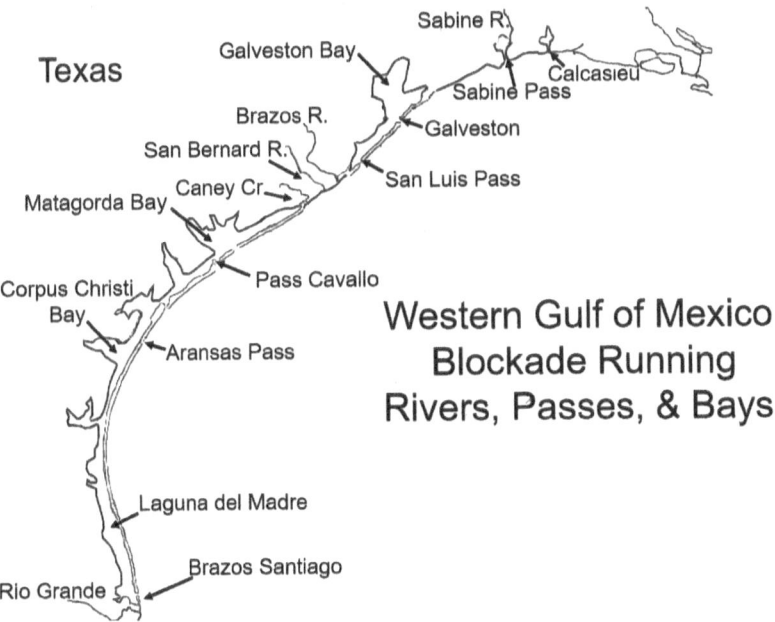

Blockade running rivers, passes and bays in the western Gulf of Mexico (author's map).

or to the few existing railroad lines. New Orleans had been the primary hub for transporting people and commodities out of Texas prior to the Union blockade. Although Texans did export some cotton from Galveston directly to foreign ports, most of it went via New Orleans with some passing through the Spanish colony at Havana, Cuba.

At the time of the Civil War, Texas had very little railroad infrastructure and these rail lines were centered on Houston. Their chief function was to connect shippers with river and ocean-going steamship lines. Connections at Houston extended east to Beaumont and the Neches/Sabine River, southeast to the deep-water port of Galveston and south to Columbia (now known as West Columbia) on the Brazos River. The western-most connection was at the once-thriving city of Alleyton. This railroad terminus was about 70 miles west of Houston, near Columbus on the Colorado River. None of these lines crossed the Texas border into a neighboring state. There was one short rail line in East Texas and another from Victoria to Port Lavaca and Indianola that had rolling stock, but no locomotives. In 1863, General Magruder had all of the rails around Matagorda Bay torn up. It seems that this little used railroad was more beneficial for strengthening the defenses against a pending invasion than it was for transportation. The general also feared that Union forces might capture and use the line to move their Army inland.[10]

Paying little attention to the situation in Texas, the contemporary Northern press derisively referred to the Lincoln administration's leaky blockade as the "Anaconda plan." Devised by General Winfield Scott, the Union's primary naval strategy was to cut off the Confederacy from all international commerce. Scott's plan called for the occupation or blockade of all Southern ports and combined Army/Navy attacks up and down the Mississippi River to separate the rebellious states. With so few ships and such a large coast to cover, the Union's initial blockading efforts were ineffective. The Confederate government and foreign dignitaries gleefully pointed out to all who would listen that the Union's attempt to stop trade with the South was a mere paper blockade that was not effectively enforced. Despite the ridicule, the blockade's immediate effect in the Western Gulf of Mexico was the suspension of all routine international commerce into and out of Texas as of May 1861. In the early days of the blockade, the presence of a single Union warship was enough to frighten owners of commercial shipping lines into keeping their vessels away from Southern ports.[11]

The impact of the blockade in Texas hit the port of Galveston the hardest. It was the state's most important interstate and international outlet and its only deep-water port. There were two channels into Galveston Bay, but only one permitted routine access for ocean-going merchant ships. It was located off the northern end of the island. There were five other Texas passes that accessed the state's large, but shallow, bays and lagoons. These passes included San Luis Pass off the southern end of Galveston Island that provided entry into West Galveston Bay, Pass Cavallo into Matagorda Bay, Aransas Pass into Aransas Bay, Corpus Christi Pass into Corpus Christi and Baffin Bays, and Brazos Santiago Pass (at the southern end of Padre Island) into the Laguna del Madre. An additional advantage of the Texas coast was its natural inland waterway. Very shallow draft vessels were able to sail from Matagorda Bay, through Aransas and Corpus Christi Bays, to as far south as Penascal on Baffin Bay without entering the open waters of the Gulf. There were four additional rivers and a creek that emptied directly into the Gulf of Mexico. The rivers included the Sabine, Brazos, San Barnard, and Rio Grande, plus Caney Creek.

The type of vessel favored by European traders attempting to run the Union blockade of the South was a fast side-wheel steamer. In the open ocean, sailing ships were simply too slow and dependent upon the winds. The most successful and popular of the blockade running steamers were propelled by paddlewheels, one on each side. The preeminent builders of these long, sleek, and fast steamers were located on the River Clyde in Scotland and on the Mersey River in England. Eager buyers snapped up and converted these steamers into blockade runners. When those were gone, blockade running merchants placed additional orders for new vessels, which led to even faster and more stealthy steamers as the war progressed.[12]

These developments in steam powered blockade runners had little impact on Texas during the first three years of the war. Until the autumn of 1864, distance alone made Texas an unattractive blockade running option. The state's large number of shallow water bays and inlets held little charm for large, ocean-going blockade runners. The new Clyde-built (or designed) steamers had drafts that were sufficiently shallow to easily enter the main channel at Galveston. For most, however, the suitability of that port was not the primary issue in the Western Gulf of Mexico. Texas ports were simply too far away.

Texas ports were the most distance of all Confederate destinations from the primary international blockade running havens at Bermuda and Nassau in the Atlantic, and Havana in the Gulf of Mexico. Even Wilmington, North Carolina, the primary Confederate port on the east coast, was closer to Havana than both Galveston and New Orleans. The sailing distance from Havana to Wilmington is 807 nautical miles; New Orleans is about 60 miles farther away, and Galveston is an additional 350

Cotton trading ports in the Gulf of Mexico and Western Caribbean, modified from "American Ports of the Cotton Trade 1861–1865" found in Texas State Historical Association, *The Southwestern Historical Quarterly*, Vol. 77, July 1973–April 1974), 195 (author's collection).

miles. Even though Galveston's sailing distance to the nearest British port at Belize is about 90 nautical miles less than the distance from Wilmington, Galveston is 300 miles farther away than New Orleans. At an average steaming speed at around 12 knots (14 miles per hour), these distances translated into hours and days of exposure at sea, and required additional coal that could not be gotten in Texas.[13]

Distance to the Texas ports would remain a major disadvantage until the Union began to occupy the other Confederate ports in the Gulf of Mexico and on the Atlantic coast. By January 1865, there were no other deep water Confederate ports available to larger blockade running steamers. During those last five months of the war, Galveston was the best and only port available to these sleek ocean-going blockade runners.

Prior to 1865, Texas also offered other unique blockade running opportunities, despite the extra challenges. Shallow-draft sailing vessels, and even small steamships that were not built for ocean travel, could hug the South Texas coast for safety and concealment. This route allowed them to avoid the tempestuous waters of the open ocean. They could virtually disappear from sight by hiding their profiles against the dark land mass. Although the tactic of sailing near the coast extended the distance to foreign markets even farther, the circuitous path had other advantages. If threatened, they could duck into one of the many coastal inlets to evade pursuing Union warships. After sailing past the Rio Grande, blockade running captains could then dart across the narrow Yucatán Channel between Mexico and Cuba and follow the same procedure along the Cuban coast. An alternative route was to simply follow the coast around the Yucatan Peninsula all the way to the British colonial port of Belize.[14]

Texas blockade runners soon turned their lack of access to deep water ports in the Western Gulf into an advantage. The shallow entrances also prevented the Navy's ocean-going steamers from freely operating within Texas' bays and rivers. Of the 226 U.S. Navy warships on blockade duty by the spring of 1862, most were unable to approach close to the Texas coast. As a result, the hydrography of the Western Gulf helped small schooners and sloops to remain a viable blockade running option in Texas throughout the war. The small boats were difficult to detect and impossible for the blockading fleet to follow inland. Some of the more aggressive Union captains tried to overcome this limitation by launching raiding parties using their ship's life boats. They filled these small craft with armed crewmembers. They sometimes added one or two short-range naval howitzers. These small cannons fired anti-personnel canister rounds that encouraged enemy sailors and soldiers to keep their heads down. If the Union sailors managed to navigate through the narrow passes undetected, they might capture or burn unsuspecting blockade runners as they rested at anchor.[15]

Prior to turning its attention to Texas, the U.S. Navy had implemented a blockade of New Orleans between the 26th and 30th of May 1861 using three of its "fastest and heaviest" warships. This looming presence was enough to completely stop the Crescent City's maritime commerce to and from the Gulf of Mexico. The subsequent capture of New Orleans in April 1862 and then Mobile in August 1864, left Galveston as the only port capable of accepting ocean-going steamers available to the Confederates in the Gulf.[16]

Adding to the U.S. Navy's challenge in Texas was the extended distance from its blockading stations to the nearest Union logistic and maintenance facilities at Ship Island, Mississippi, and Pensacola and Key West in Florida. Foraging parties from the blockading fleet found little on shore in the way of locally available food, water, or fuel. These provisions were essential for sustaining the soldiers, sailors, and their ships that were cruising offshore. The Texas landscape was as hostile toward the blockading fleet and occupying soldiers as were the Confederate armies. The advantages of the 367 mile long Texas coast made it problematic for the U.S. fleet to maintain an effective blockade of the Western Gulf. This situation remained unchanged even when most of the other Confederate ports had been captured.

As the virtual anaconda of the blockade was squeezing the life out of the other Southern states, blockade running in Texas and the trade at the Rio Grande were never shut down. In fact, the number of successful blockade runners and the amount of cotton exported out of Texas continued to grow each year. Unlike its sister states of the Confederacy, Texas was never conquered by force of arms. The greatest disruption occurred when the Union Army occupied the southern portion of its coast for about eight months beginning in November 1863. In June and July of 1864, however, they abandoned Texas, with only one exception. Federal forces maintained a tiny toe-hold on a sandy spit of land at the mouth of the Rio Grande known as Boca Chica from November 1863 through the end of the war. Despite its location, a binding international treaty prevented the garrison from stopping trade at the Texas-Mexico border at the river known as the Rio Grande del Norte, Rio Bravo, or simply, the Rio Grande.

The United States and Mexico had codified the status of the Rio Grande as a neutral waterway in the 1848 Treaty of Guadalupe Hidalgo. As far as the Union Navy was concerned, this treaty only affected trade with Texas, since it was the only Confederate state that bordered a foreign nation. A key provision of the treaty was its definition of the Rio Grande as the international boundary between Texas and Mexico. The boundary line extended three marine leagues (10.36 miles) from the center of the river and into the Gulf. The treaty also guaranteed the right of non-belligerents to conduct trade at the neutral Mexican ports on the river. The status of the Rio Grande was of little concern until August of 1862 when the Federal blockading fleet began making visits to far South Texas. The U.S. Navy's intention was to seal off the pass at Brazos Santiago and to intimidate neutral shipping that was carrying and receiving Rebel cargoes at the Rio Grande. The guarantee of unimpeded trade through the Rio Grande meant that the U.S. could not implement a blockade against neutral shipping there. Confederate vessels, crews, and cargoes were still susceptible to capture, but as long as a vessel flew a duly registered, neutral flag, the frustrated Union military forces had no legal recourse to stop it.[17]

Although the U.S. could not legally blockade the Rio Grande, its fleet managed to capture a number of blockade runners in its vicinity. The Navy's presence and some of its aggressive actions at the mouth of the river convinced local merchants and diplomats that the United States was attempting to impose a *de facto* blockade against the Texas cotton trade out of the Rio Grande. To check the occasional Federal excesses that were perpetrated against British-flagged vessels, the Royal Navy established a regular presence there. The powerful British warships provided a shield for all neutral shipping and were a great relief to the Matamoros merchants and Mexican government officials. These men depended on the commissions and tariffs from the Texas cotton trade to sustain and expand their wealth.[18]

The French Navy also maintained sporadic patrols to both hold the U.S. Navy accountable and prevent imports of war materials destined for the revolutionary Juárista forces in Mexico. These foreign warships and international diplomatic pressures forced the U.S. fleet, and its Army garrison at Boca Chica (after November 1863), into a more passive role. They had to sit and watch as hundreds of thousands of cotton bales sailed away to ports in Europe and the United States.[19]

As men and markets adjusted to these unfamiliar realities, everything about the wartime Texas cotton trade seemed different. The only constant was human nature. At each step in the process of moving cotton from the field to a market, there were individuals ready and able to lie, cheat, and steal their way into a quick profit. Even the process of selling and delivering Texas cotton to buyers in the North was an inherently deceptive business. When it came to ships and their cotton cargoes, little was actually what it appeared to be. While most of these shipments were technically legal, the person listed as the owner of a vessel or the cotton it carried was rarely the true, or beneficial, owner of either.

For example, the Texas merchant and founder of Brownsville Charles Stillman continued to conduct business with his partners in New York City even as the war complicated trade between the warring factions. The large amount of Texas commodities that Stillman transported on his British-flagged vessels between New York and the Rio Grande aroused U.S. government officials' suspicions. In response to this extra scrutiny, he and his New York partners began using Mexican and British surrogates. Soon, none of Charles Stillman's many transactions between Texas and the United States were traceable directly to him.[20]

All of Stillman's invoices, bills of lading (detailed lists of goods from a vessel sent to a consignee at its destination), and other receipts were in the names of trusted agents. These men included Santiago Yturria and Jeremiah "Jerry" Galvan of Matamoros, José Morell (aka Joseph Morrell) of Monterey, and John Crawford of Nassau and Havana. His New York partners even addressed personal letters with updates on Stillman's family in New York directly to these men, even though they were clearly intended for Stillman. The letters would only identify Stillman as "our friend." Congressional investigators were well aware of this subterfuge. They even referred to the Irishman and Matamoros resident Jerry Galvan as Stillman's "man of straw." Although U.S. officials knew what these men were doing, their allegations did not hold up in court due to lack of evidence and they could not intervene.[21]

Another example of an otherwise ethical merchant serving as the middleman between enemy citizens from the North and South was the Spaniard José San Román. San Román had moved from New Orleans to Matamoros in 1846 as a dry goods store manager. Four years later, he set up shop in Brownsville to escape the instability resulting from the Mexican War. In Texas, he expanded his business into commercial credit, trustee holdings, real estate, and during the Civil War, cotton brokerage.[22]

San Román also operated several river steamboats, sometimes in partnership with, and at other times as a competitor to, M. Kenedy & Company. This Texas–based company was a powerful partnership that included Mifflin Kenedy, Richard King, and Charles Stillman. When Union forces threatened Brownsville during the Civil War, San Román moved back to Matamoros where his business continued to thrive. Colonel John Salmon "Rip" Ford described San Román as a man "who never had an evil thought. He amassed a large fortune and was never accused of having wronged anyone in its acquisition."[23]

Men like Stillman, Galvan, Yturria, and San Román were Rio Grande residents, cotton brokers, bankers, and merchants who had many enduring business relationships. José Morell and Santiago Yturria were long-time partners and friends of Stillman, Richard King, and Mifflin Kenedy. After the war, Kenedy even adopted Morell's daughter. The influx of cotton for export gave these comparatively honest and reliable men more business than they, or the region's limited transportation infrastructure, could handle. All of these men had reliable counterparts and business associates in other blockade running destinations such as Havana, Nassau, Belize, and Bermuda. With the increased demand for their services, shipping agents and brokers were not as likely to deal as fairly with merchants who were unknown to them. For transient speculators, buyers, and sellers who were new to the Texas cotton markets their chances of getting a fair deal from either the established brokers or the many crooks that flocked into the cotton boom towns were slim.[24]

The ploy of registering vessels with a neutral country was another maneuver that both sides practiced during the war. Any captain who sailed under either a United States or a Confederate flag risked immediate capture or destruction whenever he encountered an enemy warship. Ship owners wanted to avoid the certain loss of their vessels and cargoes as well as the associated higher insurance rates. The easiest and least expensive way to achieve this goal was to register their vessels under a neutral or "false flag." As part of the registration process, the true owner would sell his vessel at a nominal cost to a citizen of a neutral country. The foreign titleholder agreed to simultaneously provide the true owner a power of attorney that granted the original owner full authority over the vessel and its cargoes. Although frequently referred to as a "sham" sale, this procedure at least offered the true owners' vessel a chance of release, escape, or government-to-government intervention in the event it was boarded or seized by a Union or Confederate warship.[25]

Of the many charlatans who participated in illicit cotton trading activities, one individual stands out. His name was Harris Hoyt. Although relatively unknown within Civil War historical writings, Hoyt's activities are well documented, if somewhat fragmented. The depth, breadth, and sheer audacity of his many scams provide illustrative examples of almost every kind of deceit inflicted upon both the overly avaricious and the unwitting victims of the Texas cotton trade. In the instances where Hoyt was not the perpetrator or co-conspirator in a specific fraud, he usually had direct contact with those who were.

Harris Hoyt was a career swindler who traveled between the Union and Confederate states during the American Civil War. He promoted the prospect of fantastic profits from the Texas cotton trade. More importantly, he was selling a dream. He promised investors that they could ensure their economic independence through self-sufficiency, provide relief for suffering souls in need, and support a noble cause that had engulfed the nation in a devastating war. Unfortunately for those who literally bought into that dream, this clever salesman peddled the same vision to both sides of the conflict. Using other people's money, Harris Hoyt would be the only investor in the scheme who achieved financial success. Instead of providing relief for their suffering, he simply added to it.

During the war, Hoyt lived and traveled through the states of Illinois, Iowa, and Texas. He also had additional stops in Indiana, Rhode Island, Vermont, Massachusetts, Connecticut, Washington, D.C., New Orleans, New York, Jamaica, Havana, and Matamoros, Mexico. He talked and manipulated his way into the confidence of politicians, military leaders, businessmen, newspaper editors, and practically everyone else he met along the way.

The Midwestern territory where Harris Hoyt began his scheming trade and even his name inspires comparisons to Professor Harold Hill, the charming charlatan of Meredith Willson's Broadway musical *The Music Man*. Just as Willson's fictional Professor Harold Hill would do, the real-life swindler Harris Hoyt collected endorsements and money while making promises that he had no intention of keeping. Willson, who was from Iowa, comically tells of a traveling musical instrument salesman from Indiana who promises to form, equip, and instruct a River City, Iowa, boy's band, complete with uniforms. Hoyt's real-life scheme was even more daring than his alliterative counterpart's. Hoyt cheated Yankees and Rebels alike and, upon being discovered, he was on the verge of being hanged, rather than just tarred, feathered, and run out of town.[26]

Harold Hill's love-interest, Marian the librarian, managed to rescue and reform the scheming swindler. The real-life scoundrel Harris Hoyt's love interest was named Marie. She also hailed from Iowa, but that's where the similarities between their stories end. It was Harris Hoyt who did the transforming and not Marie, as she eventually became his partner in crime. While there is no evidence that Willson drew inspiration from the eerily similar character of Harris Hoyt, it is possible that tales of the Iowa swindler's exploits made their way to his childhood dinner table.

The gist of Hoyt's Civil War scam was his promise to deliver Texas cotton to Northern investors and acquire Yankee-made textile machinery for the Rebels in Texas. He would deliver and install that equipment for his stockholders there. Everybody would prosper. The Yankees would get cotton for their textile mills and the Rebels would no longer have the trouble of importing their uniforms or other wool and cotton clothing material from the North. All he needed was a lot of their money and cotton to make it happen. What he lacked in cash, he made up for with ideas, charm, and determination. At the outset, his double-swindle scheme seemed too complex to succeed, especially in the midst of the wartime obstacles that complicated trade with the South, but it did.

Hoyt was 48 years old when he relocated from Illinois to Galveston, two years before the outbreak of the Civil War. This clever manipulator proceeded to work his way into the good graces and the pocketbooks of the people he encountered on both sides of the Mason-Dixon Line. Between 1861 and 1863, he collected endorsements from the Texas Legislature, the Confederate general in charge of Texas, President Lincoln's private secretary, the Governor of Rhode Island, and other prominent citizens, both North and South. Hoyt manipulated each of these endorsements to help finance the shipment of his goods into and out of Texas. His investors gained nothing but debts and damaged reputations while Hoyt made his short-lived fortune. He also avoided prison despite being caught in the act. This is the story of how Harris Hoyt and dozens of other scoundrels in the Texas cotton trade during the American Civil War were able to execute their scams and, for the most part, get away with them.[27]

2

Civil War Blockade Running

Setting Up the Scheme

Harris Hoyt arrived at Galveston, Texas, in February of 1859 from Batavia, Illinois. Located near Chicago, the small town of Batavia is the oldest city in Kane County. After the war, the town played host to Mary Todd Lincoln who was an involuntary patient at its women's sanitarium. By moving to Texas, Hoyt abandoned his failed Kane County Barrel Manufacturing Company that he had begun in 1854. He also left his business partner, Edward S. Smith, back in Batavia to pick up the pieces. Traveling with Hoyt were his third wife, the Iowa widow Marie Emma Bryant Carpenter, and three children. Hoyt's move to Texas came with hopes of re-inventing himself as a cotton broker in the port city of Galveston, the state's most active outlet for its primary cash crop, cotton.[1]

Hoyt's first wife, the former Ann Elizabeth Sayre, died in Clinton County, New York, in 1842, shortly after giving birth to her seventh child, who bore her name. His second wife, the former Charlotte E. Winchell, died in Batavia in 1852 a few weeks after giving birth to a son, Harris George Hoyt. Only five of Hoyt's ten children were still alive when he traveled to Texas. His two oldest daughters were married and remained with their husbands in Vermont and Illinois. Traveling with him to Texas were his 11-year-old daughter Harriet from his first marriage, his 7-year-old son Harris George, from his second wife, and 3-year-old Cora Louise from his third and current wife, Marie.[2]

Little is known about Hoyt's activities in Texas prior to the Civil War. He did establish a cotton brokerage business known as H. Hoyt & Co. and he traveled between New Orleans, Houston, and Galveston. He also had to defend himself against a lawsuit for an unpaid debt of $100. James Cocks claimed that Hoyt was not a resident of Texas and had left the City of Galveston with an unpaid bill for rent. Leaving town with unpaid debts would become a familiar theme for Harris Hoyt, but that aspect of his character was not clear at this early stage in his career in the Texas cotton trade. Despite the lawsuit by the litigious Cocks, by 1861 Hoyt had developed a reasonably good reputation in Texas. An auctioneer who was attempting to establish his business in Beaumont listed Hoyt and two other Galveston businessmen as prominent citizens who would vouch for his honesty.[3]

Even though Civil War hostilities had not yet reached Texas in the first half of 1861, the pending Union blockade ruined the business prospects of many small commissioned shipping agents and cotton brokers in the state. Texas was ill-equipped to transport cotton directly to its primary markets in the North and the United Kingdom. Although Galveston was not blockaded until early July of 1861, the principal path for that cotton was via New Orleans and New York. New York became off limits to all Confederate cargo and passengers as of April 1861. New Orleans followed when Union warships blockaded the port in late May.[4]

These inconvenient facts forced Hoyt to anticipate the ruination of his business. On the 17th of May 1861, Hoyt placed his wife and daughters on the last passenger steamship from Galveston to New Orleans. Like many businessmen from the North who remained in the South, he was concerned for the safety of his family. From New Orleans, Hoyt's wife and daughters continued up the Mississippi to stay with his family in Illinois and then with her family members in Indiana. Hoyt did not accompany them. He was more concerned about his property, investments, and the opportunities that he still saw in Texas. After seeing his wife and daughters off, he closed up his Galveston cotton brokerage company and relocated farther inland to Brenham in Washington County, Texas. With him were his son and some other employees who may have included his brother and father-in-law. The ambitious, smooth-talking businessman began to formulate a new scheme on how to achieve the financial success that had eluded him thus far.[5]

In Brenham, Hoyt developed a complicated gambit made possible by the turmoil of war. He then perfected a convincing pitch that promised to reduce the impact of the blockade on hard-working Texas citizens. Rather than ship raw cotton and wool to Northern mills to be cleaned, ginned, spun into thread, and woven into fabric, why not set up a cotton and wool mill in Texas and cut out the middle men? With normal trade in complete disarray for the foreseeable future, it was easy to convince investors that Texans had to become more self-sufficient. It was their best hope of overcoming the effects of the Union blockading fleet. Hoyt had a tempting solution for the trouble in the Lone Star State. Even though his ideas were mostly a confidence man's sales pitch, the trouble with trade in the Bayou City of Houston and the rest of Texas was a reality and not just a con.[6]

South Texas cotton field (author's photograph).

Early in the war, most Southerners were firmly committed to "King Cotton" diplomacy. Adherents to this policy believed that cotton was "king" when it came to leveraging political and economic dialogue. They thought that the immense demand for cotton would force European nations to break the blockade and recognize the Confederacy as an independent nation. In harmony with this belief, there was a widespread popular outcry within the South demanding the prohibition of all cotton exports. It was the public's chance to demonstrate solidarity and defiance in the face of President Lincoln's blockade proclamations. Yielding to wiser financial advice, the Confederate Congress compromised. On May 21, 1861, they enacted a law that continued to allow trade through Southern seaports; they only prohibited the overland export of cotton. Pressure from the Texas delegation convinced Congress to grant one exception to that law. It was tacked on to the last line of the final section and read, "nothing in this act shall be so construed as to prohibit exportation of cotton to Mexico through its coterminous frontier." This addition gave Texas the green light to export its cotton through Mexico. Unfortunately, the blockade, distance, and lack of transportation infrastructure meant that there was no easy way for Texans to get it there.[7]

In the midst of the fears of a complete trade embargo, Hoyt proceeded to the Texas state capital in Austin. The governor and state legislators were very receptive to his ideas about self-sufficiency. He soon obtained a charter from the Texas Congress that authorized him and thirteen fellow commissioners to incorporate and sell stock in the "Texas Manufacturing Company." Hoyt was the most active promoter of the scheme. He traveled around the cotton-growing areas of Texas in early 1861 gaining moral and financial support from newspaper editors and investors. Although he claimed that his company had capital stock of $500,000, the legislation only authorized him to raise half that amount.[8]

Hoyt later assured his Northern investors and Federal investigators that he only accepted stock subscriptions and cotton from Union sympathizers. In truth, Hoyt welcomed everybody's money. He convinced his Texas investors that he needed their financial and cotton contributions to purchase textile milling equipment. He would buy the equipment in the North and place it in operation somewhere in Texas. However, he later explained to Federal authorities that he never intended to return to Texas or set up milling equipment there. Hoyt said that he merely intended to fool Confederate officials into granting him permits that would allow pro–Union families to escape from Texas into Mexico. He just needed some cotton to help pay their expenses. This lie became apparent after he made two separate trips into Texas and put his machinery into operation on the San Marcos River.[9]

In Texas, Hoyt gathered subscriptions for the Texas Manufacturing Company's stock from planters and cotton speculators. He told Union sympathizers and Federal officials that he had been gathering intelligence and trying to organize an underground resistance force. Hoyt also claimed to have shared this intelligence with General Sam Houston, who was living in Huntsville as a civilian. Houston had been forced to resign as governor in March 1861 when he opposed secession and refused to sign a

Confederate loyalty oath. The aging Texas icon offered Hoyt a sympathetic ear, but no support.[10]

After Hoyt had sold a sufficient amount of stock, the Texas Manufacturing Company's board of directors was supposed to have sent him to the Northern states as their agent. Their instructions for him were to purchase machinery and somehow get it into Texas. Hoyt also claimed that his board wanted him to call on President Lincoln on behalf of the Union people of Texas.[11]

In April of 1862, Hoyt went to Sabine Pass looking to run the blockade with his cotton. He had a small lot of ten bales that he said had come from Union sympathizers. He needed the cotton to pay for his passage and related expenses to Washington, D.C. Sabine Pass was (and remains) a six mile long tidal inlet that forms the border between Texas and Louisiana. It connects the Sabine River to the Gulf of Mexico via a seven by fourteen mile oblong tidal lagoon that oddly resembles an outline of the human digestive tract. Until September 1862, the pass also enjoyed a rail connection to Beaumont and Houston.[12]

Hoyt was not the only person trying to ship cotton out of the Sabine. When he arrived, there were two steamers, a large schooner, and a smaller sloop preparing to run out. The small, side-wheel river steamer was the *Belle Sulphur*. It was on its way to nearby Berwick Bay in Louisiana. The much larger, 1250-ton, steamer *Matagorda* was headed to Havana, as was the schooner *Andromeda*. The relatively large ocean-going sloop was the 41-ton *Elizabeth*. Luckily, the *Elizabeth* had room for Harris Hoyt's ten bales of cotton and was bound for a British port that would have good connections to New York. Her captain was a colorful and very successful Texas blockade runner named Henry Scherffius. The sloop's owner, Alexander Gilmer, paid Confederate Customs duties of $71.14 for the *Elizabeth*'s full load of 109 bales of cotton. Among those bales were the ten that belonged to Harris Hoyt.[13]

Even though the *Elizabeth* was at Sabine Pass, the Galveston Customs House managed all clearances for the ports located between the Sabine and the Brazos Rivers. Thus, when it came time for the *Elizabeth* to depart on April 30, 1862, it was the Confederate customs officer in Galveston that collected export duties and cleared the *Elizabeth* for Havana. To reduce the draft of the heavily loaded vessel, and for his own safety, Hoyt prudently waited to board the *Elizabeth* until after she had successfully crossed over the shallow bar at Sabine Pass. He then went out in a small boat, came alongside, and embarked the sloop. The *Elizabeth*'s final outbound destination was the colonial port of Kingston, Jamaica, where Captain Scherffius could offload his cotton and finalize the *Elizabeth*'s British registry.[14]

Blockade running schooner loaded with cotton, from William Watson, *Adventures of a Blockade Runner*. London: T. Fisher Unwin, 1892, frontispiece (author's collection).

The timing of the *Elizabeth*'s departure from the Sabine was fortuitous. As Hoyt was preparing to run his cotton out of Sabine Pass, the U.S. Navy's Western Gulf Blockading Fleet under Admiral David Glasgow Farragut was concentrating its efforts on the Mississippi. On April 24, 1862, the Admiral ran his fleet past Forts Jackson and St. Philip, the Confederate bastions that were ineffectually guarding the approach to New Orleans. This daring deed led to the capitulation of the city and the surrender of the forts four days later. A few Federal steam gunboats such as the USS *Hatteras* were still lurking about the approaches to the Sabine. When the *Elizabeth* ran out, these warships were several miles to the east busily chasing blockade runners out of nearby Berwick Bay, Louisiana.[15]

After successfully running the blockade undetected out of Sabine Pass, Hoyt had a long, but uneventful passage to Kingston, where he arrived twenty-eight days later. Of the four vessels that ran out of Sabine Pass in late April–early May of 1862, only the steamer *Matagorda* and the sloop *Elizabeth* were able to reach their destinations. The *Matagorda* delivered 995 bales of cotton to Havana, but the *Belle Sulphur* wrecked coming out of Sabine Pass. The U.S. Navy captured the schooner *Andromeda* and its 597 bales of cotton off the coast of Cuba. Happy to be safely berthed in Jamaica, Harris Hoyt sold his ten bales of cotton and took passage on the British passenger steamer *Plantagenet*. After a brief stop in Port au Prince, Haiti, Hoyt arrived in New York in mid–June.[16]

With its attention focused on the Mississippi and the waters around Cuba, the U.S. fleet captured no other blockade runners that were in the vicinity of Sabine Pass until the first week of July 1862. That fateful week, three small sailing vessels fell prey to the gunboats *Hatteras* and *DeSoto*. The *Elizabeth* was one of them. The USS *Hatteras* captured the sloop on July 5th as it attempted to run back into Sabine Pass. On board were the 24-year-old Captain Henry Scherffius and Alexander Gilmer, the owner and "supercargo" (the vessel's agent or purser). Gilmer was an enterprising lumberman, ship builder, store owner, and blockade runner from Orange, Texas on the Sabine River. The loss of his sloop and its cargo was a financial setback for Gilmer. He could build another sloop, but the cargo was much more valuable and could not be readily replaced.[17]

Captain George F. Emmons of the *Hatteras* placed a prize crew on board the *Elizabeth* and was preparing to send the sloop, plus the captain and a crewmember as witnesses, to the admiralty court in Key West. Just then, the slippery Scherffius appeared to become quite ill. Fearing that the captain had a contagious disease, Emmons put him ashore near the mouth of the Sabine. Another crewman from the *Elizabeth* was left on board to continue on to Key West in his place. The wily captain's timely escape from captivity would allow the blockade running interests of Hoyt and Scherffius to intersect a few months later at the Rio Grande.[18]

Harris Hoyt was not the only one who was concocting schemes to ship cotton out of Texas with government assistance. In May 1862, just days after Hoyt ran the blockade out of Sabine Pass, four enterprising businessmen and a Confederate officer met in Houston, Texas. The men were John L. Macaulay, his brother James A. Macaulay and Robert Mott of New Orleans, the British citizen and Texas resident Nelson Clements, and Major Theodore S. Moïse of the Confederate quartermaster corps. Confederate and Union quartermaster corps officers had the task of acquiring and managing supplies and equipment for their respective armies. They also had authority to sign contracts with civilian suppliers. Moïse and other four men all agreed to a contract known as a "charter-party." On behalf of the Confederate Army, Moïse exceeded his authority and gave the four civilians the authority to use the government side-wheel steamer *General Rusk* to run the blockade out of Galveston. The men were to load the vessel with cotton, sail it to Havana, sell the cotton, and then return to Texas with a load of muskets and munitions.[19]

Before the war, the *General Rusk* had been part of Charles Morgan's Southern Steamship Company. Despite the company's name, its founder was a wealthy Yankee financier and his assets were subject to Confederate seizure. Charles Morgan's hasty transfer of the company's assets to his

The side-wheel blockade running steamer *William G. Hewes*, later renamed the *Ella and Annie* (NH 61575, courtesy Naval History and Heritage Command, Washington, D.C.).

New Orleans–based son-in-law was to no avail. The State of Texas seized the *General Rusk* in Galveston Bay and the State of Louisiana then seized five other steamers in his fleet, including the new side-wheel steamer, the *William G. Hewes*. After Texas joined the Confederacy, state officials transferred ownership of the *General Rusk* to the Army and the State of Louisiana forced Charles Morgan's son to sell the company's other five steamships to private Southern interests.[20]

Although the *General Rusk* was supposed to be subject to the orders of the Confederate Army in Texas, Major Moïse gave J.L. Macaulay complete control over the steamer's operations. Nelson Clements would act as the nominal owner to facilitate a shift in the vessel's registry from a Confederate to a British flag. Robert Mott, a prominent New Orleans lawyer, was listed as the principal partner, but all of the civilians would share in the responsibility for loading 550 bales cotton and returning to Texas with armaments from Cuba. The partners had to guarantee payment of $50,000 to the government if they were unable to return the vessel or a cargo to Texas. They also agreed to sell the weapons and ammunition to quartermaster Major Moïse at "fair and reasonable prices." In return, the men were able to use the government steamer at no charge and would share equally in 80 percent of the profits. Major Moïse would receive the other 20 percent, but did not have to put up any cash.[21]

At first, it seemed like a good investment, at least from the Confederate vantage point in Texas. The *General Rusk* escaped from Galveston though a hailstorm of 15 cannon balls fired from the USS *Santee* on June 6, 1862. The Confederate steamer arrived in Havana five days later. The *Rusk* was slightly damaged as a result of that bombardment and voyage, but could be repaired in Havana. Renamed the *Blanche* and flying the Union Jack, the steamer headed back to Texas on August 20, 1862. J.L. Macaulay, who was on board as purser (i.e., supercargo), reported his safe arrival to Brigadier General Paul Octave Hébert who commanded Confederate forces in Texas. The *Blanche* had run into Matagorda Bay and was ready to offload at Port Lavaca after a voyage from Havana of 4 days and 17 hours. Macaulay had a large load of weapons, ammunition, and medicine available for the government to purchase.[22]

Macaulay quickly offloaded the inbound cargo and filled the *Blanche* with 583 bales of cotton. He was ready for another dash to Havana from Matagorda Bay. It was at this point that the discrepancies began to show through the façade of legitimacy with the steamer's charter party contract. The local Confederate quartermaster accused Macaulay of not offering the medicines "to the Government in good faith." Civilian merchants of Matagorda Bay also were able to get their hands on some of the other supplies and were offering them to the government at twice the purchase price. Commodore Leon Smith, the head of the Texas Marine Department and former captain of the steamer, was also wondering why a fine vessel like the *General Rusk* was not in Confederate service as a gunboat. Commodore Smith's position and experience meant that his complaints carried extra weight. His input had additional impact after Major General Magruder arrived in Texas. Magruder had complete confidence in the former steamboat captain, giving him authority far beyond his appointed rank of major. These contretemps with the local military authorities in Matagorda Bay resulted in the *Blanche* being detained and delayed for a week and would lead to further investigations.[23]

When the *Blanche* was once again on its way to Havana, it was steaming along the northern Cuban coast when the USS *Montgomery* came into view. The Union warship's captain, Charles Hunter, could see the bales of cotton stacked on deck and knew that he had found a valuable prize, ripe for the taking. All he had to do was chase it back into international waters. The alternative was to risk an international incident by attacking the blockade runner within foreign territory. With the *Montgomery*'s top speed of only 11 knots, Hunter decided to roll the dice and chose the latter option.[24]

After a brief chase, Captain Hunter saw that the *Blanche* had run hard aground and could not be moved. When he boarded the steamer, Hunter knew that there was no time to remove its 583 bales of cotton. Local Spanish authorities also had boarded the *Blanche* and were well-aware of the American navy officer's illicit actions in their waters. Spanish warships had been summoned and were on their way to attack the *Montgomery*. Out of time and ideas, Commander Hunter decided to burn the *Blanche* and blame it on the crew of the blockade runner. He also forced a British passenger to sign a statement that corroborated his story. Retreating to the *Montgomery* and international waters, Commander Hunter held his British passenger for a few days and then released him. The former hostage promptly retracted his coerced statement and reported what appears to be the true situation to the British Consul in Havana.[25]

Admiral Farragut admired his aggressive ship captain and tried to brush the incident aside as a minor indiscretion. Not realizing that bad news never gets better with age, Commander Hunter and Admiral Farragut were slow to submit and follow up their official reports of the incident to the Navy Department. In the meantime, Secretary of State William Seward and Secretary of the Navy Gideon Welles were being bombarded with outraged diplomatic protests from the British and Spanish ambassadors in Washington, D.C. Secretary Welles quickly relieved Hunter of his command and had him tried at a court martial. He was found guilty and dismissed from the Navy; Hunter would later find employment in the merchant marine.[26]

As for the Confederates, they had lost a valuable ship and cargo. On the positive side of the ledger, the Union Navy had incensed the British and Spanish governments. This latest provocation gave the Rebels more false hope that Great Britain, France, and the other European powers might actually recognize the independence of the Confederate States. On a more practical level, it seemed likely that the United States would have to pay reparations to the Spanish or British government for the *Blanche* and its load of cotton. With luck, the Confederacy might be able to claim some of that money. To their embarrassment, Confederate officials would not discover their own internal conspiracy to defraud the government until later. The perfidy of Major Theodore Moïse and his partners would be one of the first but certainly not the last of the Texas cotton trade swindles, as Harris Hoyt would soon demonstrate.

3

Winning the White House
Telling a Texas Tall Tale

While his former shipmates on the *Elizabeth* were dealing with Yankee warships off the coast of Texas and the *Blanche* was still in Havana, Harris Hoyt was in Indiana. He went there to move his wife and daughter farther west, from Indianapolis to Clermont, Iowa. He would leave them in Iowa with his wife Marie's family. Along the way, Hoyt collected letters of introduction from Judge Samuel D. Lockwood and County Clerk Thomas C. Moore of Kane County, Illinois. Another endorser was General John F. Farnsworth (later a Republican congressman) of Kings County, Illinois. They were all prominent citizens who were well known to Abraham Lincoln from his time in the state. Judge Lockwood's wife, Mary Nash Lockwood, was the President's aunt. Hoyt hoped to use their influence in gaining an audience with President Lincoln in Washington, D.C.[1]

During his travels in the North, Hoyt touted himself as a delegate representing Union men in Texas. He had an audacious plan to relieve their suffering under the Confederate yoke. If he could only get permission to return to Texas, he could render aid to those in need. For himself, all he wanted was to convert his assets in Texas into cotton and return to the North along with his son and the remainder of his family and Union friends. He said that he just needed some official Federal cooperation to make this all happen.[2]

Hoyt reported that his family and other unfortunate victims of the war were stuck in Texas and needed relief. They had sent him to the North with the mission of acquiring and importing cotton and wool milling equipment into Texas. He insisted that this equipment would not materially aid the Confederacy since it would be old and of little value. The Texans would not realize that they had been duped before his Yankee friends had sold the machinery and financed their way back to Union lines. And, oh by the way, he might need to take along a few firearms and percussion caps strictly to gain credibility with Confederate officials.³

It was not uncommon for Federal officials to show compassion to certain families and individuals, particularly females, who were separated from their homes and families as a result of the blockade. Even the scourge of the South Texas coast, Acting Lieutenant John W. Kittredge, revealed a glimpse of his more charitable inclinations toward a disabled woman who was on board a captured Texas blockade runner. The 43-year-old Kittredge was a former merchant mariner who was known to be a hot-tempered, bombastic braggart. He and his bark-rigged sailing ship, the USS *Arthur*, had been terrorizing the coast between Corpus Christi and Matagorda Bay for months. But Kittredge showed his softer side when he captured the schooner *J.J. McNeil* on January 25, 1862, about 17 miles north of the entrance into Matagorda Bay at Pass Cavallo. The Texas schooner was returning to Port Lavaca from Vera Cruz with a cargo of coffee and tobacco. Its owner and supercargo, Mr. Hopper, had purchased these goods with the proceeds of about 100 bales of Texas cotton.⁴

Mr. Hopper owned a percentage of the schooner and was accompanied by his invalid wife. She was so ill that Captain Kittredge "thought it an act of humanity" to transfer her from the *J.J. McNeil* to the USS *Arthur*. He asked his boss, Commodore William McKean, for instructions on what to do with Mr. and Mrs. Hopper. McKean granted Kittredge permission to land the couple and their baggage on the Texas coast under a flag of truce. On March 3, just over a month after their capture, Kittredge returned the Hoppers to Confederate authorities in Matagorda Bay. Mrs. Hopper's illness turned out to be a debilitating form of rheumatism that prevented her from walking. Her mind was healthy, however, and she had "good use of her tongue," as she shared intelligence about the Union captain and his ship. Confederate forces would capture the audacious Captain Kittredge six months later when he led a shore expedition at Corpus Christi Bay. After his release, Kittredge received another command, but the U.S. Navy then court-martialed and dismissed him from the Navy for abusing his own sailors.⁵

Harris Hoyt knew of the government's willingness to provide humanitarian aid for suffering Union families in Texas. Playing on those sympathies, he offered a plan that required the purchase of at least two small schooners and a larger steamship. The three vessels would work in concert to export cotton purchased from his Union loyalist friends in Texas. The steamer would transport the cotton to New York, gather up another load of goods for Texas, and load the cargoes onto the schooners. The smaller vessels would then sail into blockaded Texas ports, preferably Galveston.

3. Winning the White House

All this would take money and permits to pass through the blockade that Hoyt did not have. Surprisingly, he would soon discover that money, lots of money, would be easier to obtain than permits for running the blockade.[6]

Less than one month after his return to the North, Hoyt met with Secretary of War Edwin M. Stanton in Washington, D.C. Stanton's previous political appointment had been as the Attorney General in the administration of President James Buchanan, a Democrat. As a newly minted Secretary of War in the Republican President Lincoln's cabinet, Stanton was known for being brusque and rude, but highly capable and honest. During their meeting, Stanton was unmoved by Hoyt's heart-felt pleas, but the swindler from Texas remained undaunted. Hoyt followed up his visit with the Secretary of War with a formal letter. He specifically requested a permit to pass through the blockading fleet off Texas, but received no reply. With Stanton's rebuff, Hoyt realized that he needed even more political clout to achieve his goal. Not knowing of Stanton's low opinion of Abraham Lincoln during the early stages of his administration, Hoyt thought that a letter from the President might change Secretary Stanton's mind. He hoped that such an endorsement would open other doors as well.[7]

Taking advantage of an introduction courtesy of Lincoln's friend, biographer, and U.S. Pension Office Commissioner Joseph H. Barrett, Hoyt was in the White House two days later. He met with John Hay, President Lincoln's private secretary and the future Secretary of State under Theodore Roosevelt. Hay was a trusted and reliable former law school student from Illinois whom Lincoln had added to his staff in Washington. Hoyt never actually spoke with the president, but the following note signed by John Hay would have the same effect.[8]

> "EXECUTIVE MANSION,
> Washington, September 17, 1862.
>
> Mr. Harris Hoyt, who bears this letter, is recommended to the President as a true and loyal citizen, by unquestionable authority. This letter is given to him at his request, to commend him to the confidence and kind offices of Union people on his way back to his home.
>
> JOHN HAY, Acting Private
> Secretary to the President."[9]

Although the note was signed by the President's secretary and not by Abraham Lincoln himself, the back of the letter that served as an outer envelope had the following inscription, "From the President of the United States. John Hay, Priv. Sec." It was addressed to the Secretary of War (Stanton) with a copy to Harris Hoyt. Hoyt now had an essential document in his pocket that would gain him instant credibility as he angled for investment money and permits in the North.[10]

One of the individuals who took the bait in Washington, D.C., was Governor William Sprague of Rhode Island. The thirty-one-year-old governor was in Washington as the head of the Rhode Island state regiment that he had raised and equipped. Governor Sprague had assumed the role as the colonel in command of these troops that he successfully led at the First Battle of Bull Run. During the battle, Rebel sharp-shooters missed hitting the governor, but shot his horse instead. With his uniform perforated by Confederate Minié balls, Sprague performed admirably and even heroically in his first taste of battle. Although Bull Run (known as Manassas to the Confederates) was an embarrassing and costly Union defeat, Sprague emerged as a hero. Just over a year after the battle, Governor Sprague, as well as Harris Hoyt, Major General Nathaniel Banks, and numerous other military, business, and political leaders were staying at one of Washington's finest hotels, the Willard.[11]

Hoyt met with Governor Sprague at the Willard and gave him his sales pitch. He said that the reason he approached the Governor was simply because of his high office as the result of his being "a man of means." In truth, the reasons were much broader. William Sprague happened to be a principal partner in the company that owned numerous textile mills including the largest calico cotton mill in the world, A. & W. Sprague & Co. As an added bonus, Governor Sprague was engaged to Kate Chase, the vivacious daughter of Secretary of the Treasury Salmon P. Chase. Secretary Chase was the primary government official who was authorized to issue permits to conduct trade across Union lines into Confederate territory.[12]

For his part, Governor Sprague disingenuously said that his interest in Hoyt's scheme was moved by a desire to aid the "suffering Unionists." The reality of his rationale for swallowing Hoyt's sale pitch

Portrait of William Sprague, 1862, from the cover of "Governor Sprague's Grand March," sheet music composed by E. Mack and published by Lee & Walker, Philadelphia (Library of Congress, Music Division).

was a bit more practical. A. & W. Sprague's cotton milling business required cotton. The virtual closing of trade with the South meant no more cotton for Northern mills, poverty for thousands of workers, and bankruptcy for his firm.[13]

If Sprague could somehow get his hands on a reliable source of cotton, his business not only would survive, but might even thrive during an otherwise disastrous Civil War. Sprague rationalized his actions by reasoning that Hoyt's scheme would aid Union sympathizers in Texas. It was just serendipity that he and Hoyt would derive "pecuniary advantage from his operations—motives at once politic and philanthropic."[14]

Intrigued by the prospect of a direct and inexpensive supply of cotton, Sprague invited Hoyt to meet with him at his offices in Providence, Rhode Island. But first, Hoyt needed a reliable partner to handle some of the maritime details of his plan. That person appeared on Hoyt's doorstep at the Willard Hotel, a prime Washington meeting place for the rich and powerful to intermingle and make back-room deals. Two days after his office call with John Hay, Hoyt recognized a man in the hotel lobby. He was a 41-year-old engineer named Charles L. Prescott whom Hoyt had first seen in Galveston.[15]

Knowing that Prescott had been in Texas perhaps prompted Hoyt to be a bit more candid with him than he was with his other newfound Union friends. Hoyt told Prescott that Governor Sprague had agreed to help him get permits to run the blockade. Sprague would also furnish money to purchase and equip vessels to carry out cotton from Texas. This is where Prescott fit into the scheme. Prescott would be in charge of purchasing and fitting out suitable vessels for a voyage to the Western Gulf of Mexico. Hoyt was certain "a great amount of money could be made." In an uncharacteristic moment of honesty, Hoyt

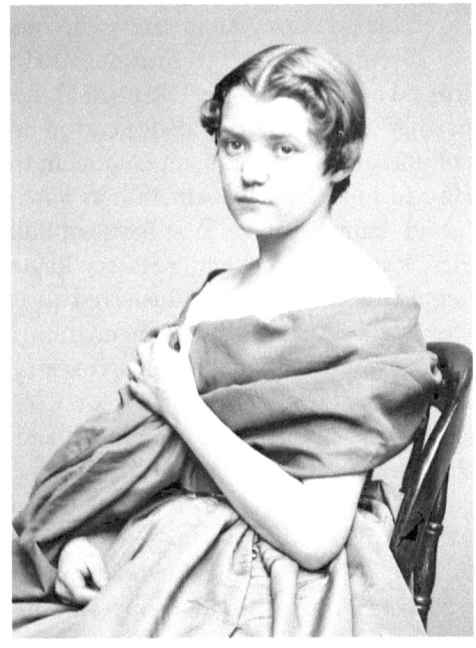

Kate Chase portrait by Mathew Brady, ca. 1860 (Library of Congress, Manuscript Division, Brady-Handy Collection).

also described his plan to get cotton out of Texas as a Union relief "dodge," a common nineteenth century term for a scam.[16]

In October 1862, Harris Hoyt traveled to Providence, Rhode Island, confident that Governor Sprague would sponsor what became known as his "Texas Adventure." Hoyt soon asked Prescott to join him in Providence where he could meet their Rhode Island benefactors. Prescott had left for his home in New York shortly after Harris Hoyt departed Washington for Providence. By the time Prescott returned home, he found a note from Hoyt beckoning him to come at once.[17]

Hoyt introduced Prescott to Sprague, who gave his assent to the plan, but the Governor handed the two men off to his 38-year-old cousin Byron Sprague. Governor Sprague later claimed that he was "too much engaged with State affairs" to take a more active role in the operation. Byron Sprague was the governor's partner in A. & W. Sprague & Co. and had served on his military staff as a colonel. It was not in William Sprague's nature to prioritize government responsibilities over his business interests, which makes his statement about his detachment from Hoyt's scheme seem spurious. The governor's real reason for giving Byron responsibility for managing the "Texas Adventure" may have been to distance himself from this dubious plan in case something went wrong.[18]

Byron Sprague then introduced Hoyt and Prescott to the governor's trusted associate Colonel William H. Reynolds. Reynolds was the general partner of his own Providence cotton brokerage firm, having resigned his commission as a lieutenant colonel in the U.S. Army four months earlier. He had fought with distinction as a major in Governor Sprague's Rhode Island regiment at the First Battle of Bull Run. While still serving with the First Rhode Island Light Artillery Regiment, Reynolds was promoted to lieutenant colonel and transferred to Port Royal, South Carolina. With Governor Sprague's recommendation and Secretary Chase's approval, Reynolds was the government's treasury agent there.[19]

Not coincidentally, Lieutenant Colonel Reynolds had the task of collecting and shipping the abandoned and seized cotton within the recently captured South Carolina territory. The cotton grown on the southern coastal islands was known as "sea island cotton." Mill owners prized this variety of cotton for its long-staple fibers and fine quality, making it particularly valuable. While Reynolds was collecting this cotton, Treasury officials encouraged him to cooperate with the missionaries there who were helping the freed slaves become more self-sufficient. Conflicts soon arose with the well known abolitionist leader of the missionary effort, Edward L. Pierce. Reynolds needed the free labor force of former slaves to collect the cotton, but Pierce was reluctant to dedicate them to manual labor.

Reynolds' dark black hair and full beard framed a high forehead and trusting, puppy-dog black eyes. Those eyes masked his single-mindedness of purpose. Reynolds' heavy handed treatment of the former slaves and his disparaging remarks about the Port Royal missionaries earned him the enmity of Edward Pierce. When Reynolds finally sold the cotton that he had collected in South Carolina for a total of $500,000 in New York, he reported a net loss of almost $75,000. Salmon Chase had had enough. Amidst charges of extensive fraud, Secretary Chase sacked him. Reynolds had served a total of eighteen months in the Army before he was forced to resign.[20]

Governor Sprague was not dissuaded by the accusations against his former artillery officer. It was his company's cotton mills (and his stock holders) that were benefiting from Reynolds' actions with the cotton from South Carolina. The proposed venture with Harris Hoyt promised more of the same, but they needed to manage the risk. The easiest method for businessmen to reduce risk when speculating in the cotton trade was to add additional investors. That is the tack that Governor Sprague and William Reynolds took with their highly speculative Texas Adventure.

Byron Sprague contacted two respectable business houses also located in Providence, Messrs. Orray Taft & Co. plus B.B. & R. Knight & Co. These men were willing to act as silent partners. Orray Taft was the principal of a large cotton brokerage company. The Knights owned a significant textile milling operation that would create the "Fruit of the Loom" clothing brand and remain in business for another 58 years. These two additions, along with A. & W. Sprague and W.H. Reynolds, formed a partnership comprising four different Rhode Island companies. Each had an equal interest in the venture as a result of their individual investment of $25,000 to finance the purchase of vessels and cargoes. Reynolds and Sprague told Hoyt and Prescott that if they needed more than this initial $100,000, it would be forthcoming. As he had done in the Army, William H. Reynolds and his brokerage company served as a surrogate for William Sprague's interests and became the most active partner in managing the daily affairs of Hoyt's Texas Adventure. Cousin Byron would take charge of the finances that he would supervise until early November of 1862.[21]

All parties agreed in principle that the Providence partners would supply the money, while Hoyt and Prescott would do the field work. In return, the two displaced men from Texas would each receive one-quarter of the profits, after first paying six percent interest to the Providence partners on the capital invested. Prescott's duties included taking charge of all nautical matters. He would select and purchase at least two schooners and one steamer. Prescott would also manage operational details and prepare the vessels for a long ocean voyage to Texas. Hoyt was responsible for procuring and accompanying items that were suitable for the Texas market. These items included arms, ammunition, bagging and ropes for bailing cotton, boots, shoes, and blankets. He also was supposed to make arrangements to get the schooners into a Texas port.[22]

Prescott immediately set out for New York in search of suitable vessels. The war had made this task considerably more difficult. The U.S. blockading fleet needed seaworthy steam ships capable of mounting heavy cannons. To meet this need, the Navy Department under Gideon Welles had to rapidly augment the nation's small fleet faster than its shipyards could produce them. The Navy secretary was searching for additional vessels that he could purchase, convert into warships, and use to seal up his leaky blockade of the Southern coast.

To better cover the Confederacy's 3,549 miles of coastline and its 180 different ports, the U.S. Navy had purchased 91 commercial vessels in the six months after the Fort Sumter attack in April 1861. The Navy Department would lease or purchase another 337 before the end of the war. While most of the Navy's new vessels were larger steamers, adventurous civilian speculators were also acquiring smaller, sea-going schooners to run the blockade in the Gulf of Mexico. Of the 226 U.S. Navy warships on blockade duty by the spring of 1862, most could not come near the shallow coastlines of the South. This limitation was particularly true in the Western Gulf. The blockading fleet was unable to patrol these shallow waters or pursue small sailing vessels as their captains dashed into a shallow inlet or simply ran their vessels ashore. Small boat raids, conducted primarily under cover of darkness, were the only option for blockading captains to catch the foxes in their lair.[23]

Byron Sprague authorized Charles Prescott to draw on an account managed by his agent in New York, James A. Suydam. With this open line of credit, Prescott could purchase the best vessels he could find without undue limitations on price. After making the purchases, he was to load them with the cargoes that Hoyt had identified as desirable for the Texas market. Hoyt, however, was not yet in New York.[24]

Upon completing his deal with William and Byron Sprague, Harris Hoyt borrowed $800 from William H. Reynolds that he said was for his family in Illinois. For collateral, Hoyt used the wedding present he had given to his wife, a diamond cluster-pin and "ear-drops," i.e., earrings. He then headed west to the home of his wife's parents in Clermont, Iowa, where Marie Hoyt and his two young daughters were staying. He uprooted them once again and deposited the family at the home of his twin brother Horace in Morris, Illinois.[25]

Hoyt's visit to Iowa and Illinois was a short one, for he had business on the East Coast. When he returned to New York, the first order of business was finding a way to acquire permits that would allow him to pass through the blockade. Permits were vital to the legitimacy of his Texas Adventure. Without them, all of the U.S. citizens involved would become criminals. It was natural for Hoyt to overestimate and oversell the ease with which he could obtain these necessary documents to bypass the blockade. He did not have them and could not get them without assistance. While he was in New York, Hoyt convinced Governor Sprague to write letters of introduction for himself and William Reynolds to Secretary of the Treasury Salmon Chase and Secretary of the Navy Gideon Welles. Hoyt had convinced Reynolds and Governor Sprague that these introductions were mere formalities to help him finalize the deal.[26]

William Reynolds accompanied Hoyt back to Washington where they planned to meet with Secretary Chase and then Welles. On the train ride south, Reynolds discovered that Hoyt had exaggerated his ability to obtain the permits. Their meetings would be more than friendly visits with their benefactors. The two men would have to convince one or both of the cabinet secretaries to sign permits that would authorize their shipments into and out of Texas. They first tried their luck with Sprague's prospective father-in-law, Secretary Chase.[27]

They had reason for optimism. In the recent past, Chase had lobbied in favor of permits for Union loyalists to pass through the blockade in the South Atlantic. Hoyt proudly showed Secretary Chase his letter of introduction from the President via John Hay. He then described his scheme to assist Union sympathizers in

Secretary of the Treasury Salmon P. Chase, portrait by Mathew Brady, ca. 1861 (Library of Congress, Manuscript Division, Brady-Handy Collection).

escaping from Texas. In return, Hoyt offered to travel throughout Texas gathering intelligence on Confederate military strength and locations. He would then pass that information along to the Federal government.[28]

When he mentioned William Sprague's involvement and support, Hoyt got an unexpected reaction. He apparently had misread Secretary Chase's relationship with the Governor. Chase "got offended" with Hoyt when he mentioned his alliance with Sprague. The Governor appeared to be leveraging his relationship with Chase's daughter Kate for political and financial favors. Although Secretary Chase would do the same in the years to come when he sought support for his candidacy for president, he icily replied that Hoyt's plan "could not or ought not to be done." Even though Chase was the only cabinet official with direct authority to issue the permits that Hoyt needed, the secretary passed the two men off to the Secretary of the Navy. Chase knew that there was no way that the acerbic Secretary Welles would accede to a blatant violation of the blockade.[29]

Gideon Welles was a Connecticut Yankee and a newspaper owner. President Lincoln nicknamed him "Father Neptune." Given his bushy white beard and grizzled appearance, it was an apt appellation. Welles was also efficient and incorruptible. He had already conveyed his feelings about deliberately allowing anyone, loyalist or not, to pass through his blockade of the Southern coast. At a cabinet meeting just a few days earlier on October 10, 1862, Welles acknowledged "the blockade caused suffering." Suffering, after all "was the chief object of the blockade." He had stopped just short of accusing Chase of issuing illicit permits as special favors to promote his political aspirations. Welles described such manipulators as "a set of bloodsuckers who propose to make use of the blockade as a money-making machine to enrich themselves." That, of course, was exactly what Hoyt, Reynolds, and Sprague were trying to do.[30]

Hoyt seemed to have been blissfully unaware of Secretary Welles' attitude or that Secretary Chase had set him up for failure. He used his letter of recommendation from Governor Sprague to meet with Secretary Welles. Hoyt argued the importance of "getting out cotton when it can be done without giving aid and comfort to the enemy." He parroted Sprague's reasoning that getting cotton out of Texas would "keep down the price of cotton" and put "bread in the mouths of our people." Hoyt contended that the advantage to the North would far outweigh any benefits gained by the South, particularly if they only traded with Union sympathizers. It was an absurd proposition. By providing manufacturing equipment to the South, Hoyt and his partners were, in effect, requesting permission to violate the articles of war by providing aid and comfort to the enemy.[31]

Welles did not directly mention Hoyt or Sprague's request for permits in his diary, but he could not, and would not, countenance any violation of the blockade. However, Welles did offer some hope that Hoyt might be able to run out a vessel from Texas that was loaded with his personal property. He would have to surrender it to the blockading fleet and ensure that it carried no contraband of war. This was not what Hoyt had in mind, but the secretary's suggestion helped him fabricate a useful cover story that he could later use when explaining his plans to Union sympathizers in Texas.[32]

Secretary of the Navy Gideon Welles, portrait by Mathew Brady, ca. 1861 (Library of Congress, Prints & Photographs Division, Civil War Photographs).

Their trip to Washington had been an unmitigated disaster. Hoyt and Reynolds failed to obtain permits for their Texas Adventure, and their names and intentions were now known to the Secretaries of War, the Navy, and Treasury. Those officials saw the request for what it was: permission to circumvent the blockade and trade with the enemy. The net effect of Hoyt's meetings with the cabinet secretaries was not a good one. If he was ever caught in the act of transporting goods into or out of Texas, it would be difficult for him or his partners to claim innocence. As events would play out, "difficult" did not mean "impossible."

Secretary Chase's rebuff was not only a professional setback for Governor Sprague, he suffered personal ramifications as well. Just after Kate Chase's father refused to give Sprague permits for his Texas Adventure, she broke off their engagement. Charles Prescott hinted that the reason for the split was Sprague's attempt to use his relationship with her for personal gain. A few months later, however, Sprague was elected to the U.S. Senate and the engagement was back on track. The perceptive Welles noted in his diary that "Governor Sprague and Miss Kate Chase called this evening. I have been skeptical as to a match, but this means something. She is beautiful, or, more properly perhaps, interesting and impressive. He is rich and holds the position of Senator. Few young men have such advantages as he, and Miss Kate has talents and ambition sufficient for both."[33]

When it became clear that Hoyt's Texas Adventure would never acquire the needed permits from Washington officials, the partners had to reassess what could be done to salvage their investment. Any attempt to run a vessel into Texas would be a clear violation of the blockade. The Providence partners, particularly Sprague and Reynolds, had no intention of going to jail. Hoyt suggested that they go to Matamoros, Mexico instead. With a slight adjustment to their paperwork, they could legally sell their cargoes and vessels there and return with cotton. Hoyt claimed that although he could not get permission to run the blockade into Texas, he did believe that he had authorization to take goods overland from Matamoros into Texas. Despite the claim, he never received any such permission, and he knew it.[34]

Prescott later testified that the reason they shifted their attention to Matamoros was "the success of the Union arms in that section to which we intended to go," i.e., Texas. Given the timing of their first voyage, he was referring to the Union's brief occupation of Galveston Bay in early October 1862. That month, U.S. naval forces occupied Galveston Harbor and placed a small Army contingent on one of its piers. They remained in Galveston until General John Bankhead Magruder and Leon Smith's small fleet of cotton-clad river steamers captured or evicted them all on New Year's Day 1863. In another, more successful operation, Union forces under General Nathaniel Banks eventually occupied the coast of Texas south of the Brazos River. That eight month long occupation did not occur until November of 1863.[35]

In reality, the dates and locations of the Union occupation of portions of the Texas coast had little impact on their Texas Adventure plans. Although the U.S. Navy held Galveston harbor as Hoyt and Prescott first prepared to sail from New York, all the other Texas ports were still available to small schooners. Even after Confederate forces had recaptured Galveston, Hoyt persisted in his plan to sail for Matamoros. Subsequent voyages of the Texas Adventure vessels continued to call at Matamoros without regard to the presence or absence of Union forces on the Texas coast. More than anything else, this revised strategy was an attempt to avoid being prosecuted for conspiracy to conduct illicit trade.[36]

Matamoros was a neutral Mexican port on the international border located about twenty miles upriver from the mouth of the Rio Grande. It was open to trade with any country. Through an international network of brokers, shippers, and agents it was possible for U.S. citizens to trade with Texas without violating the letter of the law. Hoyt and Reynolds reasoned they were only looking to "establish a legitimate trade at Matamoras [sic]."

At first, Reynolds and his Providence partners seemed to accept this proposal. They were not completely convinced, but at the time, nobody else had a better idea.[37]

The revised plan was to load two schooners with manufactured goods for the Texas market and send them into Matamoros via Havana. A steamer would then take freight from New York to Havana and follow the schooners to the Rio Grande. From there, it would lie at anchor in neutral waters awaiting the cotton that Hoyt promised to obtain from Texas. After offloading the cotton onto the steamer, the schooners would transfer another load of manufactured goods into Matamoros for further overland shipment into Texas. It was a reasonable plan, but like most wartime plans, it would soon change.[38]

4

The Texas Adventure Fleet

A Sinking Start

With the modified plan in place, all the Texas Adventure partners had to do was set it in motion. They had the money to purchase suitable sailing ships and believed that they had sufficient political influence to overcome any obstacles that the government might place in their way. It was still a complex scheme and things soon began to go awry. After a promising start, they had to overcome official delays and objections and internal dissension at almost every step in their quest to import Texas cotton. The partners' attempts to respond to changing military and political conditions would result in confusion, frustration, and a great deal of independent innovation on the part of Harris Hoyt.

While Reynolds and Hoyt were in Washington, Charles Prescott had been busy in New York. He purchased the former blockade running steamer *Ella Warley*. The Union blockading fleet had captured the 14-year-old *Ella Warley* the previous April as she attempted to enter Charleston Harbor from Havana. An American-built side-wheel steamer, she measured 220 feet in length. The *Ella Warley* was too old and not seaworthy enough for U.S. naval service, which made her available for an auction sale to private parties.[1]

The U.S. admiralty courts routinely ordered the sale of any captured vessel that it had condemned for running the blockade if it was of no use to the Navy. The vessel and its cargo would then be offered for sale at a public auction. This practice allowed the rebirth of numerous vessels as blockade runners. The blockading fleet often captured these vessels multiple times as they sailed under various names and owners. Prescott purchased the *Ella Warley* in mid–October 1862 with his winning offer of $29,000, but he decided to retain rather than change the steamer's name. He was ready to get her back into the blockade running business. Two days after purchasing the steamer, Prescott also bought the 70-ton schooner *Snow Drift* through a broker. The price was $3,500.[2]

4. The Texas Adventure Fleet   45

Prescott's first priority was to load and send out the schooner. He then planned to follow in the steamer. Finding goods suitable for the Texas market was Hoyt's job. Upon his return to New York, Hoyt hastily set about obtaining a cargo for the *Snow Drift*. The *Ella Warley* and Prescott's planned purchase of a second schooner would have to wait. Hoyt ordered lard, flour, Kentucky bagging (material for wrapping cotton bales that had been woven using Kentucky hemp), bale-rope, bleached cotton cloth, kerosene, lard oil, sperm oil, linseed oil, and cotton cards. He also wanted to buy two carding machines that he planned to install in Texas.[3]

Hand held wool and cotton cards had the appearance of wooden paddles with dozens of small, uniformly protruding nails or wires. Working in tandem, these cards were an essential tool for cleaning and preparing raw wool or cotton to be spun into thread. The carding could be done by hand, but it was a laborious process sure to leave fingers and knuckles bloodied. The carding machines like the ones Hoyt wanted to purchase would add a twist to the fiber and wind it onto multiple bobbins. They were fast and efficient marvels of the machine age.[4]

Hoyt explained that he needed this specific carding machinery to ingratiate himself with Texas officials. He intended to present himself to

Civil War–era carding machine. *Illustrated London News*, August 2, 1862 (author's collection).

Confederate authorities in the state as a legitimate blockade runner in hopes that he "would be received with open arms" as a daring Rebel patriot. He would install the old wool carding equipment in Texas "as a mere 'blind'" (another nineteenth century term for a scam or cover story).[5]

He said that this equipment would firmly establish his credibility with the Texans, especially if he promised to run the blockade again. He would return with cotton ginning equipment that could separate the sticky green seeds from the fluffy balls of cotton. With these false promises, Hoyt said that he would be able to freely move around the state. He claimed that his actual intentions were to collect intelligence about Confederate defenses and make contact with his Union-sympathizing friends. They would trade their cotton for his manufactured goods and the profits from the sales would enable these loyal families to get away from Texas. Hoyt failed to mention that he had already set up a joint stock corporation in Texas and the carding machinery would help him get that company into operation for the benefit of all Texans.[6]

Given the pretext he had used with the Texas legislature and the stockholders of the Texas Manufacturing Company, Hoyt knew that he could not return without the carding machines. Departing from New York, Hoyt proceeded to Hartford, Connecticut, where he bought two second-hand wool-carding machines and a large lot of old fashioned, handheld cotton cards from John W. Boynton. Boynton was able to claim with a straight face that he did not know where the machinery was bound, even though Hoyt told him he was acting on behalf of a group of Texans.[7]

Boynton disassembled and boxed up the carding machines and delivered them to New York. Prescott promptly prepared to load them onboard the *Snow Drift*, but Reynolds complained that the machinery took up too much room. In response, Hoyt said that he would ship them on his own account and treat the machinery as his own separate and private speculation. He promised to repay the Providence partners for everything, including freight and expenses, on his return.[8]

Before leaving New York for Matamoros, the *Snow Drift* had one last lot of cargo to load. They were items that Prescott and Hoyt had omitted from the official manifest: guns and ammunition. Among those weapons was a double barrel shotgun that Hoyt bought as a present for the Governor of Texas, Francis R. Lubbock. The governor's home was near Houston in Harris County and Hoyt probably was acquainted with Lubbock from his time as a cotton broker in Galveston. He also had obtained his charter for the Texas Manufacturing Company in Austin while Lubbock was serving as governor there. In his memoirs, Lubbock omitted Hoyt's name, but proudly mentioned the Texas Manufacturing Company as one of the achievements of his administration. The governor cited the company as an example of his efforts to promote the manufacture of cotton and woolen fabrics for home use. Hoyt planned to build upon his stock of good will with the governor and grease the process for getting Confederate permits to export his cotton.[9]

Hoyt explained to his anxious Providence partners that Texas officials expected blockade runners to carry goods for its Army. While this was a true statement when entering Texas ports, the *Snow Drift* was headed for the neutral port of Matamoros and not directly into the Confederacy. There was no such requirement or expectation of military supplies at Matamoros for neutral vessels that did not have a contract with the Confederate government.[10]

On October 27, 1862, William Reynolds bought a second schooner for the Texas Adventure through his agent Thomas W. Whitford. The purchase of the 95-ton, first class schooner *Citizen* was fully in accordance with the original plan, but nautical matters were supposed to be Charles Prescott's responsibility. The Rhode Island-built *Citizen* was in Narraganset Bay where Reynolds had his own maritime contacts. This second schooner joined the *Snow Drift* and *Ella Warley* in New York about a week later.[11]

As the key pieces of the Texas Adventure were coming together in New York, Governor Sprague penned two more letters. He still hoped that he might use the influence of his office and his wealth to offer protection to Hoyt and their Texas Adventure. He wrote a letter to the "Officer Commanding Gulf Squadron," who at the time was Rear Admiral David G. Farragut. Sprague explained that the *Snow Drift* and Hoyt intended to provide "Aid to the loyal citizens of Texas, and information for our military and naval authorities."[12]

On the same day that he wrote to Rear Admiral Farragut, Sprague composed a similar letter to Major General Ben Butler, who commanded the U.S. forces in New Orleans. Another one of the Union's political generals, Butler was a former congressman and the future governor of Massachusetts. He was particularly adept at using his position to enrich himself and his relatives. Owing primarily to the Louisiana cotton trade that he controlled while he commanded the Army in New Orleans, Butler increased his net worth over twenty-fold to over $3 million during the war. He collected some of that money from his brother and partner in crime, Andrew, who died suddenly in 1864 and left half of his $2 million estate to the general.[13]

The particular type of maritime swindle that Governor Sprague hoped to use became known as a "Butler Pass." This dodge involved General Butler giving the captain of a blockade runner a letter addressed to the "Officers of the Blockading Squadron." It declared that the owner was a loyal citizen who was cleared for Matamoros, but was permitted to bring out cotton or other supplies from a Texas port. This is exactly the type of permit that Harris Hoyt had been promising his Providence partners all along. The only stipulation from Butler was, "This course of trade should be secret of course to be successful." Unfortunately for Butler, his secret passes would soon come to the attention of the wrong government officials.[14]

The blockading fleet and Lincoln's cabinet officers got wind of Butler's blockade running scheme in the fall of 1862. In early October, the armed sailing schooner USS *Velocity* was on patrol off the East Texas coast. A former blockade runner herself, the Navy had added the shallow draft *Velocity* to its blockading fleet. They armed the schooner with two brass howitzers in hopes of extending the reach of its fleet into Texas and Louisiana coastal inlets. She was acting under the orders of Lieutenant Frederick Crocker, commanding officer of the USS *Kensington*. On October 10th, the *Velocity* discovered a suspicious schooner that was attempting to enter at Sabine Pass. The vessel proved to be the *West Florida*, a New Orleans-registered blockade runner bound from Matamoros. She had a crew of four plus a clever captain named James H. Ashby.[15]

When Lieutenant Crocker arrived on the scene with the *Kensington*, the *West Florida*'s supercargo presented his Butler pass. Crocker was astonished to learn that it specifically authorized Ashby to enter the blockaded port at Sabine Pass to trade for cotton. Captain Ashby was a well known blockade runner. He had been at Sabine Pass as captain of the schooner *Andromeda* at the same time that Harris Hoyt and the sloop *Elizabeth* were preparing to run out. Ashby was captured on the *Andromeda* off the coast of Cuba, resulting in the condemnation of the schooner and its load of cotton for a total prize money award of $127,727.96 (well over $3.3 million in 2020). Given Captain Ashby's past, Crocker had good reason to doubt the document's authenticity. He placed a prize crew on board and sent the blockade runner to Pensacola, Florida, and dutifully reported the incident to Admiral Farragut.[16]

Crocker's report to Farragut set off a chain of letters. First, Admiral Farragut wrote to General Butler, explaining what had been done with Ashby and his schooner, and his intent to strictly enforce the blockade. As Farragut would later learn, not only was the Butler Pass genuine, there were many more. The *West Florida* just happened to be the first vessel that was seized while attempting to use one. In May, Butler had given Eli H. Skaggs a similar permit to sail "the steamer *Indian No. 2*, from the mouth of Sabine to this city [New Orleans] with a load of cattle and provisions." Skaggs was a "professed gambler and speculator" and Louisiana plantation owner who managed to flummox the captain of the USS *Hatteras* with his Butler Pass. The captain allowed the steamer to continue on its way to Texas after taking a portion of its inbound cargo as security. By 1863, the *Indian No. 2* (also known as the *Indian Queen No. 2*) was back in Confederate service on the Red River.[17]

General Ben Butler realized that he had some explaining to do about the *West Florida* and his passes, especially since he and his brother were using these permits to line their pockets. Butler hastily explained to Secretary Chase that he was just trying to "open trade in cotton through the Rebel lines." He thought his actions were "consonant with the wish of the Government." He went on to complain that he had not been able to capture much cotton in Louisiana because the cagey Confederates were burning it before he could get his hands on it. He feigned disbelief at the disapproving attitude of Admiral Farragut and Navy Secretary Welles.[18]

Sounding much like Harris Hoyt, General Butler avowed that his motives were pure when he allowed the *West Florida* to pass through the lines. Not only were his passes beneficial to Northern cotton mill workers, they were a military necessity. He thought it was "infinitely of more importance to get the cotton even for our sails and tents than whether A or B loses or gains in the exchange of commodities." Butler glossed over the fact that "A" and "B" were two countries at war with each other. By assuming control of the illicit Texas cotton trade, Butler felt he was cutting out the middlemen and preventing "the Jews from gathering up all the gold in the country to exchange it with the Confederates for cotton." The general's derogatory comments reflected his attitude toward cotton speculators other than himself, and Jews in general.[19]

Using his civilian brother, Andrew Jackson Butler, as a front man, General Butler was well-experienced at enriching himself at the expense of the Army and the citizens of Louisiana. For example, the general banned the sale of liquor to his soldiers, but allowed his brother to buy up the entire inventory at discounted prices. The general then reversed the policy and helped his brother, and himself, make yet another fortune selling this same liquor to his soldiers. Additionally, his harsh confiscation practices against Confederate citizens who owned property within Union-occupied territory was akin to the wanton confiscation of Jewish property in World War II. There is little reason to doubt that General "Beast" Butler's motive for issuing his blockade running passes, while dressed in a humanitarian façade, was corrupt at its core.[20]

To prevent a potential whistleblower backlash from the owners of the

West Florida, Butler asked to have the schooner released and be permitted to proceed on its voyage. Secretary of War Stanton recognized the logic of that argument and informed General Butler that his request would be granted. Stanton reasoned that the *West Florida*'s owners had acted in good faith, expecting that the blockading fleet would honor the bogus Butler Pass. He then ordered General Butler to desist from issuing any future passes without first receiving permission from Washington. That kind of permission was never granted.[21]

Unaware of this negative change of policy in Louisiana, Prescott and Hoyt vigorously proceeded with their plans to obtain cotton from Texas. On the same day that the *Citizen* sailed for New York, Charles L. Prescott and Harris Hoyt drafted and signed an agreement documenting their 50–50 split of the profits with the four Providence partners. Surprisingly, the principal investors in the Texas Adventure never signed this nor any other contract with Hoyt or Prescott. As a result, Hoyt was about to set out on his Texas Adventure with a $100,000 investment in vessels and cargo, but no specified obligations on his part. It was an ideal contract.[22]

On November 6th, the Texas Adventure lost one of its members. On the day before the *Snow Drift* cleared New York Customs for Havana, Byron Sprague resigned from A. & W. Sprague & Co. He departed the company under a cloud. Although the reason for his departure was never specified, it may have been Byron's mishandling of the Texas Adventure accounts. Dishonesty or greed on Byron Sprague's part might explain the lack of any signed contract with Hoyt and Prescott. Distrust of Byron Sprague may also clarify why William Reynolds did not follow the agreed upon process for acquiring vessels when he bought the *Citizen* directly instead of having Byron handle the finances.[23]

On November 7, 1862, amidst the drama of Byron Sprague's withdrawal from the venture, the *Snow Drift* gained its clearance to Havana from the New York Custom House. The 30-year-old Joseph C. Witham was the captain and William Reynolds' agent, Henry B. Brastow, was the supercargo. The cargo was consigned to Charles L. Prescott, who was also listed as the nominal owner. Hoyt was onboard as a passenger.[24]

Prescott had spent a total of $5,500 to purchase the *Snow Drift* and get everything ship shape for a long voyage. Hoyt invested another $11,500 of the Providence partners' money on the cargo. She was only cleared as far as Havana for a number of practical reasons. The *Snow Drift* needed to stop in Havana for logistical purposes. There, she could replenish food and water for the crew before continuing on to Matamoros. More importantly, New York Customs officials were already becoming wary of vessels that openly declared that their destination was Matamoros, which actually meant that they were trading for Texas cotton.[25]

In 1861, only three brigs and six schooners had cleared directly from New York to either Matamoros or Brazos Santiago, the Texas port of entry for Brownsville. By the end of 1862, the annual total of vessels to these ports would grow to thirty-three. Even though their manifests and invoices said otherwise, it was obvious that the cargoes within these vessels were destined for—and the outbound cargoes originated from—the Rebels in Texas. To minimize the extra scrutiny from suspicious Union officials, many shippers used a broken voyage strategy. They would sail to a neutral port and then continue to their actual destination, in this case, the Spanish colonial port at Havana, Cuba before proceeding to Matamoros, Mexico.[26]

Prescott had paid duties on the *Snow Drift*'s cargo at the New York Customs House and Captain Witham had his clearance in hand. Unfortunately for them, John A. Kennedy, the New York City Chief of Police, got wind that something was amiss. There were certain items onboard the schooner that indicated the cargo was bound for the Confederacy. Those articles included the bagging and rope for baling Texas cotton. Plus, there were other items that were not even listed on the manifest that the U.S. considered contraband of war, especially the "revolvers, guns, and rifles, cartridges, caps, &c." Percussion caps were the small brass or copper cylinders that contained shock-sensitive explosive material used to ignite the powder in muzzle loading rifles and muskets; they were included among the list of contraband items that were generally categorized as arms and armament.[27]

The invoice of contraband goods that were not on the *Snow Drift*'s manifest specifically included six double barrel shotguns, ten Wesson's rifles, two pistols, twenty-one Colt revolvers, thousands of percussion caps, and rifle and pistol cartridges. Despite Hoyt's protestations that the arsenal of guns were for his personal use, Police Chief Kennedy seized the *Snow Drift* and took out the revolvers and other armament. Hoyt was only able to retain one or two guns and pistols that did not appear to be intended for resale. Prescott offloaded and packed the offending armament into trunks. Only after Prescott paid the Customs House for bonds that guaranteed the delivery of the designated goods to Havana, did Kennedy release the *Snow Drift*.[28]

The *Snow Drift* finally sailed for Havana on November 13, 1862, under Captain Joseph C. Witham. After a voyage of sixteen days, she arrived in Havana with Harris Hoyt as a passenger and Reynolds' agent Henry B. Brastow still listed as the supercargo. The looming presence of Castle

Morro (*Castillo de los Tres Reyes Magos del Morro* or Castle of the Three Magi Kings of the Moor) guarded the entrance to Havana. Initially constructed in 1589, Castle Morro was a monstrous fortress with tall towers, a lighthouse, and "teeth of guns." Inside the harbor, the crew had to weave their way through a forest of masts that formed a belt along the edge of the city. All the ships that were moored at the piers had their bows pointed toward the street. They were packed in "like horses at their mangers." The vessels that rode at anchor were so densely packed that they almost blocked passage to the Gulf.[29]

After entering the harbor, a Spanish health officer greeted Captain Witham and certified that the ship carried no infectious diseases, especially the dreaded yellow fever. The next Spanish official to board was the customs officer. He met with supercargo Henry Brastow to compare the passenger list with the passports and check the bills of lading. Only when all was pronounced clear could the passengers or cargo leave the schooner.[30]

The exotic port city of Havana was almost as bustling with activity as New York, but the political climate was considerably different. A letter written to a Houston newspaper editor in early 1863 describes the pro–Confederate sentiments of the Cubans at the time of the *Snow Drift*'s arrival. Havana's Hotel de Cuba was a "great resort for all rebels." Another "Confederate club room" provided the latest intelligence from all over the world to help them manage their blockade running and cotton trading business. As for the attitude of the Cuban residents, a Confederate correspondent observed that "The whole soul of the Spaniard is with us, and they are as anxious after the news of the Confederates' prosperity as we can possibly be."[31]

The cause of these amicable feelings had little to do with fraternal or cultural bonds between the Cubans and the South. War meant business. The Yankees were trying to stop all trade with the South, while the Confederates and their supporters were creating it. As an example of the blockade-driven boon to the Cuban economy, Henry Brastow sold the *Snow Drift*'s cargo to the Havana firm of Ulrici & Barroso. This sham sale was intended to document the delivery of the cargo to Havana and disguise the true ownership of the contraband that was intended for Texas via Matamoros. Despite the nature of the sale, Ulrici & Barroso collected their full fees.[32]

The cotton trade was rife with eager opportunists who naively entered the potentially lucrative blockade running business as novices. These gullible persons were susceptible to the many con artists who flocked toward the chaotic cotton trade. The market was ripe for manipulation and thievery, making the selection of a reputable shipping agent difficult. Given the amount of new business passing through the primary blockade running havens at Bermuda, Nassau, Havana, and Matamoros, finding an honest agent was a difficult challenge. Even the reputable Civil War era shipping agents were often inconsistent in the fairness of their dealings. Large, established customers had a better chance of getting a consistently square deal than newcomers to the business.

The 31-year-old Galveston blockade running captain and ship owner J.T. Burkhardt experienced some of the difficulties faced by small-time players in the Texas cotton trade at Havana. Burkhardt had completed a successful winter run from Galveston to Havana via Tampico, Mexico, in his sloop *Little Carrie*. After he arrived in Havana, Burkhardt wrote to his wife Anna in Texas. He told her that the prospect of running the blockade was so poor that he would delay another attempt until the upcoming fall or winter seasons. In addition to relaying depressing news about "this dreadful war," he asked his wife to warn other blockade runners that the Havana agent Gresser & Co. was "a swindling house." He had to remain in Havana where he could monitor their dealings closely to ensure they did not steal his cotton. Sadly for Anna Burkhardt, her husband's letter never arrived. When the blockading fleet intercepted the steamer *Isabel* as it attempted to run into Galveston Bay in late May, his letter was part of its captured cargo of arms, gunpowder, and medicine.[33]

After supercargo Brastow placed his trust in the more reliable Havana agents Ulrici & Barroso, he submitted a request to the American consul to transfer the schooner's ownership to Harris Hoyt. However, there were problems with the *Snow Drift*'s papers. The registered owner was Charles L. Prescott of New York. Although Hoyt identified himself as the *Snow Drift*'s supercargo, he was not. When the schooner arrived in Havana, the official documents only listed Hoyt as a passenger. Henry Brastow was the supercargo.[34]

Brastow's request immediately aroused the suspicions of U.S. Consul (and later Rear Admiral) Robert W. Shufeldt. On December 1st, the consul fired off a letter to Admiral Farragut advising him, "I think the Rio Grande deserves your attention next. The American schooner *Snow Drift*, of New York, arrived here lately from that port, and from certain mysterious movements and from the character of her cargo, I am inclined to think is bound to Matamoras [*sic*]. If you fall in with her, I am quite sure she would prove a legal prize. She seems to be one of those cases which renders it necessary to be watchful of our friends."[35]

Hoyt's intent became clear when Brastow applied for a clearance to Matamoros. The connection of Prescott and the *Ella Warley* with Hoyt and the *Snow Drift* led Consul Shufeldt to correctly surmise that both vessels were part of a scheme to run merchandise into and out of Texas. Unlike the Providence partners, Shufeldt quickly saw through Hoyt's deceitful character and the true nature of his Texas Adventure. However, Shufeldt, like all American consuls, had no legal authority to prevent shipments to this neutral Mexican port, even though he was certain that the cargo was destined for Texas.[36]

Shufeldt found another way to delay Hoyt and his schooner. There was an additional problem with the *Snow Drift*'s paperwork. Brastow's power of attorney to sell the vessel had not been notarized. The consul might have overlooked this technicality under normal circumstances. However, because the *Snow Drift*'s cargo included "contraband of war," Shufeldt denied the sale. Prescott had paid a bond in New York certifying that the cargo would be delivered to Havana which gave the American consul additional leverage. He forced Brastow to unload all of the bonded cargo, which meant that he had to pay additional customs fees. This inconvenience would at least delay the process and add to their expenses. As an added benefit, the forced delivery at Havana padded Shufeldt's personal pocketbook with extra tariff duties. The only cargo that remained onboard the *Snow Drift* was Hoyt's two old disassembled carding machines.[37]

Shufeldt also sensed that the intended voyage of the *Snow Drift* signaled a quickly developing trade route from New York to Matamoros and Texas via Havana. He reported to the U.S. Secretary of State, William H. Seward that "The principal trade now with the Confed. States is carried on through that Port [Matamoros] & it will be engaged in soon by more of our own vessels from Havana unless I am authorized to place upon it such restrictions as the Government may deem adequate." That restrictive authorization never came and the Texas cotton trade through Havana and Matamoros continued to flourish.[38]

Back in New York, Prescott was preparing the steamer *Ella Warley* for its voyage to Havana. In the previous month, Prescott had briefly considered leasing the *Ella Warley* to Commodore Cornelius Vanderbilt while the Texas Adventure partners were awaiting the permits from Washington, D.C., that never came. The steamer would have sailed as part of General Nathaniel Banks' expedition from New York to New Orleans, but Vanderbilt wanted an open-ended lease at a bargain rate. As a result of Prescott's decision to keep his steamer in New York, the *Ella Warley* was available to sail for Havana almost immediately. At the time, it seemed fortuitous that Prescott had not leased the Texas Adventure's steamer to Commodore Vanderbilt and General Banks.[39]

The *Ella Warley* was available to carry the rifles, revolvers, cartridges

4. The Texas Adventure Fleet   55

and percussion caps that Police Chief Kennedy had removed from the *Snow Drift* and take them to Havana. With Prescott's assistance, Hoyt had packed the firearms and ordnance into trunks. Prescott loaded the trunks on board the *Ella Warley* and listed them on the manifest as passengers' personal baggage. In addition to the 10 Wesson rifles and 21 Colt revolvers, Hoyt added another 34 hand guns for a total of 55 Colt revolvers. With the help of "a little gold persuasion with the custom house officials," the *Ella Warley* cleared customs without incident.⁴⁰

The Port of New York customs agents were among the most notoriously corrupt swindlers of the Civil War. In an era when the Federal government's primary revenue source was customs tariffs imposed on imports and exports, Treasury Department officials held important and lucrative jobs. It was a plum assignment both at home and abroad. The best assignments were most often doled out as a reward for political patronage. Much like the tax collectors of ancient times, a customs official could make as much money as the commercial traffic would allow. It was common practice for shippers to add a little extra "grease money" to lubricate the wheels of the bureaucracy, if the legal five percent cut was insufficient for prompt or advantageous clearances.⁴¹

President Lincoln had appointed Hiram Barney as head customs revenue collector in New York. Barney was a former law partner of Major General Ben Butler, but his primary qualification for the job was an I.O.U. from Treasury Secretary Salmon Chase for $45,000 that the secretary never repaid. Barney was not up to the task of managing so large an organization, particularly one with an institutional history of graft, abuse of public accounts, and an expectation of individual profit. He compounded his shortcomings by attempting to simultaneously manage his personal business that frequently required out-of-state travel. Following a Treasury Department investigation against several of his subordinates, Barney eventually resigned.⁴²

Governor William Sprague had a personal and professional relationship with Hiram Barney and the two men maintained a regular correspondence. The governor had invited the customs collector "and any other friends" he wished to invite to a "clambake" at Newport, Rhode Island in the summer of 1861. While Sprague was in the field with his Rhode Island troops during the Union siege of Yorktown, Virginia, he wrote Hiram Barney another personal letter. This one responded to a thank you note from the customs collector for a photograph that the war hero colonel had sent to Barney's admiring daughter. Sprague complained that he had "neither duties or [sic] responsibilities" under Brigadier General William Barry. He also confided the unsolicited observation that General George

McClellan "has alienated from him almost every prominent man in the army." Sprague was evidently referring to himself and his other prominent friends.[43]

Although there is no direct record of William Sprague asking the head customs collector of New York City for a favor, it is unlikely that such a request would have been placed in writing. It is clear, however, that somebody within Barney's New York Customs House received a bribe that allowed Hoyt's contraband armaments to proceed to Havana. Sprague's relationship with Hiram Barney may explain why Police Superintendent Kennedy and not the New York Customs Office seized the contraband cargo of the *Snow Drift*. Prescott steamed away from Pier 37 on the North River on the *Ella Warley* at noon on December 13, 1862. Although he was the supercargo, Prescott made the unlikely claim that he was unaware that the illicit arms were on board the steamer until after he saw Hoyt in Cuba. Perhaps he was distracted from his duties by personal concerns, for among the *Ella Warley*'s 12 passengers was Prescott's wife Frances. Their four children, aged from eight to sixteen, did not travel with them.[44]

Within a week, the *Ella Warley* arrived in Havana and Prescott sold its cargo to Ulrici & Barroso. Not surprisingly, this was the same company that was handling Hoyt's consignment and it was a firm that had excellent business contacts in Matamoros. Prescott then set about helping Hoyt with his problems with the *Snow Drift*. As the owner of record, Prescott transferred nominal ownership of the schooner and her cargo to an "Englishman" rather than to Hoyt. It was a typical sham sale.[45]

For a mere $100, Hoyt and Prescott now had their schooner under the protection of the British flag. The *Snow Drift* also had a new name: the "*Cora*." Hoyt selected the name in honor of his six-year-old daughter Cora Louise. Through a power of attorney, the nominal British owner had absolutely nothing to do with the management of the schooner and no share in any profits. Hoyt was now calling the shots, or so he thought.[46]

Hoyt's rationale for this change of name and registry varied depending on his audience. He told Union investigators that the reason for the sale was that the *Snow Drift* drew too much water to cross the shallow bar at Matamoros when fully loaded. Hoyt said the sale fell through at the last minute. He then said that because of the failed sale, Reynolds authorized him to receive the proceeds from the sale of the *Ella Warley*'s cargo.[47]

At another time, Hoyt said that the name change was "more to mislead the confederate [sic] spies in Havana and Matamaras [sic]." This was an absurd statement. The only officials who would have opposed taking contraband or milling equipment into Texas would have been the Yankees. The real reason for the sale had nothing to do with the schooner's draft, or misleading the Confederate spies.[48]

Before he even had left New York for Havana, Hoyt had intended to register the *Snow Drift* as a British-flagged vessel and sail it to Matamoros. Changing the registration of a vessel to a neutral flag was a standard practice for both sides during the Civil War. In a more candid moment, Hoyt confessed that he hoped that a British registration would make the *Snow Drift* "less liable to capture by the rebels if under the English flag." The change of colors, however, was not an act of patriotism for either side. Confederate owners also used the Union Jack to protect their vessels from the U.S. Navy's blockading fleet.[49]

Much to the Providence partners' chagrin, Charles Prescott also assigned a portion of the proceeds from the *Ella Warley*'s cargo to Harris Hoyt's account. Hoyt loaded the unsold portion of the steamer's cargo onto the *Snow Drift*. As a result, the Providence partners ended up owing additional money to Ulrici & Barroso. Although their partners in Providence lost money on these transactions, Prescott and Hoyt turned a profit. Ever on the lookout for an opportunity to "invest" other people's money, Hoyt tried to persuade Prescott to trust him with his share of profits. He proposed using the money to buy low cost slaves in Texas on Prescott's behalf.[50]

Hoyt also tried to negotiate another side deal while he was in Havana. He approached Addison Cammack, an agent for the steamer *William G. Hewes* that was laid up in Havana Harbor. Before the war, the *W.G. Hewes* had been part of Charles Morgan's fleet of steamers. Like the *General Rusk*, the steamer had been a frequent visitor to Texas ports. Also like the *General Rusk* (aka *Blanche*), the *W.G. Hewes* was rumored to be preparing to run the blockade.[51]

Cammack was a bear of a man, appropriately nicknamed "Ursa Major," who was well known for his brusque personality. He was also a partner with the Macaulay brothers and Robert Mott in the Confederate Bank of Louisiana. He may have assisted those men with their blockade running ventures involving the steamer *General Rusk/Blanche*. An opportunistic Rebel, Cammack had sponsored a Confederate ball on board the luxuriously fitted-out *W.G. Hewes* just before Hoyt's arrival in Cuba. The party was held to honor the new Spanish Captain-General of Havana, much to the great annoyance of the U.S. Consul General, Robert Shufeldt, who detested any recognition of the legitimacy of the Confederacy.[52]

The celebration on board the *W.G. Hewes* was only one of a series of events designed to sway international opinion in favor of the Confederacy in Havana. On December 15th, the Confederates hosted another grand ball at the home of Major Charles Helm, the Confederate procurement agent in Havana. Helm was well qualified for his job. He had fought in the Mexican war and served one term in the Kentucky legislature. Immediately prior to the war, he had been the U.S. consul accredited to both St. Thomas, the capital of the Danish Virgin Islands, and Havana, Cuba. Robert Shufeldt was the man that Secretary Seward had sent to take Helm's place.[53]

With his new allegiance to the Confederate States, Major Helm's job responsibilities included obtaining credit, removing trade barriers, making purchases, and influencing public opinion in favor of the Confederacy. He was very good at it, especially with the Spanish and British leaders in Havana. Among the guests of honor at his home were the officers of Her Britannic Majesty's men-of-war *Vesuvius*, *Immortalité*, and *Steady*. The Royal Navy reciprocated his kindness by supplying their ships' bands to provide music for dancing and entertainment. The office and home of Major Helm would become a "regular resort for all rebels." From this favored position, Helm was able to monitor the diplomatic tsunami that was rippling from the shores of Cuba, to the Potomac, and across the Atlantic to the Iberian Peninsula, and English Channel.[54]

When the *Snow Drift* first arrived in Havana, Vice Consul Shufeldt was still dealing with the political fallout over the USS *Montgomery*'s egregious violation of Spanish sovereignty. It was less than two months earlier that Captain Hunter had boarded and burned the Texas blockade runner *Blanche* after running it aground in Cuban waters. Spanish officials remained livid over this deliberate disregard of international law and insult to their flag.[55]

It is instructive to note that Consul Shufeldt discussed Harris Hoyt and the *Snow Drift* in the same report to Admiral Farragut that described the problems he was having with the Spanish over the USS *Montgomery* and SS *Blanche* incident. He appeared to be spending as much time trying to thwart Hoyt as he was trying to mollify the Cuban officials.[56]

The arrival of the *Snow Drift* in Havana also marked the time frame when Confederate officials were becoming aware of the scandalous conduct of one of their own quartermaster corps officers in the *Blanche* affair. With large amounts of cash passing through their hands, there were many opportunities for quartermaster mismanagement or outright corruption that would be familiar to modern auditors and inspectors. Such was the temptation that Confederate Major Thomas S. Moïse could not resist. Major Moïse's actions had complicated the Confederacy's prospects for restitution payments.

The contract that Major Moïse had signed the previous May called for his civilian partners to pay the Confederate government $50,000 in the event the *General Rusk* (renamed the *Blanche* at Havana sometime between June and August 1862) or its cargo were lost. However, when the *Blanche* went up in smoke, Major Moïse's civilian partners refused to pay. They argued that because the Confederate government had detained the *Blanche* at Port Lavaca in Matagorda Bay for a week after she had her cargo on board, they were not liable for the loss. Despite losing their steamer, the captain of the *Blanche* had salvaged some of the partially burned cotton, and sold it for $30,000. The real reason that the partners withheld payment to the government had little to do with their ability to pay; it was far more devious. The contract was not only a bad one for the government, it was illegal and fraudulent. It seems that Major Thomas S. Moïse had no authority to sign a charter party contract for the vessel. It was his own, private arrangement.[57]

Even if the partners had agreed to pay the $50,000 bond, the government would have recovered only about one third the value of the *Blanche*. The clever civilian speculators from Louisiana paid no rental or lease fees for the use of the vessel and crew, and there were no freight charges for hauling their cargoes. In effect, Moïse gave them free use of a government blockade runner that hauled their cotton and other cargo at no charge. The partners had then purchased munitions of war and medicines in Cuba and sold them to the Confederate Army in Texas at a profit. Even worse, as far as the Army was concerned, the profits from the first voyage all went directly into the pockets of the individual parties to the contract. No payments ever made their way into Confederate government accounts. However, Major Moïse was able to purchase a $25,000 home in Alexandria, Louisiana, with his personal 20 percent share of the profits.[58]

Like Commander Charles Hunter of the USS *Montgomery*, Major Thomas Sydney Moïse of the Confederate States Army Quartermaster Corps was found guilty at a court martial and dismissed from the service. Although not directly accused in the investigation, Moïse's commanding officer, Brigadier General P.O. Hébert, was also implicated. Hébert had been the Governor of Louisiana prior to the war. Soon after he assumed command in Texas, the general brought Moïse to Texas to be his assistant quartermaster. An ethnic Jew, Moïse was best known as a successful portrait artist whose subjects included Henry Clay, Andrew Jackson, and his boss, Brigadier General Hébert. Moïse was habitually in debt and often painted a portrait as payment for his overdue bills.[59]

Three of the other parties to the conspiracy, John and James Macaulay, and Robert Mott, also had come to Texas from New Orleans. The only participant in the *General Rusk/Blanche* contract who did not have a Louisiana connection was Houston resident Nelson Clements of the United Kingdom. Before the war, Clements had offices in New York and Galveston, but he retained his British citizenship. Initially, Clements escaped condemnation. He later became involved in a number of other dubious contracts that turned out badly for himself and the Confederacy. His predilection for shady government deals suggests that he was complicit with, rather that victimized by, Major Moïse and his partners. Clements would repeatedly prove that he had no qualms about using the courts to advance his personal agenda and would continue to press his claims against his partners in the *Blanche* affair after the war.[60]

General Hébert was removed from his command of Confederate forces in Texas on the day before the *Blanche*'s capture. The date of his relief was also just two days after the Union Navy's occupation of Galveston Harbor. Although Hébert's failure to defend Galveston was distressing, the timing of his departure appears to be coincidental and not directly connected to the illicit *Blanche* contract or the loss of Galveston. His replacement, Major General John Bankhead Magruder, was already in Texas preparing to relieve Hébert before the Union Navy entered Galveston Bay. General Robert E. Lee had exiled Magruder to Texas for his lack of aggressiveness during the Seven Days Battles in Virginia. It was a mistake he would not repeat.[61]

Brigadier General Paul Octave Hébert, portrait attributed to his quartermaster, Major Theodore Sydney Moïse (courtesy Collections of the Louisiana State Museum).

The tall, handsome, and always immaculately groomed "Prince John" Magruder was quite a contrast to his predecessor in demeanor, if not in appearance. Hébert was already unpopular with the troops for his autocratic manner. Similarly, the Texas Governor and merchants disliked his interference in the Texas cotton trade. Hébert had implemented a plan that required overland cotton shippers to purchase export licenses that had to be approved by General Hamilton P. Bee in Brownsville and the Governor of Texas. Shippers also had to agree to return to Texas with military stores. Texans were also unhappy with Hébert's strict enforcement of conscription laws. The investigation into the government's contract for the *General Rusk/Blanche* that led to the arrest and dismissal of Major Moïse may not have been the reason for Brigadier General Hébert's replacement, but it probably played a role in hastening his departure.[62]

In Richmond, Confederate Secretary of State Judah P. Benjamin hoped that Spain would collect reparations from the United States for the value of the *Blanche* and its cargo. The total came to about $200,000. In Havana, Charles Helm did not expect Major Moïse's fraudulent transfer of the *General Rusk* to John L. Macaulay to affect the Spanish claim. Helm was confident that he could collect the payment, especially if Spain ended up recognizing the independence of the Confederate States. It was another case of misplaced hope and confidence in the willingness of a friendly European power to risk creating an enemy by betting on the underdog Confederacy. The U.S. State Department said that it regretted the violation of Spanish waters and meant no disrespect to their flag, but rejected their claim for reparations.[63]

The controversy about the *Blanche* was still swirling around Havana as Harris Hoyt awaited clearance for the *Cora* to depart for Matamoros. With time on his hands to develop new schemes, Hoyt was undeterred by the loss of the former Charles Morgan steamer. Confident that he could do better, he contacted the former New Orleans–based shipping agent and cotton speculator, Addison Cammack. Hoyt's intent was to obtain a lease for Cammack's idle steamer, the *William G. Hewes*. The State of Louisiana had forced Morgan's Southern Steamship Company to sell this steamer to Addison Cammack and his partners in May of 1861. Unable to profitably operate the steamer themselves, the Louisiana partners were ready to sell, but not to Harris Hoyt. The Exporting Company of South Carolina eventually bought the *William G. Hewes* in April 1863, sailed the steamer to Nassau, and renamed her the *Ella and Annie*. Under that name, she made four successful round trip runs through the blockade.[64]

From his residence in Havana, Cammack was also the agent for the Confederate blockade running steamer *Matagorda* (renamed the *Alice*). The SS *Matagorda* was the steamer that had successfully run the blockade out of Sabine Pass at the same time as Hoyt and the sloop *Elizabeth*. The *Matagorda* would end up running the blockade at Mobile ten times and the Texas coast another eight. Hoyt's clumsy attempt to independently expand his blockade running operation on the cheap never got underway.[65]

Typical of a con artist, Hoyt consistently exaggerated the amount of money he controlled and he accentuated what could have been and not what actually happened. He boasted that he had refused an inflated offer of $60,000 in gold for the *Snow Drift* and its cargo. He also claimed that he had another offer of $8,000 in gold for just the vessel. These tales carried no weight in Havana. Hoyt had no funds of his own. Gold and silver were the only currencies that had any value in blockade running ports. As a partner of the swindling trio of Robert Mott and the Macaulay brothers of the *Blanche* conspiracy, Addison Cammack clearly recognized a fellow scoundrel when he saw one.[66]

Although he lacked Addison Cammack's insight, Charles Prescott declined Hoyt's proposition to purchase Texas slaves on his behalf. Instead, Prescott quickly reloaded the *Ella Warley* at Havana and departed for New York on Christmas Day, 1862. Hoyt expected to see him again at Matamoros within a few weeks. The *Ella Warley* and the schooner *Citizen* were supposed to meet him there. However, when Prescott returned to New York on New Years' Eve, the plan had changed once again.[67]

The Providence partners had decided to shift the Texas Adventure's port of entry from Matamoros to New Orleans. They believed that Major General Nathaniel Banks planned to invade Texas at the Rio Grande, which they presumed would cut off the Matamoros trade. Banks was preparing to relieve General Ben Butler and launch his operations from New Orleans. It made sense to sail the *Ella Warley* there as well.[68]

General Banks was a former Massachusetts congressman and governor who grew up working as a bobbin boy in a textile mill. It was his job to fetch fresh bobbins for the women at the looms and then collect the full bobbins of spun cotton or wool thread. Banks appreciated the importance of cotton to the North's economic well-being. He also had large personal debts with Governor Sprague. The general's indebtedness gave the Providence partners hope of gaining a favored position when it came to acquiring permits to trade cotton along the Texas coast. Governor Sprague's network of friends worked behind the scenes to help General Banks understand the advantage of granting permits. The fact that Banks had no legal authority to issue them and that General Butler had just been reprimanded for doing the same thing did not seem to factor into their reasoning. The ever-optimistic Texas Adventurers expected to get "a good slice" of the business by giving Banks a partnership in their scheme.[69]

Hoyt learned of this change of plans in mid–January 1863 via a letter from Reynolds' agent Henry Brastow who had returned to New York. Hoyt decided to ignore the agent's order. He had no intention of applying for a customs clearance to New Orleans. He had just gotten Consul

Robert Shufeldt's certificate confirming that he had landed all the bonded goods from the former *Snow Drift*. This certificate would allow the owners to recover the New York Customs' bond payment. After all the difficulties he had encountered with the American consul to clear for Matamoros, Hoyt had no inclination to alter his plans. Plus, it was much easier to cross goods directly into Texas from Matamoros rather than out of New Orleans.[70]

Hoyt reloaded most of the *Cora*'s goods that he had landed at Havana as a result of Consul Shufeldt's diligence. He complained that "The American consul has given us all the trouble he could and put us to all possible expense."

Portrait of Nathaniel P. Banks, 1862, from the cover of "General Banks' Grand March," sheet music composed by E. Mack and published by Lee & Walker, Philadelphia (Library of Congress, Music Division).

Hoyt also transshipped goods from the *Ella Warley*, and a few other items purchased in Havana, onto the *Cora*. Those items included a large amount of gunpowder. Hoyt's subsequent explanation for this additional contraband cargo was that he "could do nothing without such things" when it came to dealing with Confederate authorities.[71]

Hoyt's plans had to overcome resistance from the *Cora*'s captain. At first, Joseph Witham did not recognize Hoyt's authority over the schooner. Prescott was able to assure the captain that the *Cora* was indeed under Hoyt's "full and absolute authority." With the reluctant captain on board both literally and figuratively, Hoyt finally obtained a Spanish clearance and the *Cora* set sail from Havana for Matamoros about the 15th of January 1863. What should have been a layover of less than a week had stretched into a delay of almost two months in Cuba.[72]

Back in Providence, Rhode Island, the partners were not happy with Charles Prescott or the progress of the Texas Adventure. By the time

Prescott returned to New York on the *Ella Warley*, he and Harris Hoyt had been cut out of the steamer portion of the deal. The two men would only receive profits, if any, from the two schooners. Prescott believed that he had held up his end of the bargain, but had been wronged by both Hoyt and Reynolds. Prescott would not soon forget his treatment at their hands or their insinuations that he had cheated them.[73]

The revised plan called for the *Ella Warley* to sail to New Orleans under the direct management of W.H. Reynolds & Co. She would act as the consort for the smaller schooner *Citizen* and perhaps the *Cora*. They would use New Orleans, rather than Matamoros, as a base. Despite the change, Prescott still had an interest in the *Citizen*. He had participated in outfitting the schooner for a voyage before he departed for Havana in the *Ella Warley* in mid–December. The *Citizen* had remained in New York until after Prescott sailed for Havana.[74]

For most of the month of December, the *Citizen* sat idle at the pier in New York awaiting permits from either Washington, D.C., or General Banks in Louisiana. On December 23, 1862, ten days after the *Ella Warley* had cleared for Havana, the *Citizen* cleared for Matamoros, but it did not sail. The reason became apparent six days later, when she cleared for New Orleans instead.[75]

The captain's orders were to take the 95-ton *Citizen* up the Mississippi River and remain there without "breaking cargo." Reynolds wanted to leave the *Citizen*'s customs seals unbroken to avoid paying port duties for delivering the goods at New Orleans as Hoyt and the *Snow Drift* had just done in Havana. Governor Sprague and William Reynolds had brokered a gentleman's agreement with Major General Banks. The general would grant permits to trade directly with Texas if his campaign was successful in "opening some Texas port." In return, the Providence partners would charter their steamer to General Banks. If the *Citizen*'s cargo remained unbroken, New Orleans would become an interim stop, and not the destination of the goods. The captain could deliver the cargo in Texas as if it had sailed directly from New York. Prescott would have nothing further to do with her.[76]

Sprague and Reynolds hoped that New Orleans could serve as their operating base for trading with Texas. If not, it was unlikely that they would be able to profitably sell their cargo and purchase a load of cotton on the Mississippi River. The New Orleans market was focused on shipping cotton to Northern buyers, not selling the commodity at low prices to the universally vilified speculators.[77]

William Reynolds wanted Henry B. Brastow to manage the *Citizen*'s affairs in conjunction with the *Ella Warley*, just as he had done with the

Snow Drift. Brastow once again set sail as a supercargo from New York City, this time aboard the steamer *Ella Warley*. In the event there was no cotton to be had, Brastow's orders were to send the *Citizen* to Matamoros and buy cotton there. Reynolds specifically authorized his agent to sell the schooner if needed. Reynolds wanted the *Ella Warley* to remain "in New Orleans or its vicinity, if she can be profitably employed, either by a charter to the Government or for [the] owners' account." In New Orleans, Brastow could consult with William's brother Francis W. Reynolds, who was traveling with him as a passenger on the *Ella Warley*.[78]

At about 3 p.m. on February 9th, the side-wheel steamer sailed from New York for New Orleans under Captain George R. Schenck. Eight hours later, tragedy struck. The *Ella Warley* collided with the SS *North Star* off the coast of New Jersey. It was a bitter irony for the Texas Adventure partners. The *North Star* was one of the vessels that Cornelius Vanderbilt had chartered on behalf of General Nathaniel P. Banks. She was returning from New Orleans where the 1,867-ton side-wheel steamer had delivered the general and his staff plus a group of Unionist sympathizing Texans, and a large number of cotton speculators. If Prescott had accepted Commodore Vanderbilt's offer, the *Ella Warley* might have been part of General Banks' fleet rather than a victim of it. The *North Star* struck the smaller side-wheel steamer on its starboard side, forward of its paddle-wheel housing. The *Ella Warley* sank in twenty minutes. The human cost was seven lives and her cargo, valued at $29,600, was a total loss "without a dollar's insurance."[79]

For the Providence partners, their carefully woven plans for the Texas Adventure were now completely unraveled. The plan had been relatively simple up to this point, but when it came to execution of this portion of the plan, nothing was easy. Police and consular officials had constantly delayed and obstructed their shipments. The treasurer of the scheme had resigned from the partnership under a cloud. Most importantly, they had lost their steamer and its cargo that they had hoped to run into Texas and trade for cotton with the assistance of General Banks. The remaining elements of their plans were also in disarray. Harris Hoyt had defied their orders to sail to New Orleans and had taken off on his own. For Hoyt, however, his objectives remained clear. He had a ship, crew, cargo, and some cash at his disposal. All he needed to do was get into Texas, sell his goods, collect more money from the citizens there, buy cheap Texas cotton, get it to New York, and make a financial killing. Given the wartime situation, this daunting task would have been impossible for a less resourceful person, but Harris Hoyt was not to be denied.

5

Hot, Dirty, and Full of Fleas
At the Rio Grande

The Texas Adventure plans for coordinated steamer and schooner operations went down with the *Ella Warley*. The partners still had two schooners, but no steamer. Due to Hoyt's obstinacy, both he and his Providence partners were operating independently. Harris Hoyt and his partners were also ignorant of each other's movements and intentions. At about the same time that the *Citizen* arrived at New Orleans in late January 1863, Harris Hoyt and his newly renamed *Cora* were approaching and preparing to enter the Rio Grande. The schooner *Cora* arrived off the coast of Texas and Mexico and anchored amidst a virtual flotilla of ships. They filled the anchorage near the mouth of the Rio Grande (known as the Boca del Rio) with a thick maze of masts that covered the water for several miles out. While Hoyt's schooner lingered in the Gulf of Mexico, there were over forty merchant vessels offshore, plus an assortment of warships and lighters.[1]

Some of the anchored vessels and their captains were impatiently waiting for their agents to send them a load of cotton. The lucky ones were loading and unloading from lighters when weather permitted. These small craft were dedicated to transferring cargo to and from the deep draft vessels anchored off shore. They would then carry their freight over the sand bar protecting the entrance to the Rio Grande. A few of the lighters were steam powered, most only had sails, but they all had shallow drafts. Lighters usually offloaded their inbound cargoes at Bagdad, Mexico on the banks of the Rio Grande. Most inbound and outbound cargoes traveled to and from Bagdad by ox and mule carts. There were also several smaller river steamers that were able to navigate the notoriously crooked Rio Grande between Matamoros and Bagdad. Those river steamers included at least two of Richard King and Mifflin Kenedy's steamers that were capable of crossing the bar and steaming all the way to Matamoros.

5. Hot, Dirty, and Full of Fleas   67

Bagdad, Mexico, and the Rio Grande anchorage, gateway for the Texas cotton trade, by Myrna Ellison (author's collection).

After offloading their inbound goods at Bagdad or Matamoros, the lighters then loaded their cargoes for export. During the Civil War, those cargoes primarily consisted of compressed cotton bales. The lighters then re-crossed the shallow Rio Grande bar for a return trip to the waiting vessels at anchor, where the process was repeated in reverse. Weather was a major factor in the ability of the shallow draft vessels to efficiently go about their business. The anchorage had no protection from the elements, making it a hazardous one. The open waters of the Gulf combined with the volatile geo-political situation at the border often slowed or stopped the movement of lighters entirely. As a result, the vessels waiting offshore often had lain at anchor for months before they could complete the process of offloading cargoes and embarking outbound bales of cotton.

When Harris Hoyt arrived off the Rio Grande, he was among the many who worried about the process of getting his cargo safely ashore at

Bagdad, transporting it to Matamoros, and then crossing it into Texas. As expected, the heavily loaded *Cora* could not pass over the shallow bar guarding the Rio Grande. Her legitimate manifest showed a cargo of machinery, cotton cards, oils (kerosene, lard, linseed, and sperm), rope, gunny cloth and twine (for bagging and baling compressed cotton), hoop skirts, bleached and printed cloth, thread, needles, nails, tin, butter, mustard, candles, soap, patent medicines, pain-killers, copper, alcohol, brandy, and claret. The *Cora*'s secret manifest included weapons and ammunition, plus shirts, socks, drawers, pants, coats, jackets, fishing tackle, and ale, for a total invoice value of about $17,000.[2]

It was fortunate that the *Cora* was flying the Union Jack of the United Kingdom. Confederate soldiers and sailors were on the lookout for any vessel that was flying the Stars and Stripes. These vessels were easy prey for armed Confederate boating expeditions that launched from the shore. While Hoyt and the *Cora* were at the Rio Grande, a group of men that included the local Confederate Marshal Edward Martin decided to capture the U.S.-flagged schooner *General C.C. Pinckney*. The men waited for the schooner's captain to go ashore into Bagdad before making their way to the anchorage in a small boat. They surprised and overpowered the crew before running the schooner onto the Texas beach just north of the Rio Grande on a stretch of sand called Boca Chica. The men filed a successful claim for capturing and salvaging the vessel and its cargo of flour, corn, and coffee.[3]

After the schooner was refloated and safely anchored at Brazos Santiago just inside the Laguna del Madre, the profit-minded Confederate marshal offered the *General C.C. Pinckney*'s services to anyone who would give him and his partner an "interest in the adventure." A willing buyer could obtain the services of the schooner by giving a bond for $1500 in Confederate dollars, which was equivalent to about $150 to $185 in specie, i.e., gold or silver. John W. Jockusch and two other men from New Orleans decided to accept the marshal's offer.[4]

J.W. Jockusch was a naturalized citizen and a partner with the firm of R. & D.G. Mills of Galveston. He had been the Prussian Consul there since 1848 and would later return to Galveston in that capacity. Although the well-established Brownsville merchant Charles Stillman did not trust him, Jockusch became a successful shipping agent on the Rio Grande. Unfortunately for him, his gamble on the *General C.C. Pinckney* did not pay off. The schooner ran aground coming out of the lagoon as it attempted to cross the bar at Brazos Santiago between Padre Island and Boca Chica, and was a total loss. Jockusch was responsible for covering the $1500 bond on the schooner plus $28.50 in court costs. As the only partner still located in South Texas, a Confederate court forced him to pay the full amount in gold and silver rather than devalued Confederate dollars. The Confederate marshal and his partner pocketed the money, effectively netting an additional $1,350 through manipulation of the currency exchange and a friendly court.[5]

With the *Cora* and its crew safely under the protection of the British colors, Hoyt did not have to worry about a similar misfortune as he rested easy at the anchorage. However, they were still at the mercy of the wind and wave. The captain had to lighten the draft (depth of the keel below the waterline) of the *Cora* so it could pass over the bar and enter the port of Bagdad. Hoyt contracted with a lighter named the SS *Mexico* to ship a portion of the schooner's cargo. Earlier in the war, the *Mexico* had been part of Richard King and Mifflin Kenedy's steamboat fleet. They sold it to a Mexican citizen named Benito Vinas for the sum of $7,000 in June of 1862. Vinas used the steamer both outside the river and between Bagdad and Matamoros. Although Benito Vinas may not have been the true owner, this sale was a legitimate transaction. M. Kenedy & Co. would also sell and reflag, but retain beneficial ownership of five other Rio Grande steamers, the *Matamoros, Mustang, James Hale, Alamo* (as of October 31, 1863), and *Grampus No. 2*. With the SS *Mexico*'s assistance, the *Cora* was sufficiently lightened and Captain Witham was able to get the schooner over the bar and into Bagdad near the mouth of the Rio Grande.[6]

The Mexican City of Bagdad was "a mushroom city" that had sprouted up almost overnight to accommodate the cotton trade. The former fishing village now sported a multitude of rough wooden shanties that passed for hotels, boarding houses, and billiard-saloons or "rum mills," as they were called. These hastily knocked together buildings were no more than sheds. They were in danger of collapse whenever the sudden, gale-force winds rolled in from the north in a weather phenomenon known simply as "northers." Most of Bagdad's crude restaurants were even more flimsy. They were open to the elements. Their only protection from the sun and weather was courtesy of tarpaulins, loosely spread over poles to form a roof that was constantly flapping in the wind.[7]

This beachfront paradise was home to about four thousand transient souls and at least twice as many fleas. The presence of the human element of the population on those insidiously blowing and shifting sands was due to a single factor: endless bales of cotton destined for markets in Europe and the Northern states. While there was nothing exotic about the appearance of Bagdad, its population was "as heterogeneous as the dwellings."[8]

Bagdad had become a cosmopolitan collection of speculators, draft dodgers, merchants, and adventurers, all in "a whirlpool of business, pleasure and sin." In the streets, teamsters cracked their whips over teams of mules and oxen, and "horsemen, booted and spurred, galloped hither and thither." In the midst of this bustling frontier boom town, there were hundreds of opportunists out to make a quick dollar, some by hard work and others through moral or fiscal corruption. For the naive and inexperienced, "prospects of an advantageous trade in that direction were entirely visionary." As the novice blockade runner William Watson observed, everyone was trying to "grab what they could, and many schemes there were to make money out of the crisis."[9]

One of the first things Harris Hoyt did when he reached Bagdad was to find somebody he could trust, his twin brother, Horace. His brother was a recent widower from Morris, Illinois, and was in Mexico with his youngest son, the 17-year-old Thomas. Harris had placed his wife Marie and his two daughters at Horace's home in Illinois before heading back to Texas. Horace was operating "a cotton-pressing business at the mouth of the Rio Grande." The cotton press was a large wooden device with a vertical screw powered by steam or a team of horses or mules. As the animals walked in a circle, they turned the screw that had a plunger at the bottom. The crude plunger then forced the cotton into a rectangular box. After backing the plunger out, men would wrap and tie the compressed cotton with bagging and ropes. The baled cotton would then be marked with a unique brand to identify the owner. The concept was similar to cattle branding, but the cotton wrangler used India ink dye instead of a hot iron to make his mark.[10]

Although the minimum British standard weight for a bale of cotton at this time was only 400 pounds, Texas cotton was compressed into bales that typically weighed between 450 and 500 pounds. Cotton was sold by the pound and valued according to quality. The reason for compressing the bales was to make them as small and compact as possible. Smaller cotton bales were better able to fit into the tight confines of the holds and on the decks of the merchant vessels that carried them to market. One technique for boosting the apparent weight of the bales was to add wet cotton and rocks into the mix. This type of fraud typically would not be "discerned until it reached the manufacturers ... and was opened for use." While there is no direct evidence that Horace was falsely tipping the scales, events would show that he shared his brother's swindling propensities.[11]

Shortly after the *Cora* departed Havana, Hoyt's shipping agents in Havana Ulrici & Barroso, wrote a letter to José San Román. A native of Spain, San Román was a prominent and respected merchant and cotton broker who had offices in Matamoros and Brownsville. By the time the *Cora* reached Bagdad, San Román's clerk, Simón Celaya, handed the letters to Captain Joseph C. Witham and supercargo Harris Hoyt that he had been holding for them. Ulrici & Barroso had forwarded the letters to them from Havana via San Román. Although Hoyt never revealed the contents of the letters, they probably informed the men about the loss of the *Ella Warley* and Reynolds' continuing desire for Hoyt and the *Cora* to go to New Orleans. His Havana agents may have expected Hoyt to use San Román as his agent in Matamoros, but he did not. Hoyt's brother Horace must have had a different recommendation. Harris decided to consign the cargo to a British merchant named John P. Maloney, the principal owner of the Matamoros firm of Hale & Co. Maloney was probably the true owner of the steamboat *Mexico* that was registered in the name of the Mexican citizen Benito Vinas who served as the nominal owner.[12]

In this frenetic frontier environment, Harris Hoyt needed a broker like Maloney who was not likely to cheat a swindler like himself. Matamoros agents were well known for "the many acts of extortion practiced upon strangers ... in the general confusion of business." One of Hoyt's problems was that he did not have enough hard cash to purchase a full load of cotton for an outbound trip. He needed to sell his cargo to finance his purchases. Unlike most supercargoes, he was not looking to generate cash to purchase cotton in Matamoros for the benefit of his partners. He had his own uses for the money in Texas.[13]

According to the astute British military observer Lt. Colonel Sir Arthur Fremantle, Mr. Maloney was one of the most hospitable men in Matamoros. He welcomed visitors, "treating them to good wine and food." Maloney's home was a haven in a place that one U.S. consular agent described as "hot, dirty, & nasty, full of fleas" ... that was ... "over run with emigrants [*sic*], rebels, and other black legs [another nineteenth century term for people who steal from or cheat a gullible person] seeking to make fortunes as if by magic & ... will find themselves woefully mistaken." Perhaps more importantly, Maloney "was one of the principal and most enterprising British merchants" on the Rio Grande. Under his leadership, Hale & Co. had become one of the largest and most successful shipping agencies and steamboat companies on the river.[14]

John Maloney was one of the small group of men that Col. John Salmon "Rip" Ford had called together in March of 1862 to discuss how to respond to the *de facto* U.S. blockade of the Rio Grande. Other trusted participants in that meeting included Charles Stillman, his partner Mifflin Kenedy, Confederate District Judge Thomas Devine, José San Román, British Consul Louis Blacker, and George Oetling. Described as a "very nice fellow," Oetling was also the Prussian consul at Matamoros and a principal with Droege, Oetling & Co. throughout the war. He and his firm were among the most prosperous cotton brokerage houses in the Lower Rio Grande Valley.[15]

Their initial plan had been to sell the Texas Rio Grande steamers to Droege, Oetling and Mr. Maloney on behalf of Hale and Co. Some of the steamers were probably transferred to these men under Mexican flags, but M. Kenedy & Co. decided on an independent course of action. King, Kenedy, and Stillman had their own Mexican allies and registered their steamers in name of José San Román. All of the Texans retained beneficial ownership of the steamers for themselves. Instead of losing their vessels to Union forces, these men and their surrogates would sell, lease, and operate them for the benefit of all combatants. This strategic decision netted great profits for the Rio Grande ship owners during the American, French, and Mexican participation in the two Civil Wars fought on both sides of the river.[16]

Mr. Maloney was able to sell most of Hoyt's cargo quickly, receiving payment in gold. He also agreed to ship Hoyt's other merchandise to Texas. The official paperwork indicated that the goods belonged to Hale & Co., but the agreement stipulated that Hoyt would take possession when they reached Alleyton, the railroad terminus located west of Houston. Hoyt took this precaution to keep his name out of the shipping record and to ensure that he would have a claim against Hale & Co. if the shipment was lost or seized in transit. This load of commodities bound for Texas included his wool carding machinery, arms and ammunition, seven cases of bleached goods, one case of prints, another of hoop-skirts, thirty boxes of cotton cards, and some bagging and rope for baling cotton.[17]

When speaking with Union officials, Hoyt only admitted to taking a double-barreled shotgun with him into Texas (the gift for Governor Lubbock), plus a revolver and a rifle. With the exception of those personal weapons, Hoyt swore that he "never took any arms into Texas." This statement may have been technically correct, despite the fact that Hoyt sold the revolvers, ammunition, and caps to Confederate Colonel Philip N. Luckett at Brownsville. While it was Hoyt who sold the arms to Colonel Luckett, Maloney was the party who was responsible for transporting the weapons into Texas, and not Harris Hoyt.[18]

Hoyt's decision to purchase the Colt revolvers for the Texas market was no accident. It was well known that the Texas Rangers had favored the Navy Colt as their weapon of choice in dealing with renegade Native American Indian tribes. During the Mexican War, Luckett had served in Rip Ford's Texas Ranger Company as a surgeon. Prior to the Civil War, the Texas Secession Convention selected Doctor Luckett as one of three commissioners who successfully negotiated the surrender of U.S. Army

Colt 1851 Model Navy revolver presented to Texas Ranger John Coffee Hays (author's collection, courtesy Robert Swartz).

equipment and facilities in Texas. In appreciation for his work, the Bexar County Committee of Public Safety presented him with an engraved model 1851 Navy Colt revolver. The State then appointed Luckett as a colonel and assigned him to once again serve under Colonel Ford at the Rio Grande. By the time that Hoyt arrived at the Rio Grande, Luckett had succeeded Ford as commander of all Confederate forces at the border.[19]

Other than Luckett's assumption of command, all of these developments would have been known to Hoyt before he departed Texas in April of 1862. The *Cora*'s invoices and manifests do not specify the particular model of Colt revolver that Hoyt brought to Texas. However, the six-round .36 caliber, 1851 Model Navy Colt is the most likely candidate. This model remained in production until 1873 with over 272,000 built, many of which were sold to civilian clients. A few weeks after Hoyt sold the colonel his arms and ammunition, Luckett was promoted to brigadier general and was briefly transferred to Galveston and the Brazos River, where he could easily testify to Hoyt's claims of loyalty and his substantial support for the Southern cause.[20]

Although he was not mentioned in any of the contemporary travel-related documents, it appears that Hoyt's father-in-law, Samuel S. Bryant, may have accompanied Hoyt from New York. It is also possible that Bryant, along with Harris Hoyt's twin brother Horace, was already in Matamoros when Harris arrived on the *Cora* in late January or early February of 1863. During his two month stay at the Rio Grande, Harris Hoyt bought a pair of horses and a buggy for himself and his father-in-law with a portion of his profits. They rode as part of an ox cart train that carried his goods as well as other merchandise to Alleyton via Victoria, Texas. Fittingly, Hoyt's caravan began their trek on April Fool's Day, 1863.[21]

While Hoyt had been busy in Matamoros selling the goods that his Providence partners had bought and paid for, William Reynolds' agent, Henry Brastow, was following behind him to clean up the mess. When Hoyt left Havana in January, the accounts for the *Ella Warley* and *Snow Drift/Cora* were in arrears. The Providence partners still owed $1,333.32 to Ulrici & Barroso. The Havana commission agents informed Reynolds that the amount that he owed was too large for them to await the return of the schooner *Cora*. It is more likely that they correctly assessed the character of Harris Hoyt and never expected to see him again. They wanted their money up front.[22]

Reynolds also heard "Hoyt was raising the devil" in Matamoros and had taken off "on a private speculation into Texas." In response, he sent Brastow to the Rio Grande via Havana to investigate. He also directed Captain John Lancy to sail the schooner *Citizen* from New Orleans to join Brastow in Matamoros. Brastow's instructions were to sell the *Cora* and *Citizen* and whatever remained of their cargoes. His orders were to "close up the concern."[23]

Brastow tied up all the loose ends that Hoyt had left in Havana and, like Hoyt, continued his journey on April 1, 1863. After an uneventful voyage of almost two weeks, he arrived at the mouth of the Rio Grande aboard the British bark *Herbert*. At Bagdad, he found and took possession of the *Cora*. By the end of April, he had the *Citizen* as well. In Matamoros, Brastow confirmed that Hoyt had taken or sold all of the *Cora*'s cargo for his own use. Brastow then traded the *Cora* for an invoice of medicine. The new owner of the schooner was a person that he vaguely described as a Matamoros resident.[24]

There was good reason for Brastow's ambiguous identification of the buyer. The *Cora*'s nominal owner was a British citizen from Belize, but the true owner was the German immigrant and notorious blockade runner from Texas named Henry Scherffius. Scherffius was the same captain who had spirited Harris Hoyt out of Sabine Pass on the sloop *Elizabeth* back in April of 1862. The elusive Scherffius was reputed to have run the blockade 23 times. He would make several of those runs into Texas on the *Cora*. Over the next year and a half, Scherffius successfully delivered Texas cotton to the ports of Matamoros, Belize, and Vera Cruz.[25]

Captain Scherffius was so confident in his ability to sail the *Cora* through the blockade that before he departed Galveston on February 6, 1864, with 125 bales of cotton, he invited his friends to attend his wedding in Houston that was scheduled for May 5th. True to his word, he ran past the blockading fleet on the dark and cloudy evening of April 29th and came to anchor in Galveston Bay. On the day of his wedding, he showed

5. Hot, Dirty, and Full of Fleas

up with a huge cake that he brought with him from Vera Cruz, Mexico, especially for the occasion. Scherffius eventually sold the *Cora* in November of 1864. The next month, the blockading fleet captured the *Cora* and her new, less skillful captain. They had run out of Galveston Bay bound for Belize with another 175 bales of cotton on board.[26]

Back in Bagdad, it is unclear whether Brastow was aware that Harris Hoyt's twin brother, Horace, was still at the Rio Grande when he first arrived at Bagdad from Havana. Horace had decided to return to Illinois and was quitting the cotton pressing business. Upon his departure on May 24, 1863, Horace had control of 26 bales of cotton, 20 of which belonged to his brother. Harris Hoyt had purchased those bales with funds from the partial sale of the *Cora*'s cargo. Harris said that the cotton was intended for the Providence partners, but first, he had to repay his brother Horace for the extra fees he had paid to the lighters for loading his cotton (known as "lighterage") and seaborne freight charges from the Rio Grande to New York.[27]

Horace and his son Thomas Hoyt cleared from the mouth of the Rio Grande, aboard the British bark *Thomas H. Terry*. Three weeks later they were back in New York with their 26 bales among a load of 105 bales of cotton. Instead of delivering the cotton to William Reynolds, Horace sold it in New York and gave his brother "credit for the net proceeds" minus expenses still owed to Horace. The Hoyts rationalized their actions by claiming that Reynolds had treated them so poorly that the brothers deserved the money and not him.[28]

Even though the Hoyt brothers were probably upset by Reynolds' sale of the two schooners that would no longer be at their disposal, it does not justify their thievery. They could not have reasonably expected the two schooners to sit idle while Hoyt tarried in Texas. Harris Hoyt claimed that he did not learn of Brastow's intent to sell the *Cora* and *Citizen* until November 1863 when he was about to return to New York. However, Horace almost certainly wrote to Harris about the sale of the schooners at the border prior to his departure for New York in May. Brastow was the representative of the true owners of the schooners and it was his prerogative to sell the schooners especially since Hoyt had taken all the profits from the *Cora* for his own use. Additionally, Harris Hoyt had departed the Rio Grande for the interior of Texas over seven weeks before his brother Horace departed for New York. Harris may not have had enough money remaining in his account to cover expenses, but he took plenty of extra cash with him into Texas. Horace's sale of the cotton in New York netted a substantial profit that could have covered any excess expenses upon arrival. In short, it was William Reynolds & Co., and not the Hoyt brothers who were the aggrieved parties in these transactions.[29]

Salvaging what he could from the situation, Brastow sold the medicine he got from Scherffius in Matamoros and bought cotton for shipment to New York in the spring of 1863. Rather than using Hale & Co. or José San Román, Brastow consigned the *Citizen*'s cargo to Labatt & Joseph. These Matamoros merchants then sold the *Citizen* and most of its cargo for hard currency that Brastow used to buy more cotton.[30]

The *Citizen* departed the Rio Grande on June 13 under a different captain. It was loaded with 65 bales of cotton and six passengers that included a lady and her children. Among the adult male passengers was one named Henry Hoyt. He may have been related to Horace and Harris, or perhaps to the lady and her children. However, he was not identified in any of their letters or statements. It is also unclear whether any of the *Citizen*'s cargo of cotton belonged to Reynolds & Co. Nonetheless, Henry Hoyt and other passengers of the *Citizen* and its 65 bales of cotton arrived in New York Harbor on July 13, 1863. Upon setting foot on dry land, they found themselves in the middle of a maelstrom known as the New York City Draft Riots.[31]

The deadly riots were a working-man response to the Enrollment Act of 1863. It was an unpopular piece of legislation that authorized the registration and conscription of draft-eligible men. Two provisions in the act fed the prevailing sentiment that the conflict with the South was a rich man's war, but a poor man's fight. Congress had retained the clauses in the legislation that allowed wealthy men to pay for a substitute to take their place. Alternatively, draftees could simply pay $300 to the government for an exemption. New York's men of high standing, like Theodore Roosevelt, the father of the future president, took advantage of the first provision and hired a substitute. In Roosevelt's case, he paid his substitute $1,000 for the duration of the war. From a military and financial perspective, it was a successful piece of legislation that drafted thousands of men for the Army and raised over $12 million in exemption payments for the Treasury.[32]

The working men of New York City did not see it that way. The three days of riotous violence and burning only came to an end on July 16 with the deployment of the Army. Soldiers then fired live volleys into the angry mobs. Contemporary analysis put the toll at 400 to 500 killed, most of them innocent African Americans who were hanged or assaulted. Among those seriously injured was John A. Kennedy, the police superintendent who had delayed the sailing of Hoyt's schooner, *Snow Drift*. Kennedy was nearly beaten to death while trying to quell the violence.[33]

As the passengers and crew of the *Citizen* were dodging the mobs in New York City, the 35-year-old Brastow was eager to leave the Rio Grande Valley. It observed that it was "getting quite sickly here and as hot as they

5. Hot, Dirty, and Full of Fleas

make it." He had not, however, been able to sell all of the *Citizen*'s cargo. There was little demand in the market for the remaining "boots and brogans [a coarse, stout leather shoe], sperm oil, [and] blankets."[34]

The only way he could "close them out now would be by selling at auction at a low figure." Since Labatt & Joseph allowed him to use their warehouse at no charge, Brastow told William Reynolds that they should delay the sale until the fall. He believed that the market for these cold weather items would improve in a few months as long as "the Rio Grande is not occupied by federal forces." Brastow would prove to be a poor prophet.[35]

With no word from Hoyt and little prospect for profitable business in the near term, Henry Brastow departed sweltering, dusty Matamoros for New York. He left the unsold portion of the *Citizen*'s cargo in the hands of Labatt & Joseph. Brastow gave his agents instructions to dispose of the entire lot as soon as the market recovered, buy cotton with the proceeds, and forward the bales to New York. Before departing, he also made arrangements to ship another small lot of cotton. It was part of the 195 bales loaded on the British brig *Emma Dean* that cleared from Matamoros in late September and arrived in New York twenty days later.[36]

The *Emma Dean* was one of Charles Stillman's steamers. It had been making regular runs between New York and the Rio Grande since before the war under the name *"John Jewett."* Stillman and his New York agent had registered the steamer under the British flag. They also renamed the vessel in honor of Emma Dean Smith, the widowed wife of a longtime New York partner. That summer, Stillman and his surviving New York partners had avoided jail when congressional investigators could not directly link Stillman to the Texas cotton trade. He had sufficiently insulated himself from all the official documents and his alcoholic New York agent, John H. Donahue, had conveniently disappeared. For this trip of the *Emma Dean*, Charles Stillman rejoiced when there was a replacement in the New York Customs House. As a result, the partners were able to "bring a good deal of influence to bear on him." The owners of the steamer included Stillman and his son, along with Mifflin Kenedy, who had a one-eighth interest.[37]

By the time the *Emma Dean* arrived with his cotton, Henry Brastow was back home in Providence. He could point with pride to the job he had done in selling off the two schooners and a large portion of the *Citizen*'s cargo. The cotton that he shipped to New York as a result of those sales had a total value of between $60,000 and $70,000. He had not, however, been able to recover any money from Hoyt's sale of the *Cora*'s cargo. He told Reynolds that, in his opinion, Hoyt was "a great scoundrel."[38]

He may have been a scoundrel, but Harris Hoyt appeared to be on the verge of accomplishing the impossible. He had gotten his carding machinery for the Texas Manufacturing Company and armaments for the Confederate Army into Texas from the North. He had some cash in his pocket thanks to his Providence partners in the Texas Adventure and to Colonel Luckett who had already purchased his guns and ammunition for the Army. Now, all Hoyt had to do was set up the equipment, sell it, raise some more money, buy cotton, and ship it to the North. He would again discover that none of this would be easy, but it was all possible, as long as he remained flexible with the truth.

6

Double Dealing Cotton in Texas

After the delays and frustrations of Havana, the Rio Grande portion of Harris Hoyt's Texas Adventure had gone extraordinarily well. As he set off across the Texas coastal deserts and plains, he had to be filled with optimism. If this portion of his scheme went as well, he would soon be a rich man. In addition to the cash that he had earned from the sale of the *Cora*'s cargo, Hoyt also was carrying a significant amount of Confederate money that he had purchased at discounted rates in Washington, D.C. He knew that much of it was counterfeit, but the fake bills were printed using better quality paper than the genuine.[1]

While Brastow had been in Matamoros diligently tending to the *Cora* and *Citizen*, Harris Hoyt was equally busy advancing the Texas components of his plan. After a brief stop in Victoria, he made his way to a settlement on the San Marcos River named Prairie Lea. General Sam Houston had named the place for his wife, the former Margaret Lea. More importantly, it was the site of a gristmill and sawmill owned by Thomas Mooney.[2]

Upon his arrival in Prairie Lea, Hoyt immediately made arrangements with Mooney to set up the carding machines at his mill. Within three weeks of his departure from Brownsville, Hoyt took out an ad in the Houston *Tri-Weekly Telegraph* titled "Notice Extraordinary." Hoyt proudly announced the impending operational status of "two suits of Double Wool Carding Machines and Picker" located at "Prairie Lea, in Caldwell county, at the mills of Mr. Thos. Mooney, on the San Marcos river [sic]."[3]

In the same paper, Hoyt cited his charter from the Texas Legislature that authorized the formation of his Texas Manufacturing Company. The charter bolstered his credibility and gave him the confidence to announce that he had made arrangements to obtain another "cotton and woolen mill of any size or capacity desired." All he needed was cotton to pay for it.[4]

Hoyt told Texas planters that in return for their cotton, he would deliver the equipment and his manufacturing charter at their par value, i.e., its listed value of $250,000. His only desire was to help Texans become "more self-reliant ... manufacturing plantation goods, and producing in our glorious Confederacy every necessary of life we require." The newspaper's editor then echoed Hoyt's production claims and added the following enthusiastic endorsement: "We sincerely hope he will receive the encouragement he deserves in his enterprise."[5]

In a final patriotic exhortation, Hoyt's ad said, "With the sword in one hand and the plow and spindle in the other, and God on our side, we will conquer our Independence, and by economy, industry and temperance and the productions of our soil, the Confederate States of America may become one of the wealthiest—most independent and powerful nations on the globe, for if God be for us, who can be against us." Hoyt later told Reynolds that his traitorous, and some would say blasphemous, statements in the Houston paper were "a blind to the confederates [sic]" and did not represent Hoyt's true loyalties.[6]

Hoyt predicted that his wool carding machines would produce enough material to "keep one thousand hand spinning wheels going, supplied with rolls, and furnish filling for two thousand yards of plantation goods per day." This mechanical carding process yielded spools of wool that could be hand-spun into thread at a rate of ten cents per pound. The person operating the machinery was Hoyt's father-in-law Samuel Bryant. It took about three months for Bryant to actually get one of them started, but he injured his right hand in the process. He never got the other carding machine into operation. With a single device, Bryant was able to card about 50 pounds of wool per day.[7]

While his father-in-law toiled away in Prairie Lea, Hoyt traveled around Texas collecting Confederate money. He later claimed that he had gotten the money from his debtors and generously redistributed it to Union sympathizers in return for cotton. In fact, he was soliciting investment in his milling business and was buying cotton for export and resale. There is no evidence that he ever "redistributed" any of this money except for his own purchases. After he had collected over $80,000, he sold the wool carding machinery and charter to Wilson Bell (on behalf of Thomas Mooney) for another $84,000 in Confederate money, which was quite a bit less than its stated par value of $250,000. With that money and the profits from his sales of the *Cora*'s cargo, he bought about 270 bales of cotton.[8]

The only problem now was how to get the cotton out of Texas. The simplest and most direct method was to run the blockade or make maximum use of Texas' inland waterway. This system of interconnected coastal bays and lagoons was very shallow. The inland waters were also relatively

6. Double Dealing Cotton in Texas 81

calm due to the protection of a series of long, narrow sand islands. These islands formed a protective barrier from the more turbulent waters of the Gulf of Mexico. Water transport through this corridor was much faster and cheaper than hauling it all the way to the Rio Grande by land. During the early years of the Civil War, small sloops and schooners with retractable centerboards could navigate from Matagorda Bay to the southern reaches of Corpus Christi Bay. Major General Magruder described the importance of this maritime route "which makes us independent of the blockade as long as we can hold these passes [Cavallo and Aransas]."[9]

Centerboard schooners were ideally suited for these waters. They were equipped with a pivoted wooden extension that the crew could lower through its keel. It reduced sideways movement when they were in deeper water and captains could raise the centerboard when passing through shallow channels and bays. Vessels like this with very shallow drafts of less than three feet could sometimes sail past Corpus Christi as far as Penascal. A transshipment point for goods bound for Brownsville, Penascal was located at the southern entrance to Baffin Bay. It was the southernmost point of the inland waterway and was equipped with an extended pier for loading cargo.[10]

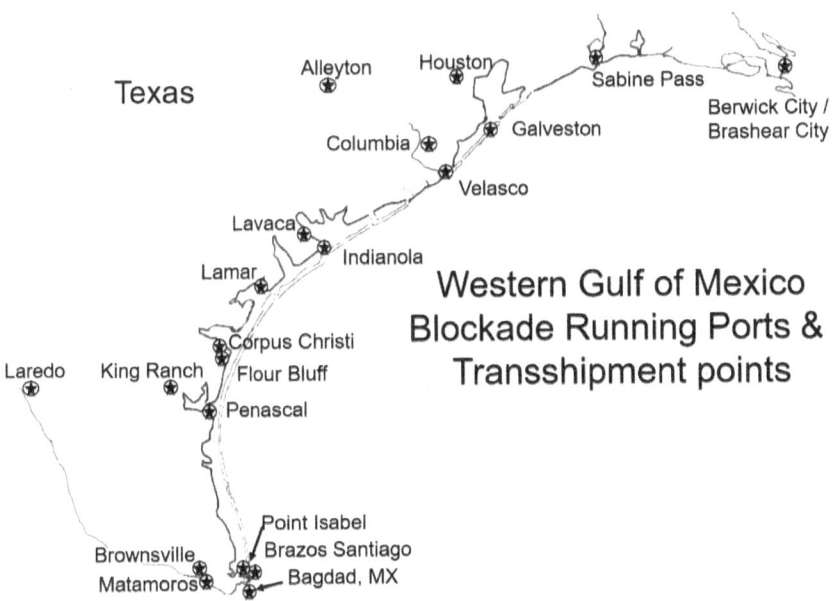

Western Gulf of Mexico blockade running ports and transshipment points (author's map).

Unfortunately for Texans and the Confederacy, not even vessels with drafts of less than three feet could go any farther than Penascal. If a shipper did not want to risk running the blockade, all cotton transported via the inland waterway had to be loaded onto wagons at some point and then hauled overland to the Rio Grande. In March 1862, the Texas State Military Board designated Richard King's Santa Gertrudis Ranch, located about 45 miles southwest of Corpus Christi, as an official depot for receiving, storing, and shipping cotton. The King Ranch was the last vestige of civilization before making the 125 mile trek across the Wild Horse Desert to Brownsville.[11]

This overland leg was the most difficult and dangerous portion of the trip. Practically every creature in this sandy wasteland threatened to bite or sting the teamsters and their animals. For those who did not first die of exposure, thirst, or starvation, there were plenty of bandits and renegades eager to steal their cotton at the point of a gun or knife. The route out of San Antonio was no less dangerous. Shortly after Union forces occupied the South Texas coast (November 1863–June 1864), Major General Napoleon J.T. Dana issued a deadly secret order. It was Dana's "desire to make the road from San Antonio to Eagle Pass and Laredo so perilous that neither Jew nor Gentile will wish to travel it. Please make this known, confidentially only, to good, true, and daring men. I wish to kill, burn, and destroy all that cannot be taken and secured." The hardy few who made it past these obstacles to the Rio Grande earned every penny of their wages and often left a malodorous trail of dead mules and oxen in their wake.[12]

Hoyt said that he purchased an unnamed inland waterway sloop at Matagorda using his own funds. He never seemed to acknowledge that he had no funds of his own. He was only able to generate income by selling goods purchased by his Providence partners. Hoyt said that he used this unnamed sloop to transport 34 bales of cotton from Matagorda Bay to Flour Bluff, a port on Corpus Christi Bay. His purported intent was to deliver the cotton to United States troops there, which was another manifestly absurd assertion. Federal troops did not occupy that portion of the Texas coast until mid–November of 1863, after Hoyt and his cotton were on their way out of Texas and into Mexico. It is more likely that Hoyt's cotton made the overland haul of over 120 miles from Flour Bluff to Brownsville and the Rio Grande via the King Ranch.[13]

The fastest, least expensive, but highest risk option for exporting cotton was blockade running. Hazardous gambles appealed to Hoyt's nature, so it was natural that he planned to accompany his cotton during the attempt to run it through the blockade. In June of 1863, the blockading fleet had eight vessels available to cover the Texas coast. Two of those eight

6. Double Dealing Cotton in Texas 83

were dedicated to the main channel out of the northern end of Galveston Bay. These few warships were not enough to effectively blockade the Texas coast. After a blockade runner had loaded its cotton and obtained the necessary permits, its captain could reduce the risk of capture by waiting for a night when the coast was clear of warships or the visibility was low. It was an advantage that made it very difficult for the eight ships of the blockading fleet to detect a vessel as it departed port.[14]

Before a vessel could attempt to run out of a blockaded port, the ships' captains first had to pay the appropriate customs fees and receive the necessary health and military permits, just as they had done in peacetime and at neutral port destinations during the war. The same customs and permitting process applied to overland trade when merchants exported goods across the Rio Grande and into Mexico. Maritime commerce in the presence of a blockade was difficult and dangerous, but the government still collected import and export fees. If the vessel was captured there were significant financial consequences for the owners of the vessel and its cargo, but not because they were breaking the law by engaging in smuggling.

The United States could not legally charge the owners of a vessel or its cargo with smuggling if they had paid the requisite customs duties at the vessel's port of origin and destination. Blockade runners to and from Confederate ports usually paid all of these fees, and they had the appropriately stamped customs clearance forms to prove it. A blockade is a belligerent act that can only be declared against another country; it is not a device that a nation can use against its own citizens. Therefore, when President Lincoln declared a blockade against the South, the international community automatically recognized the Confederate States as a belligerent nation-state. The contemporary rhetoric from Union authorities, however, refused to officially acknowledge the "so-called" Confederate States. In the eyes of Union officials, the insurrectionary states were in rebellion. There was no Civil War and the Confederacy was not a legitimate country. They knew better, but it did not serve the Union's political purposes to publicly acknowledge the fact.[15]

This contemporary narrative regarding blockade running has muddied the more modern understanding of the distinction between blockade running and smuggling. The term "smuggling" refers to the illegal movement of goods into or out of a country. Blockade running is an act of defiance against a barrier maintained by force of arms. If a neutral vessel attempted to pass through the blockade without a permit, it was breaking no law, foreign or domestic. When the United States declared a blockade against the Southern states, it committed an act of war against a *de facto* belligerent nation. Contemporary international law stipulated three basic requirements for a blockade to be legitimate. The aggressor nation, i.e., the United States, had to properly announce the blockade, enforce it with a credible deterrent of armed forces (usually warships), and continuously maintain it at the relevant ports.[16]

While blockade running was not smuggling, there were legal and financial consequences for those vessels and their cargoes and crews if the U.S. blockading fleet captured them in the process of running the blockade. A captured vessel and members of its crew that were suspected of running the blockade were brought before an admiralty court for adjudication. Whenever the court ruled that a captured vessel was guilty of attempting to violate the blockade, the finding was condemnation. If the vessel and cargo were condemned, the government would temporarily confine its neutral crew members. Through the local U.S. marshal, it would seize both the vessel and its cargo and then sell them both at public auction. There were variations and degrees of condemnation when only a portion of the cargo was condemned. The courts would sometimes release a vessel and its cargo but refuse to pay the owners any reparations for extra expenses. In these cases, the evidence had convinced the judge that the blockading fleet had a legitimate justification for seizing the vessel, but insufficient evidence to condemn it.[17]

Captured sailors who were citizens of the Confederate States could be imprisoned or exchanged as belligerents, while U.S. citizens were subject to being tried as traitors. Blockade running crewmen or owners were not, however, charged with smuggling. While there were numerous instances of smuggling into and out of both the Union and Confederacy, most of the cotton trade out of Texas and the rest of the South did not constitute smuggling.

If a vessel successfully evaded the blockade, its owners and their agents were free to conduct business in any neutral port. They also were not subject to future seizure or prosecution due to past blockade running activities. To avoid legal problems for trading directly with the enemy, American ship owners and merchants had to use intermediaries. As long as the vessel's papers could verify that the owners of the vessel and its cargo were citizens of neutral countries, there would be no violation of the laws of the United States.

For an admiralty court to uphold a seizure, there had to be sufficient evidence of enemy ownership of the vessel or cargo or that it had originated from or was bound to a Confederate port or buyer. Neutral vessels, crews, shipping agents, and ports provided an artificial, but technically lawful conduit for trade between the North and South. Although this process added layers of cost and obscured the true nature of the transaction, most of the Confederate cotton that departed Texas and was destined for a United States port, did so quite legally, if somewhat surreptitiously.

The legal aspects of blockade running did not deter men like Harris Hoyt. The key to success was to avoid being caught, and that required a good sea captain. As he prepared to run his cotton through the blockade, Hoyt sent a special request to Major Simeon Hart on July 24, 1863. Major Hart was the Confederate War Department's cotton agent in Texas. Hoyt hoped that Major Hart could obtain a furlough for William R. Evans, who had been conscripted into the local Galveston Coast Guard Company. Hoyt had made arrangements with Evans to take charge of a schooner that was now loaded with his cotton. Hoyt planned to take personal charge of another schooner that was in the process of loading, but he needed Evans right away for his first schooner.[18]

A competent captain was a necessity and not just for his ability to ensure the safety of the vessel, cargo, and crew against the dangers of the sea. In peacetime, a really good captain had to be skilled at keeping water under the keel and paint on the sides of his vessel. During the Civil War, he had to be adept at eluding and escaping from the Union blockading fleet as well. As illustrated by the capture of the schooner *Cora* after Henry Scherffius had sold her to another captain, there were numerous instances of blockade runners that made multiple successful runs until a new captain took command. The new captain often found himself in the clutches of a U.S. gunboat on his first voyage.[19]

Darwinian survival principles helped eliminate the incompetents, but there was another type of poor sea captain: one who lacked integrity in the face of temptation. William Watson, the owner of the schooner *Rob Roy*, discovered this unfortunate truth after he had successfully run into the Brazos River from Matamoros in September of 1863. Watson had purchased his center-board schooner at New Orleans that spring and sailed it to Belize to obtain a permanent British registration. From Belize, he stopped at Matamoros in an unsuccessful attempt to acquire some cotton that he could haul to Havana.[20]

The trusted captain who had sailed Watson's *Rob Roy* to Belize and the Rio Grande was Henry Laverty, a 45-year-old Irishman. Standing only 5 feet 5½ inches, Laverty had been dutifully practicing his maritime trade out of New Orleans since 1849. The *Rob Roy* was the second schooner that he had commanded since the outbreak of the Civil War. The 109-ton schooner *C.P. Knapp* was the first. On Laverty's second wartime voyage on the *C.P. Knapp* in August of 1861, the U.S. blockading fleet captured him as he sailed the British-flagged schooner from Brashear,

Louisiana, to Havana. The Navy prize crew took him and his schooner to the Admiralty Court in Key West. Fortunately for Laverty, he was soon released. By October he was back in command of the *C.P. Knapp* and once again on his way to Havana. He then sailed her to the Rio Grande in January 1862 and loaded the *C.P. Knapp* with 150 bales of cotton bound for Havana.[21]

Laverty stayed with the *C.P. Knapp* through September of 1862. He then signed on as the captain of the *Francis Marguez, Jr.*, and sailed the smaller, 48-ton schooner to the Rio Grande late that winter. He returned to New Orleans with 23 bales of cotton on April 4, 1863. On May 19, Captain Laverty again cleared his schooner from New Orleans, but this time there was a new name painted on the stern, the *"Rob Roy."* Laverty was headed for Belize with a cargo of molasses, pork, lime, nails, tar, shingles, and seven packages of general merchandise. Sailing with him was the new owner and supercargo, a British citizen and former Confederate soldier named William Watson.[22]

From Belize, the Henry Laverty sailed the *Rob Roy* to the Rio Grande in July 1863. When he arrived, he wrote to José San Román. He told the Brownsville and Matamoros merchant that the *Rob Roy* was ready to take eighty bales of cotton to Havana. The captain agreed to ship the cotton at a rate of 2½¢ per foot, provided that San Román had it ready to load within eight days. Laverty made it clear that he was writing on behalf of the *Rob Roy*'s owner, a man that he identified as "William Watson."[23]

When it became clear that neither San Román nor anybody else at Matamoros would provide him with a load of cotton for Havana, Watson decided to try his luck running the blockade into Texas. Henry Laverty appears to have had enough of blockade running and Yankee prize courts through his experience with the *C.P. Knapp*. He and most of his crew understandably refused to stay with the *Rob Roy*. Watson was forced to hire a new captain in Matamoros and take on a new partner to help pay expenses. Unfortunately for William Watson, the pickings of available captains were limited. He eventually found a suitable candidate in another Irishman, a powerfully built man who had served as first mate on a British-flagged bark. The man was qualified as a ship's master, able to recruit a crew, and willing to run the blockade. After he had signed the shipping papers, Watson received a warning that his new captain was a man of poor character, but it was too late to make a change. There were no other available options.[24]

Shortly after departing the Rio Grande for Texas in mid–September, the new captain became seriously ill with yellow fever. The pugnacious first mate, and former shipmate of the captain aboard the British bark, took command of the *Rob Roy*. William Watson, who knew how to use a sextant and chronometer, took over the navigation duties. When a Union Navy warship stopped the *Rob Roy* off the coast of Texas, the boarding officer beat a hasty retreat when he learned that the dreaded yellow fever was on board. The next day, as the *Rob Roy* approached the Brazos River and headed toward shore, a different Union gunboat opened fire. One of the shots ricocheted and skipped across the water several times before it struck the *Rob Roy* at the waterline. Despite taking on water, the schooner safely made it over the bar, past the forts, and into the river with the remnants of her original cargo, plus a small consignment of wine.[25]

After salvaging the undamaged goods upriver at the railhead city of Columbia, Watson had to make several trips to Houston and Galveston to meet with the agent who had arranged the *Rob Roy*'s cargo consignment and with Confederate customs officials. While he was away making arrangements to acquire a load of cotton, Watson discovered that the Confederate Army had taken control of his schooner. They were using the *Rob Roy* to install obstructions to prevent the Union Navy from entering the Brazos River. It took the intervention of the British consul at Galveston, Arthur T. Lynn, but Watson eventually managed to recover his schooner a few weeks later.[26]

Having repaired and loaded the *Rob Roy* with cotton, Watson went to Galveston for a customs clearance. When he returned, he found his schooner resting at the bottom of the river. It had sunk at the pier. His captain, only identified as "Captain J.," had fully recovered from his illness and saw an opportunity to capitalize on Watson's misfortune. Captain J. and his co-conspirators had gotten a corrupt official to declare the schooner as "abandoned." The *Rob Roy* was now facing condemnation to be sold at auction. Captain J. then offered to buy the schooner from Watson at a fraction of its value. The burly Irishman strongly advised him to accept the offer. Watson refused and soon had the schooner afloat and ready for sea on his own. Captain J. was furious. He drunkenly attacked Watson with a knife, but failed to kill him. Thanks to the timely and forceful intervention of a "Captain S.," Captain J.'s cutthroat friends were unable to come to his aid. Captain "S." may have been Commodore Leon Smith of the Texas Marine Department, but he was most likely Harris Hoyt's former benefactor, Captain George Henry Scherffius, who was in the area during this time. Captain Watson sent Captain J. scurrying away, and took command of the *Rob Roy* himself.[27]

While William Watson was dealing with his scheming Captain J., Harris Hoyt was pleased to have the much more reliable 28-year-old William Evans as his captain. Evans, like Watson's Captain J., was originally from County Cork in Ireland. Unlike his devious countryman, Evans' reputation was sterling. He had just moved to Galveston from New Jersey with his wife and two young daughters less than a year before the outbreak of war. He quickly established himself as a merchant and employed two clerks as part of Evans & Co. He was an active participant in community activities and was a founding member of Galveston's Young Men's Christian Association. The six-foot-tall Evans had performed well while under hostile fire during the Battle of Galveston on New Year's Day 1863. He had been part of a small, hand-picked company of trusted bodyguards for Major General Magruder during the attack.[28]

Evans was also a friend of the Confederate Customs Collector James Sorley, who had been his co-founder of the Galveston YMCA. It was an important relationship that the politically astute Harris Hoyt would exploit. The 43-year-old James Sorley was a former Galveston City alderman (equivalent to a councilman representing a specific district of the city) and a principal partner in one of the largest commission merchant firms in the South. He was Galveston's collector of customs for the duration of the Civil War and assistant chief of the Texas Cotton Bureau for the Confederate States. In the latter position, Sorley was responsible for holding all public funds collected in the state for the Bureau. He was so prominent in the city that when the Confederacy seized the Union Revenue Cutter *Henry Dodge*, they renamed it the *Mary Sorley* in honor of his wife.[29]

Hoyt, who was no seaman, pleaded with Major Simeon Hart for Captain Evans' services immediately. Since the moon was on the wane, Hoyt wanted to take advantage of a moonless night at the end of the month. When Hoyt wrote his request for Evans' services on July 24, 1863, the moon was actually waxing. The full moon would appear on July 30th. To strengthen his case for procuring William Evans as his captain, Hoyt also related the Southern version of his oft-told story that highlighted his altruistic motives.[30]

Hoyt reminded the major that he had a charter for a cotton factory and had returned to Texas from the North with his carding machinery. He added a few treasonous details to the letter that he omitted when speaking with his Union friends and inquisitors. Hoyt claimed credit for getting both the *Cora* and *Citizen* into Matamoros with cargoes for Texas and for providing arms and ammunition to Colonel Luckett. He promised to return to Texas with cotton ginning equipment that he would add to the wool carding operation at Prairie Lea. He also offered to honor any shopping list that the Texas Quartermaster's Office might have for him.[31]

Harris Hoyt had learned his lesson from William Watson's infamous confrontation with Captain J. and his own dealings with Captain Joseph Witham of the *Snow Drift/Cora*. He knew that it was important to select a trustworthy and loyal captain. Blockade running was a risky business, particularly for those who gambled with their lives aboard the ship. Ship captains who were willing to accept that kind of risk often had no problem bending the truth and cheating their bosses as well. Unlike William Watson's Captain J., most never tried to kill the ship owner, but many would seize any opportunity that came their way if it meant personal profit at little risk to their own safety. Even experienced merchants like Charles Stillman and his New York partners were subject to the fraudulent dealings of their captains.

In October 1863, Stillman and his partners contracted with Captain G.B. Maggio of the 502-ton Italian sailing ship, *Carioca*, to carry 905 bales of their cotton to New York. With Jerry Galvan acting as their surrogate, they chartered all of the ship's cargo space. The agreed upon shipping rate was 2¾¢ per pound of freight that was payable in greenbacks (a "greenback" was the U.S. paper currency of American Civil War era that was printed in green ink on the back). Captain Maggio, however, got a better offer while he was ashore in Bagdad. Another shipper was willing to pay him 4¢ per pound in gold for hauling 100 bales of cotton. At the going currency exchange rate, 4¢ in gold was worth about 6¢ in greenbacks.[32]

The lure of an extra $1,600 in his pocket was too great for Captain Maggio to refuse. He left 100 bales of Stillman's cotton on the Mexican beach in early November 1863 and arrived in New York Harbor twenty-three days later. When Stillman discovered the deception, he retrieved his cotton from Bagdad and shipped it out on his own full-rigged sailing ship, the *Banshee*. Fortunately for Stillman, his partners also discovered the discrepancy when the *Carioca* and Maggio arrived in New York. Communicating through another surrogate, José Morell, the partners informed Stillman that they had refused to pay Captain Maggio until he reimbursed them the difference in the freight charges for his unauthorized cotton exchange, the full $1,600. They also forced the captain to forfeit his charter and planned to claim any difference in market prices when the remainder of their cotton arrived in the *Banshee*.[33]

The captain, however, was not pleased at this turn of events and had a "nice little rattle" with the New York businessmen. They were prepared for a long legal battle, and they were confident that they could outlast the Italian captain. The partners told Stillman "You know this is fighting times and we are bound to have a fight from him [Captain Maggio]." Fortunately for Captain Maggio, the price of cotton was higher when the *Banshee* arrived and they managed to settle all accounts by early March of 1864.[34]

Hoyt's false sense of urgency for getting Evans underway in his schooner was of no matter. It took almost three weeks for his letter to make its way through the Confederate bureaucracy, traveling from Houston to San Antonio, and back to Brazos County. Hoyt did, however, gain the necessary approvals from five different officers, including three generals. Two of them were Brigadier General William R. Scurry, Commander of the Eastern Sub-District of Texas, and Brigadier General Elkanah B. Greer, Chief of Conscription. A veteran of the New Mexico campaign and the Battle of Galveston, General Scurry was camped northeast of Houston at Millican City as General Magruder's representative. General Greer was from Marshall, Texas, but served with Kirby Smith in Louisiana. The third and most senior endorser was Lieutenant General E. Kirby Smith, who was the overall commander of the Trans-Mississippi Department. Hoyt's letter also had endorsements from Captain Charles G. Wells, the Cotton Bureau's quartermaster agent in Houston, and Major Simeon Hart in San Antonio.[35]

The two schooners that Hoyt mentioned in his letter to Major Hart turned out to be the *America* and the *Lehman*. William Evans would captain the *America* and Hoyt would follow with his father-in-law, Samuel Bryant, in the *Lehman* as supercargo. When word filtered back to Rhode Island about Hoyt's blockade runners, there was some, probably deliberate, confusion about vessels' names. At various times, Hoyt's partners named the two schooners as the *Lamon*, *Lamar*, *Zara Gorsher*, *Zeragona*, and *Zaragossa*. The *Lamon* and *Lamar* were probably misspellings of the more fully documented schooner *Lehman*. There was a Texas sloop named *Belle of Lamar* operating in Aransas Bay in 1862, but it was the wrong type of vessel and there is no indication that it was still in service by July–August 1863. The schooner *Lehman* that would carry Hoyt's cotton had arrived in Galveston via Lake Charles, Louisiana, Tampico, and Matamoros. Daniel Goos of Louisiana and Samuel Loeb of Galveston were joint owners.[36]

The antecedents of the *America*, however, are less certain. There is no record of any vessels with the names *Zara Gorsher*, *Zeragona*, or *Zaragossa*, or their phonetic equivalents operating along the Texas coast during this timeframe. It is possible that one of those names belonged to the schooner *America* at some point, but it is more likely that Hoyt's partners were simply confused or misled. There was a Dutch bark with a somewhat similar name of *Geziena Hilligonda* that was captured off the Rio Grande in December 1864 (and eventually released), but Hoyt had nothing to do with the Dutch bark, it was the wrong type of vessel, and their paths did not overlap. Contemporary records also fail to mention a Gulf Coast schooner named *America* until Harris Hoyt became involved with it in August 1863.[37]

Of Hoyt's two blockade running Texas schooners, the *America* was the first to sail. Despite the nighttime illumination of an almost full and waxing moon, Captain Evans ran the blockade in late August 1863. He passed over the shallow bar at Caney Creek, a small stream that fed directly into the Gulf just south of the Brazos River. During the war, the Confederates had dug a shallow canal through a swampy marsh that connected Caney Creek to the far northern end of Matagorda Bay. The *America*'s draft must have been too great for the schooner to attempt using the inland waterway from that point, forcing it out into the open waters of the Gulf.[38]

The *America* was headed for Matamoros with 55 bales of cotton on board. The schooner made it as far south as Corpus Christi Bay. On August 27, the fast sailing bark USS *William G. Anderson* captured her as a prize of war about 50 miles off shore. The captain of the 8-gun *W.G. Anderson* was an enterprising Acting Volunteer Lieutenant named Frederic S. Hill. Before the war, Hill had been a merchant mariner for 17 years and then a U.S. Customs agent. At the outbreak of war, he was a newspaperman in Boston. As a result of his maritime background and the great need for experienced mariners, he received a direct commission as a Navy officer in 1861. After serving on the USS *Richmond* and participating in the capture of New Orleans, Hill was promoted to Acting Lieutenant and given command of the *W.G. Anderson* in February 1863.[39]

Captain Hill placed a small complement of his most reliable sailors and an officer on board the *America* to serve as a crew for his prize. After giving chase to a different blockade runner, Captain Hill took the *America* in tow. That night during the midnight-watch, the schooner gave a "broad sheer." It turned broadside to the wind and wave and then capsized. Hill was able to rescue his prize crew, but the *America* was now floating bottom side up.[40]

At daylight, the crew of the *W.G. Anderson* could see some of the *America*'s 55 bales of cotton floating away from the wreck. Captain Hill lowered his boats and picked up 14 bales of the drifting cotton. When all efforts to refloat the schooner failed, he had her decks cut open. After laboring for two days, his crew recovered another 30 bales of cotton from the *America*'s cargo hold. Some of the bales were so wet that the sailors had to cut them open so that the cotton could dry on deck. After drying and packing the cotton into bags, Captain Hill was able to save a total of about 43½ of the bales.[41]

Ten days after the capture of the *America*, the *W.G. Anderson* shifted its blockade station to the mouth of the Rio Grande. There, Captain Hill sent Evans and the crew of the *America* ashore along with the crew of another captured blockade runner, the *Mack Canfield*. When the *W.G. Anderson*'s lifeboat was unable to safely navigate across the bar, Hill transferred the captured sailors to a nearby merchant brig whose captain generously helped the men make their way back to Texas. Captain Hill's decision to release all of his prisoners was an unusual action, since the admiralty court usually needed the testimony of two or three captured crewmen to make a condemnation ruling.[42]

Frederic Hill described these events much differently in his memoirs. He claimed to have left his position off the inlet to Corpus Christi Bay at Aransas Pass at his own initiative. Captain Hill also said that he needed to replenish the *W.G. Anderson*'s stock of fresh fruit and vegetables at the Rio Grande. His men were showing signs of scurvy and they needed something else in their diet besides salt-beef. It was at this point that his sea story strayed from the truth and became a fairy tale. While he was still at anchor off the Rio Grande, Hill said that he spied a schooner heading toward the Mexican side of the river. He quickly set about disguising his warship as a merchant ship by running in his guns, closing the gun ports, and using his sails and rigging to give the appearance that he was loading cargo. He then dropped two of his small boats over the side and "like a tiger springing upon his prey," the *W.G. Anderson* succeeded in capturing the schooner while it was still in Texas waters. Hill said that this vessel was named the *America*.[43]

He said that the *America* had 111 bales of Texas cotton on board that he sent to the Key West admiralty court for adjudication. While his story had several elements of truth, Hill changed a several important details to better fit his narrative. U.S. District Court and official Navy records confirm that the capture he described in his memoirs was that of the schooner *Mack Canfield* and not the *America*. Hill captured the *Mack Canfield* at the Rio Grande on August 25, 1864, two days before the *America*. The schooner had 133 bales of cotton and not 111 as he reported in his memoirs. He also sent the *Mack Canfield* to New Orleans rather than to Key West, where the admiralty court condemned the vessel and its cargo for a net total of $30,416.98 in prize money. Hill made no mention of the *Mack Canfield* or the actual capture of Captain William Evans and the schooner *America* in his memoirs. That capture occurred two days after the *Mack Canfield*, about 50 miles north of the Rio Grande. Hill omitted any reference to his forced removal from command, court martial, or reprimand from Secretary of the Navy Gideon Welles. He merely said that he was relieved in the spring of 1864 while the *W.G. Anderson* was in New Orleans refitting.[44]

Hill also conveniently skipped over his return to the Rio Grande where he released the *America*'s captain and crew. As for William Evans, he was

6. Double Dealing Cotton in Texas   93

happy to be a free man once again. He remained in Matamoros where he continued his exploits as a blockade runner, but with mixed results. His wife Ophelia and their namesake children, a 2-year-old son, William Jr., and 6-year-old daughter, known as Fillie, soon joined him in Matamoros. While there, Evans purchased the schooner *Caroline* and sent her to New Orleans where U.S. Marshals seized it in June 1864 for lack of proper clearance. Customs officials released the *Caroline* two months later, but as the captain attempted to enter the Rio Grande, she ran aground and was a total loss. Some of her cargo was salvaged when it washed ashore. This was just another in a series of cruel blows for William Evans. He had lost one of his two daughters in 1862 and his only son, William, died that August. Evans had been captured running the blockade, two of his precious children had died, and his finances were suffering due to the sinking of his schooner.[45]

If the Irishman's grey eyes were sad, it was not for lack of activity. William Evans stayed busy pursuing additional blockade running adventures from his new home in South Texas. While he was at the Rio Grande, Evans gained the trust of Richard King, the future cattle baron. King's primary occupation during the war was as a steamboat owner, shipping agent, and, with his partners Stillman and Kenedy, the chief supplier of Confederate forces at the border. King needed a competent captain for his steamboat, the SS *Cora* (not to be confused with the schooner that was also named *Cora*). Evans would lead a crew of twelve sailors. Four of them were "negroes," who were probably slaves on hire from their masters.[46]

Captain King wanted Evans to navigate the SS *Cora* from Matagorda Bay to Corpus Christi via the inland waterway, just as King had done with another river steamer, the SS *Alamo*, prior to the Union occupation in November 1863. From there, Evans would run the SS *Cora* into the Gulf and deliver the steamboat to the Rio Grande. Like the SS *Alamo*, she would join the King and Kenedy fleet of river steamers. But first, Evans had to get past the blockading fleet. He almost did. The heavily armed steam warship *Quaker City* intercepted the *Cora* within sight of Brazos Santiago and seized her as a prize of war. Due to the fragility of the river steamer, the Union Navy convened an admiralty court at Brazos Santiago rather than taking the risk of sailing her to New Orleans. Since the SS *Cora* flew the Confederate flag, it was a clear cut case of blockade running. The court condemned the *Cora* and took her into the Union Navy as a military river transport.[47]

The man who first delivered William Evans to Matamoros, Captain Frederick Hill, had signaled his deceptive intentions by releasing Evans and his crew there. Hill did report the capture of the *America* and its cargo of 55 bales of cotton to Secretary Welles and Admiral Farragut. However, Hill's report did not mention that he had sent the schooner's crew members ashore near the Rio Grande. He told the secretary that when the vessel capsized, his crew was able to save "several bales of cotton ... in a very wet and damaged state." He argued that since his men had "worked up to their necks in water to save this portion of the cargo," he thought the government should "allow them the benefit of it as drift cotton." Unfortunately for Hill, it is at this point that the allure of the fluffy white gold commodity clouded his judgment. His release of all the *America*'s crew showed that he had made up his mind to keep all the cotton for himself and his hard-working sailors.[48]

Acting Lieutenant Hill failed to report exactly how many bales his crew recovered and he did not wait for a positive response to his request. All of the captured bales should have been delivered to the admiralty court at New Orleans for adjudication, even when the blockade runner itself had sunk. By releasing all of the *America*'s crew, there were no witnesses to provide the Admiralty Court testimony about what he had done with the cotton. To compound his offense, Acting Volunteer Lieutenant F.S. Hill had all records of these events erased from the log slate and never entered them into the ship's official logbook.[49]

The *W.G. Anderson* reached the South West Pass of the Mississippi River about a month after the *America*'s capture. Hill transferred the 43½ bales to the merchant bark *Sol Wildes* and consigned the cotton to the respectable Boston banking and brokerage house of Blake Brothers & Company. The *Sol Wildes* departed New Orleans with the cotton on October 19th, but made an unscheduled stop at Havana, reportedly due to the illness of several crew members. The captain of the *Sol Wildes* either sold the cotton at Havana, transferred it to another vessel, or simply did not declare it when he arrived in New York on November 11, 1863.[50]

After the sale, Lieutenant Hill and his paymaster, Louis L. Scovel, eventually went to Boston to collect their share of the profits. They distributed the money among themselves and the other officers and crew of the bark *W.G. Anderson*. The U.S. Treasury Department did not receive its normal 50 percent split of the net proceeds.[51]

Admiral Farragut discovered this deception several weeks later when he reviewed the *William G. Anderson*'s log book. He noticed that there was no mention of the *America*'s captured cotton. After getting confirmation from the ship's executive officer, Farragut reported Lieutenant Hill's fraudulent conduct to Secretary of the Navy Gideon Welles.[52]

Hill's court martial convened at the Philadelphia Navy Yard nine months after the incident. The charge was "Scandalous conduct tending to the destruction of good morals." Although the officers of the court found him guilty as charged, they let Hill off with a reprimand and forfeiture of the $900 he personally received from the sale of the cotton. The court generously reasoned that Lieutenant Hill's actions were "attributable to a misconception of his duty" rather than any desire to act fraudulently.[53]

Frederic Hill's chicanery provided Harris Hoyt with another example of how his "honest" efforts to export Texas cotton for his Providence partners were thwarted by forces beyond his control. His honest efforts always seemed to involve the cotton that never arrived and belonged to other people. When Hoyt became aware of his fellow swindler's actions, he accused Lieutenant Hill and the U.S. Navy of stealing his cotton. This was another of Hoyt's ridiculous claims. The only parties who did not receive their lawful payments were the senior officers in Hill's chain of command and the U.S. Treasury Department, not Harris Hoyt or his partners. Hoyt lost all claim to the cotton when the *William G. Anderson* captured it. Admiralty courts would never issue a ruling that awarded or returned the condemned cargo from a blockade runner to its Confederate or Union owners.[54]

While Captain Hill and his crew were was busy dealing with the cotton from the *America*, Harris Hoyt was preparing to depart Galveston Bay on his other schooner, the *Lehman*. He had a verbal contract with one of the vessel's owners, Samuel Loeb, to place up to 200 bales of cotton on board as freight. Hoyt said that it was Thomas Mooney who loaded the *Lehman* with cotton at Houston, Texas. In reality, it was cotton that Mooney had traded to Hoyt for his carding machinery.[55]

Hoyt would later brag to Charles Prescott that he also had a $400,000 contract with the Confederate government. He said that he had agreed to import much needed supplies such as firearms, ammunition, blankets, shoes, leather, and oil. If he delivered the goods on a steamer, the government would pay for all of it in cotton and give Hoyt a permit that exempted him from paying export duties. He also said that James Sorley would provide the money and that General Magruder had given him authorization to act on his behalf. Although he may have had an agreement in principle to import military provisions, it is unlikely that Sorley advanced Hoyt any money to carry out his scheme. General Magruder did, however, sign a special order that authorized Hoyt to run the blockade in the *Lehman*.[56]

The Texas phase of Hoyt's Texas Adventure was proceeding according to plan, or at least almost according to plan. He had gained the confidence of the leading military and civilian officials in the state and many of its wealthy investors, sold his carding machinery, purchased cotton, and was well on his way to getting at least some of it out of the state. The loss of the *America* was unfortunate, as was the loss of the *Cora* and *Citizen*, after Henry Brastow sold them at the Rio Grande. These difficulties would help him explain to his Providence partners why they did not receive any return on their investment. As for himself, Hoyt still had the *Lehman*, most of his money, and a lot more cotton to ship.

7

Escape from Texas

Just four days after General Magruder authorized Harris Hoyt to run the blockade out of Galveston, Hoyt was on board the schooner *Lehman* with his cotton. He accompanied Captain Maynard who was taking soundings at the San Luis Pass channel at the far southwestern end of Galveston Bay. Experienced mariners knew that shifting sands could change the hydrography of the sandbar protecting the bay overnight. A prudent captain like Maynard needed timely, first-hand information about the depth of the channel and its approaches before he made his dash into the open waters of the Gulf on a dark night. As Maynard maneuvered the *Lehman* toward San Luis pass, he received a message ordering him to return to Galveston. Harris Hoyt was under arrest.[1]

Hoyt and his father-in-law had planned to run the blockade out of Galveston Bay on the schooner *Lehman*, but they wanted to avoid the main channel at the northern end of Galveston Island. The Navy's vigilance at the narrow San Luis Pass was less stringent than at the wider and deeper entrance north of the island. The two passes were also separated by over 27 miles, making it impossible for one U.S. Navy warship to cover both exits at the same time.[2]

Hoyt had told his Union sympathizing friends that he did not intend to actually run the blockade or proceed directly to a neutral port. Instead, he would "take the schooner to the blockading fleet off Galveston." Deliberately surrendering to the Union fleet would have been a difficult achievement without the unlikely cooperation of the ship's captain who owed his loyalty to his Confederate owners. Hoyt had probably gotten the idea for this deception from his meeting with Secretary of the Navy Gideon Welles in Washington, D.C. It was, however, a believable line that he fed to the Unionists living in Texas.[3]

The *Lehman*'s captain, W. Maynard, had received customs clearance for the *Lehman* to depart Galveston Bay on September 9, 1863. There were 187 bales of cotton on board that were bound for Matamoros. Although

Civil War blockade runners at Galveston piers (G-2274.2 FF4, courtesy Rosenberg Library, Galveston, Texas).

the new moon had passed on September 12th, the *Lehman*'s captain was still awaiting an opportunity to run out two weeks later. A patient blockade runner, Maynard was waiting for the right combination of wind, weather, visibility, and tide to maximize his chances of a successful escape.[4]

Twelve days after the *Lehman* received its clearance, General Magruder had issued an unusual directive that he also published in local newspapers. His "Special Order No. 266" authorized Thomas House, Marx Levy, and Harris Hoyt to send out blockade runners with cotton. The Special Order also specified some other men of questionable loyalty who would not be extended that privilege. In addition to Hoyt, the men who were entrusted with the privilege of running the blockade included Mr. Thomas House. A former baker, Thomas House was a founder of the Galveston Navigation Company and a prominent Houston businessman with interests in numerous blockade runners. The second man was Marx Levy, a hardworking and ambitious 16-year-old Polish Jew. He was a clerk for Benjamin Weil and Samuel Loeb who were also part-owners of the schooner *Lehman*.[5]

General Magruder prevented Hoyt's departure and delivered an arrest warrant to the *Lehman* while it was at the far end of Galveston Bay. The general had this capability thanks to his control of the Galveston Harbor Police and its small fleet of schooners like the *Lecompt*. The Confederate Marine Department had first chartered the *Lecompt* for service as a guard, dispatch, and supply vessel in Matagorda Bay. It was acting in that capacity when the former Coastal Survey steamer USS *Sachem* entered Matagorda Bay in October 1862 and captured her. The *Sachem* towed the *Lecompt* to Galveston Bay where it served in the same capacity for the U.S. Navy during its occupation of Galveston Harbor from October through December 31, 1862.[6]

General Magruder's forces recaptured the *Lecompt* on January 1st, 1863 during the battle of Galveston, and it once again served as a Confederate guard and dispatch boat. This time, it was in Galveston Bay under the command of the Chief of Harbor Police, Thomas Chubb. Chubb's immediate commander was Commodore Leon Smith, the head of the Texas Marine Department. Among the duties of guard boats like the *Lecompt* was to board and check the papers of all vessels passing up or down the Bay. The Harbor Police paid special attention to the blockade runners that were about to depart. Chubb's men ensured that outbound blockade runners had paid all custom duties and received the proper military clearance before they were allowed to leave the harbor. In the case of Harris Hoyt and the *Lehman*, their clearance had been revoked and the *Lecompt* would have escorted the schooner back to Galveston.[7]

Hoyt told his Yankee associates that he had no idea why he was detained, but speculated that his arrest could be attributed to a letter that he had written and had been captured on board the U.S. Navy warship, *Clifton*. His explanation was plausible, if he had only been telling the truth. The day before the *Lehman* had gotten its customs clearance, a small Confederate force at Sabine Pass disabled and captured the steam gunboats USS *Clifton* and *Sachem*, the same warship that had captured the *Lecompt* a few months earlier. Hoyt claimed to have smuggled out an intelligence report to the *Clifton* sometime prior to that battle. His report supposedly detailed a Confederate Army mutiny at Galveston.[8]

There had been a brief mutiny in Galveston during the second week of August 1863. The men of the Third Texas Infantry had refused to drill and the men of Cook's 1st Heavy Artillery Regiment disobeyed orders by remaining at their batteries. The men were protesting poor food and unreliable pay. Brigadier General Luckett calmed the situation by promising better rations, and suspending all drills until the food improved. While the situation was real and references to a mutiny found their way into the newspapers, there is no mention of Hoyt's communication in any of the official records. The letter was probably another figment of Hoyt's fertile imagination.[9]

As usual, it did not serve Harris Hoyt's interests to tell the whole truth. The actual situation regarding his arrest would have jeopardized his position with Union authorities and can only be discovered within contemporary Confederate sources from Texas. Unfortunately for Hoyt, the tale that he fed to his Union friends about delivering the cotton to the blockading fleet had leaked to Confederate military officials. General Magruder called witnesses to testify regarding Hoyt's traitorous plans to surrender the *Lehman* to the Yankees. Based on the accusations against him, he had to be either a Confederate traitor, a Yankee spy, or just a lying swindler.[10]

In his defense, Hoyt's only available course of action was to solemnly swear that he was a loyal Southerner. That testimony would have exposed him as the swindler that he was, at least to his former Texas supporters and investors. He confessed that he had no intention of turning his schooner over to the Union blockading fleet. He was simply a dishonest businessman who was trying to cheat Union loyalists out of their money. His passing of counterfeit Confederate currency did not help his case with the Confederates, but provided a handy explanation for his troubles when talking with Yankees. Hoyt described the counterfeit notes as better than the genuine bills which were of lighter weight than the counterfeits. As a result, "he came near being seized as a swindler." Since Hoyt's Northern partners and inquisitors did not have access to his Confederate court documents, they found out too late that he was swindling them as well.[11]

While Hoyt tried to untangle his legal problems, the *Lehman* continued to languish in Galveston Bay. The local ship owners, Weil and Loeb, were stuck with mounting expenses that included having to pay the idle captain and crew. On October 19th, Samuel Loeb wrote to General Magruder in hopes of getting him to release his schooner. Loeb explained that Louisiana parties were the principal owners of the schooner, but he failed to mention that he also had an ownership interest in the vessel. Given Magruder's recent experience with the *Blanche* and its Bayou State swindlers, it is not surprising that the general failed to be impressed by Loeb's plea on behalf of his Louisiana partners.[12]

Loeb said that he understood that there were some charges against Hoyt and, as a result, he was willing to remove Harris Hoyt from the equation. Loeb offered to buy the cotton, pay all the expenses, and send the *Lehman* on its way. The schooner would then return with suitable goods for the Confederate government. Loeb pleaded for a timely resolution, or else he would have to sell the *Lehman* just to cover expenses. In late October 1863, Loeb reported to his partner in Matamoros, Benjamin Weil, that he had to neglect all his other business "to attend to the schooner *Lehman*."[13]

In Hoyt's version of the same story, he claimed that Magruder forced Thomas Mooney to sell the *Lehman*'s cotton to one of the general's friends. It was a believable tale that could have been true, but in this case, probably was not. In Galveston, manipulation of ownership papers was common. William Watson of the schooner *Rob Roy* related how his Galveston-based partners, Robert & David G. Mills, attempted to take ownership of his entire load of 198 bales of cotton. Thomas House, a more reputable merchant, advised Watson that the Mills brother's scheme was "a right down swindle." R. & D.G. Mills failed in their attempt to wrest ownership of the *Rob Roy* and its cotton away from William Watson, but it did not mean that they would not try again in the future.[14]

In describing his transaction with the *Lehman*, Hoyt said that he never received any money from the sale of the cotton he had placed on board. This story appears to be just another lie. He was simply shifting blame to General Magruder. His story rationalized his reasons for not sharing his profits and proving how his Yankee loyalties got him arrested in Texas.

The *Lehman* did finally run the blockade in early November, but without Harris Hoyt on board. However, Hoyt's father-in-law, Samuel Bryant, remained embarked as a passenger where he could look after Hoyt's interests.[15]

After General Magruder granted his release, Hoyt arranged to have his remaining cotton shipped overland to Matamoros. For himself, he went to Brenham and purchased two pairs of horses, an "ambulance" (a type of light, covered wagon), a buggy, and provisions. The cost was $4,000 in Confederate dollars. On Sunday morning, November 1, 1863, he headed south for Mexico. With him were three unidentified women, four children, his 12-year-old son, Harris George Hoyt, and one man to drive the second team. Hoyt said that after he had

Robert Mills, engraved portrait from a Southern Cotton Press and Manufacturing Company stock certificate, 1858 (MS23-5199008, courtesy Rosenberg Library, Galveston, Texas).

started out, General Magruder recalled him and his cotton. Rather than returning his cotton to Brenham, Hoyt said he burned it all in defiance.[16]

This explanation also seems unlikely and contradicts his other statements. Hoyt's departure for Mexico began just two days before the Union invasion of South Texas. To prevent capture, Confederate officials did burn several dozen bales of cotton, most of it in Brownsville. Some of Hoyt's cotton may have been burned, but based on his other claimed and documented shipments of cotton, it is more likely that all or most of it made its way to the border.[17]

When Hoyt reached Laredo in late November, General Hamilton Bee was in command of the small band of retreating Confederate forces. Bee's quartermaster, Major Charles Russell, was also in the border town. The major had evacuated Brownsville with General Bee and shifted his base of logistic operations to Laredo. Russell was in charge of paying the freight on Confederate cotton crossing the river there. In the Army's haste to escape from the invading Yankees, the general ordered the cotton supplies in the city burned. The resulting conflagration spread to Fort Brown and ignited the stored gunpowder. The fires eventually consumed a large portion of downtown Brownsville. The change in the city was dramatic. Just a few months earlier, Brownsville had been a "mercantile Mecca," where "Pretty females ... made their pilgrimage ... across the desert and over the lonely road from here to Goliad, driven to the journey by the necessity of the times." After the Confederate retreat, most of the city was a smoldering ruin.[18]

Immediately after the Army fled from Brownsville without a fight, the Confederate commercial agent Richard Fitzpatrick accused Major Russell and General Bee of burning the cotton to cover up their misdeeds. The 71-year-old Fitzpatrick had been the U.S. consul to Matamoros from 1858 until he accepted the same position for the Confederate States in November 1862. He reported to Secretary of State Judah Benjamin that "The whole movement of setting fire to the town and burning of cotton and goods was no doubt intended to cover up the stealings of Russell and company of cotton." Fitzpatrick's official report reflected the popular sentiment among Southern loyalists that probably inspired Hoyt to make up his story about burning cotton.[19]

Major Charles Arden Russell had first come to Texas via Canada, New York, Massachusetts, and Michigan as an 18-year-old U.S. Army private during the Mexican War. Unaccustomed to Army discipline, Russell deserted the Army for about eight months before returning to his unit. He completed his enlistment and received an honorable discharge in January 1846 at Corpus Christi, Texas. His intention was to return to New York

State, but when he missed the boat bound for Galveston, he decided to set out on horseback. Fate intervened when he crossed the San Antonio River. He stopped at Goliad to have dinner with the local ferryman and his daughter. Russell traveled no farther. A year later he married the ferryman's daughter, Emeline Brightman, and remained in the area as a tax assessor and collector, post master, notary public and then a lawyer specializing in real estate law in the newly formed Karnes County. On the eve of the Civil War, he was a delegate to the Texas Secession Convention with Colonel Philip Luckett. Both men also served with Colonel Rip Ford's frontier protection forces. Russell then accepted his current position as General Bee's quartermaster along the lower Rio Grande.[20]

Major Russell's boss, Brigadier General Hamilton P. Bee, had been in Texas since arriving with his family from South Carolina in 1836. As a youth, Bee had been the clerk for the future Civil War Governor of Texas, Francis R. Lubbock. He then held a number of important state positions including the joint U.S.–Texas boundary commission, a peace treaty council with the Comanche tribes, a state treasury agent, and secretary of the Texas Senate. During the Mexican War, Bee served with the prominent Texans Benjamin McCulloch and Colonel John Coffee Hays of the Texas Rangers, and the future President of the Republic of Texas, Mirabeau Buonaparte Lamar. General Bee then won election as a state congressman from Laredo that included a two-year term as speaker of the house. The General had property and family connections around Corpus Christi and was well acquainted with Major Charles Russell before he joined the general's staff in South Texas.[21]

Hoyt had made the overland trip from Brenham to Matamoros through territory that was still, more or less, controlled by General Bee's Confederate forces in exactly one month. His direct route to

Major Charles Arden Russell, Confederate States Army, date unknown (courtesy Carolina L. Lawson).

Matamoros was a distance of about three hundred fifty miles, but Hoyt said it was more like five hundred. The extra mileage is attributable to the Union occupation of Brownsville in the second week of November. His and many other mule and ox trains that were loaded with cotton had to detour to the west to avoid marauding Union troops.[22]

By this stage of the war, most of the two-wheeled Mexican ox carts, or *carretas*, had been replaced with four-wheeled freight wagons. Each of these wagons had a team of ten oxen and could carry 10 to 16 bales of cotton. The ox trains normally comprised ten to fifteen wagons. The trains sometimes had only four to six carts carrying lesser loads, depending on availability of carts, cotton, and the distance. The preferred Rio Grande crossing for the ox and mule trains was at Laredo where they could avoid Yankees patrols that were in search of cotton. The mule and oxen wagon train drivers were an unruly lot. Much like the cattle-driving cowboys of a later era, whenever they rolled into town, a general riot would ensue, with drinking, fighting, and shooting. For Hoyt and his train of over 100 bales of cotton, it was a hard trip with hard men under trying conditions. Both man and beast had to sleep "in the open air night after night, at times suffering for the want of provisions."[23]

Hoyt's hardships were not over when he reached the river. He had to pay the necessary fees and show the proper government permits to load the cotton onto one of the ferries into Mexico. Unlike modern Texas, the State did not operate any free ferry services and there were no bridges across the Rio Grande. Private entrepreneurs like M. Kenedy & Company received government concessions to manage river ferries on an exclusive basis. In addition to the normal fees, business ledgers frequently had a column designated specifically for bribes paid to ferry operators and Custom House officers. Hoyt also had to be careful about his permits and bills of sale.[24]

Even Major Simeon Hart fell victim to a clever Mexican shipper who crossed a wagon train into Laredo that included 114 mules, two mares, and four horses. When Major Hart purchased the entire train, the owner returned to Mexico and redeemed the $272 customs bond he had paid for crossing into Texas. Hart then loaded the wagon train with his cotton and crossed the Rio Grande. He had to pay the $272 even though it was a government shipment.[25]

One persistent shipper manipulated the system to recover his entire wagon train of cotton that a Confederate agent had seized as it was on the road to Laredo. When the agent seized his cotton, all the shipper received was a receipt that could only be exchanged for payment in deflated cotton bonds. The aggrieved Texan waited until the government agent had gotten all the necessary permits, paid the customs fees, and crossed his cotton from Laredo into Mexico. At that point, the Texan presented his original bill of sale to the Mexican officials. His papers confirmed that he was the sole owner of the appropriately branded bales of cotton. He recovered the whole lot in Mexico without having to pay any fees. There was nothing the Confederate official could do but fume.[26]

One of the State officials that allegedly helped Hoyt get his cotton into Mexico from Laredo was James Sorley of Galveston. This claim may have been technically correct, since Sorley was the chief customs agent in Texas and the Assistant Chief of the Texas Cotton Bureau. Without a permit from Sorley or another member of the Cotton Bureau, Hoyt would have been unable to export his cotton. The creation of the Cotton Bureau in the Trans-Mississippi Department was part of an ongoing, but futile series of attempts to effectively manage its only cash crop. The Confederate government and its military needed the cash from cotton sales to finance the war effort.[27]

In 1861, Texas Governor Francis R. Lubbock made an initial effort to control speculation in the cotton trade by requiring all shippers to purchase a license in order to haul cotton. When this program proved to be unwieldy, the state legislature established the Texas State Military Board. Led by the governor as its chairman and two other commissioners, one of the Military Board's first acts was to issue cotton bonds. They were supposed to pay 8 percent interest in hard currency. These state bonds had a much better yield than those issued by Richmond. Lubbock intended to use the money to equip his state militia forces. Unfortunately, the state did not have that much specie (i.e., gold or silver) on hand and its agents could pay no more than 10 cents per pound for cotton, which was far less than the market rate. In another seemingly altruistic move that only invited corruption, the Military Board's agents received no pay for their work. Their only compensation was reimbursement for expenses. The state was also unable to protect teamsters, their wagons or animals, from being drafted into the Confederate Army, once again placing the state agents at a distinct disadvantage against the cotton speculators.[28]

In the midst of the confusion and bureaucratic wrangling over cotton, the Confederate War Department decided to enter the competition for Texas cotton in the fall of 1862. Richmond commissioned its own purchasing agent in Texas in the person of Major Simeon Hart. Major Hart was the official that Harris Hoyt had asked to release William Evans from military duties so that he could run the blockade in the *America*. Among his duties, Hart was supposed to be entrusted "with the exclusive power of purchasing cotton" in Texas. Richmond's goal was to supply munitions and quartermaster's stores for Lt. Gen. Kirby Smith and his forces in the Trans-Mississippi Department. Unfortunately, Major Hart's authorities and finances were woefully inadequate to accomplish such a daunting task.[29]

There appeared to be no prospect for cooperation in the Texas cotton trade, but the events of July 1863 forced General Smith's hand. He summoned the civilian political leaders of the states within his Department to a mid–August conference at the Northeast Texas city of Marshall. The immediate impetus for the meeting was the loss of Vicksburg and Port Hudson on the Mississippi River. These devastating Union conquests severed overland and river communications and commerce with the Eastern portion of the Confederacy. General Smith had to take bold action to bolster the defense of the Confederate West and find a way to bring order into the chaotic cotton trade. The area within Smith's department included Texas, New Mexico and the Indian Territories, plus the portions of Missouri, Arkansas, and Louisiana that were west of the Mississippi River. The Confederate armies and citizens in this region were now on their own and had to manage their own affairs with no expectation of assistance from Richmond. The Texas delegation to the conference included Governor Francis Lubbock and Governor-elect Pendelton Murrah. One of the primary topics of the conference was cotton, specifically General Smith's authority to buy, sell, seize and transport it.[30]

The civilian leaders at the meeting all agreed to give General Smith extraordinary powers to act as the *de facto* Confederate War Department west of the Mississippi. They also endorsed his department's Cotton Bureau that he had formed earlier in the month. The Cotton Bureau's mission was to manage "the purchase, collection, or other disposition of Government cotton." General Smith and the other leaders recognized that cotton was the only viable means for his Army to obtain vital military supplies. The general asked for their help in devising the best method of "securing the cotton of the department without causing opposition on the part of the people." Back in Richmond, the Confederate government quickly acknowledged the reality of the situation and reluctantly agreed with most of Smith's initiatives.[31]

Lt. Col. William A. Broadwell, a New Orleans cotton broker (known as a "factor"), headed the Cotton Bureau from his base in Shreveport, Louisiana. Since most of the department's cotton had to travel through Texas for export, Smith appreciated the need for a Cotton Bureau office in Houston. He established the Texas Cotton Bureau in November 1863 under Lt. Col. William Hutchins. Colonel Hutchins was the former Mayor of Houston, a well-respected businessman, and one of the wealthiest men in the State. Among his four assistants was James Sorley, who acted as the depository and treasurer for the funds that the bureau collected and disbursed within Texas.[32]

On its surface, the joint state resolution appeared to give General Smith full authority to buy or impress all of the cotton west of the Mississippi, except for small amounts needed to sustain private owners. However, the non-binding resolution did not include provisions that would allow Smith's Cotton Bureau to buy imported goods, control speculators, or stabilize the currency. These omissions intensified the competition for control of the cotton trade between and among Richmond, Smith's Trans-Mississippi Department, and the State of Texas.[33]

Further adding to the confusion and frustration, Confederate military officials like Generals Hébert, Magruder, and Bee periodically and arbitrarily issued and inconsistently enforced cotton trade regulations. Accusations of corruption and abuse abounded. Most were unfounded, but appear to be justified in the case of Governor Murrah's chief cotton agent in Galveston, Ebenezar B. Nichols. Agent Nichols pocketed over $130,000 after selling 8,102 bales of cotton that were supposed to be for the benefit of the state. Perhaps Nichols thought of it as a repayment, with interest. He had loaned the state $58,000 of his own funds while serving as a member of the Secession Convention with Colonel Luckett and Charles Russell in March 1861.[34]

Texas citizens bitterly complained about the Cotton Bureau's impressment policies and the artificially low prices that the government paid for cotton. It amounted to official thievery. In December 1863, Governor Murrah, in his role as chairman of the Texas State Military Board, devised a new plan to appease the cotton planters and speculators. The governor's plan called for the acquisition of 60,000 bales of cotton for state militia forces using 7 percent bonds to purchase cotton at fair market prices. The state would also solve the transportation problem by assuming responsibility for transporting the entire shipment for anyone who would sell half of their cotton to its Military Board. Since the state would have title to the cotton while it was in transit, all of it would be exempt from impressment by other authorities. This plan would put General Smith's Cotton Bureau agents out of business since it effectively exempted up to 120,000 bales of cotton, offered better prices, and guaranteed delivery.[35]

Governor Murrah finally abandoned his competitive fight for cotton in July 1864. While the Yankee offensive along the Red River in Louisiana was in progress, General Smith convinced Murrah of the Army's desperate need for cotton. However, before the ink had dried on the governor's conciliatory proclamations, Richmond abolished the Smith's Cotton Bureau and replaced it with the Trans-Mississippi Treasury Agency. Despite this administrative change, the operations and practices of the Cotton Bureau and endemic mismanagement continued unabated. The lack of effective administration opened the door for fraud and bribery, exemplified by speculators who illegally obtained export licenses and paid for the services of draft-exempt teamsters.[36]

Amid this bureaucratic confusion, the shift of trade to the Rio Grande using overland routes created a great demand for ox and mule carts and the teamsters who drove them. Even when carts could be found, there often were not enough able-bodied men to drive them. The manpower shortage presented opportunities for boys who were too young for conscription and men who were too old. One example is the German-born, 16-year-old August Santleben and his 52-year-old father, Christian. Although the younger Santleben found the teamster work not to his liking and led him to enlist in the Union Army, his father continued to drive Confederate ox trains throughout the war.[37]

To stabilize the availability of teamsters, the Confederate Army granted conscription exemptions to drivers who hauled government cotton. This practice was fine in theory, but it was inherently corrupt in practice. As one Brownsville correspondent reported in May 1863, "The teamsters come here and report to officials as loaded for [the] Government, yet these officials have no advices, and presently some citizen comes forward to claim the consignment."[38]

Private shippers who had obtained their export licenses and a contract for draft-exempt teamsters could still find themselves with no means of transporting their cotton. One such speculator made it as far as the King Ranch in May of 1863 only to lose his ox carts and teamsters when General Magruder ordered them back to the railhead at Alleyton. Even cotton that did arrive at the Rio Grande still could be lost at the whim of the teamsters. Although the Mexican drivers generally were reliable, some of the conscript-exempt German-born teamsters deserted at the Rio Grande and sold their cotton to Union speculators.[39]

Even if a shipper experienced no problems with export licenses, teamsters, ox trains, or thievery, the expenses were exorbitant. The Civil War ledger of William Pitt Ballinger recorded the following expense categories for shipping 160 bales of Texas cotton via Matamoros to Liverpool: freight, labor, drayage (overland hauling fee), lighterage, repairs (on cotton bales), teamsters, bagging, rope, tax ("State, County & City"), weighing, export duties & fees, rolling downhill (on the Texan and Mexican sides of the river), cartage to ferry & lighter, ferry, Custom House papers, import duty, commissions, portage, and interest. Additionally, Ballinger had to pay "bribes [to] ferry & Custom House Officers $50.00." He also deducted the expense for bales of cotton lost to the 20 percent "Confederate Government forced loan," one bale stolen in Brownsville, and one bale lost in repairing. Even with all of these losses and expenses, Ballinger's cotton found a favorable market in Liverpool. The net return in British pounds sterling was the equivalent of over $30,000 in June 1864, a sum that would amount to about a half a million dollars in 2020.[40]

Harris Hoyt had successfully maneuvered his way past the various Texas cotton agencies, but he could not avoid the exorbitant expenses. He experienced and complained about the costs of moving his cotton from Central Texas to Bagdad. Although he had been able to buy cotton at eight cents a pound in Texas, it cost him nine cents per pound to haul it to Mexico, and another nine cents for transport downriver via shallow draft steamers. He also paid the four-to-six cent fee for lighterage to the waiting merchant vessels and their inflated wartime freight charges, as well as the other charges listed in the Ballinger ledgers.[41]

Like all shippers, Hoyt bemoaned his payments to the Confederate government. He told his Northern partners that he had to hand over "as many bales as they brought out," which was another of his fabrications. Unscrupulous Confederate agents, like one at Eagle Pass, Texas, did occasionally seize half of the cotton for the government in the summer of 1863. However, by the time that Hoyt's cotton reached the Rio Grande in November and December 1863, the tax on cotton, otherwise known as the "Confederate Government forced loan," was 20 percent. At this point in the war, the 50 percent requirement generally applied to the amount of cargo space allotted to the government on blockade runners that were outbound from Texas ports. Vessels that cleared from the neutral port of Matamoros were technically not blockade runners and were not subject to the 50 percent requirement. General Smith did not issue his order for planters to sell 50 percent of all cotton to his agents in Texas until June 1, 1864, well after Hoyt and his cotton had departed Texas.[42]

Still, "after all the risk and trouble, they [Hoyt and his agents] could buy it [cotton] in Matamoras [sic] as cheap as they could get it out of Texas." In addition to the hassles Harris Hoyt and all shippers had as they tried to navigate the Confederate permit system, his complaint about expenses resonates with a faint ring of truth. The price of cotton purchased in Matamoros had increased five-fold from the 1862 price of sixteen cents a pound, but buying the cotton at the border avoided the pitfalls and costs of transporting it across the Texas plains.[43]

Hoyt was not exaggerating the other hazards involved in transporting cotton overland into Mexico. Not only was it a long, arduous journey, there were plenty of thieves and fraudsters besides himself along the way. A Confederate soldier who served at the Rio Grande derisively referred to the general in charge of South Texas, Hamilton P. Bee, as "General Wasp." He accused the general of amassing over $100,000 in his personal accounts through robbery and swindling with help from his quartermaster, Charles Russell. Along with the Confederate War Department's cotton agent, Major Simeon Hart, Russell and Hart were the unpopular faces of Confederate policies in South Texas that called for the impressment of cotton, teamsters, and laborers for government use. They also forced Texas citizens to accept payment for goods and cotton in bonds or inflated paper money at a fixed rate and then sold the cotton for gold in Mexico.[44]

The contradictory Confederate management of the Texas cotton trade presented additional opportunities for misunderstandings and corruption. As historian Tom Lea aptly observed, "Honest confusion overlapped with dishonest greed." This tangled web of authority kept Majors Russell and Hart working at cross purposes. Each thought he was operating within his authority. Hart was a respected Mexican War veteran and El Paso flour miller who would remain in Texas after the war. Restrained by his own honesty and naiveté, Hart was out of his depth in managing the unmanageable Texas cotton trade.[45]

Richmond acknowledged "the jealousies and invidious rivalries of other parties" who were causing Major Hart difficulties. The bureaucrats at the Confederate capital could not, however, offer any substantive assistance. They were too far away to remove the many obstacles and embarrassments that prevented Hart from acquiring the cotton he needed to fulfill his contracts. Most of these difficulties emanated from his chief antagonist and counterpart at the Rio Grande, Major Charles Russell. Major Russell routinely took credit for Major Hart's successes and confiscated Hart's War Department cotton to cover his own command's debts. Some reports also suggest that Russell accepted bribes from Mexican firms and personally profited from his cotton deals.[46]

While Harris Hoyt was working much smaller cons in Matamoros, Major Russell was helping the cunning Irish-born merchant, Patricio Milmo confiscate $16 million in Confederate dollars. These treasury notes had arrived in seven large cases just a few days before Hoyt's schooner *Lehman* anchored off the Rio Grande in November 1863. Milmo captured the Confederate paper notes in mid–December and held them as a ransom for unpaid government bills for military supplies and commissary stores. As the business partner and son-in-law of the Mexican Governor Santiago Vidaurri, Milmo's action instigated a diplomatic confrontation.

7. Escape from Texas111

The standoff finally ended when the Confederacy agreed to repay Milmo in full.[47]

Shortly after the Milmo affair, the dispute between Majors Hart and Russell came to a head. General Kirby Smith ordered an investigation after Russell directed a series of accusations against Hart. In response to the charges, Simeon Hart offered all of his accounting books and his full cooperation. As for Major Russell, things had gotten too "warm" for him in Matamoros so he quietly headed south to Monterey, Mexico. An impartial audit proved that Hart had been treated unfairly and that Russell was personally profiting from his Matamoros contracts.[48]

After reviewing the evidence against Major Russell, the South's chief agent in Northern Mexico, José Agustín Quintero, remarked "It is a misfortune for our Confederacy to have so many fools or scoundrels in charge of our interests." Although Russell may have been working at the behest of General Bee and considered Quintero a friend, the Cuban-born Confederate agent had the ear of Confederate President Jefferson Davis. By February 1864, Russell had been reassigned to Houston where he was granted a sixty-day leave of absence due to "general muscular rheumatism."[49]

In the midst of the internal Confederate battle over control of the cotton trade, the schooner *Lehman* arrived off the Rio Grande from Galveston. Benjamin Weil confirmed the arrival of the long-delayed schooner to his partner Samuel Loeb on November 10, 1863. By this time, the number of merchant vessels offshore numbered over 50, despite the presence of the Union Navy and Army forces at Brazos Santiago and along the Rio Grande. The *Lehman* was "in distress but escaped from the Yankees." Rather than being thankful for the schooner's successful run out of Galveston Bay and through the blockade, Benjamin Weil chastised Loeb. He accused his partner of being duped, saying "these men played off on you." Weil could not understand how his partner got stuck with paying the expenses of the vessel and crew for three months. He went on to observe, "Without money we are nobody. ... Money makes the mare go. Patriotism don't pay very well." Loeb and Weil said they were never "able to collect one dollar" from the sales of the *Lehman*'s cargo.[50]

Weil did admit, however, that he eventually received $137 from Hoyt. He also had a promissory note that Hoyt's Matamoros agent, William Compton, would cover if and when he was able to settle the account. Due to the lack of cash, business was bad and Weil was desperate, "If we don't get cotton out, we are all gone." As an interim measure, Weil hired out the *Lehman* as a lighter to load and unload larger vessels off the mouth of the Rio Grande. Unfortunately for Loeb and Weil, the *Lehman*'s papers indicated that another man, nicknamed "The Doctor," was the owner of the vessel. As a result of his manipulation of the ownership papers, "The Doctor" was collecting all of the money. Weil realized that the man was "tricky," but the captain (who was probably Captain Maynard) managed to sail the *Lehman* to Tampico. According to Benjamin Weil, the man escaped with all the money to England. Given Hoyt's later claim that he had cotton in Tampico, the captain may have been operating under the direction of Hoyt or his father-in-law Samuel Bryant who had remained with the *Cora* on its voyage from Galveston.[51]

Leaving Weil in Matamoros, Hoyt made the dangerous 20-mile trip to Bagdad. When he arrived, he was reunited with his father-in-law. Hoyt claimed to have found the schooner *Cora* there as well. He also said that he first learned about Henry Brastow's sale of the *Cora* upon his return to Matamoros in December of 1863. This is another convenient, but unlikely, story. Henry Scherffius had run the *Cora* into the Brazos River that summer. On September 1st, Scherffius paid the export fees and got clearance from the Galveston Customs House for the *Cora* to sail for Nassau or Belize. Hoyt and Weil obtained their clearance for the *Lehman* at the same custom house just eight days later. The previous July, Hoyt revealed his knowledge of Brastow's activities in his letter to Major Simeon Hart, when he took credit for the *Citizen*'s arrival at Matamoros and delivery of supplies to Texas. In short, Hoyt had known about the *Cora*'s status for several months before his return to Bagdad in November 1863.[52]

Harris Hoyt and his father-in-law remained in Mexico for just a few days. They departed for New Orleans on one of the many small schooners that continued to trade and carry passengers between the two ports. In New Orleans, they boarded the large passenger and cargo steamship *George Washington* in mid–January and arrived in New York on January 22, 1864.[53]

Hoyt had escaped from Texas with cash in hand and with cotton on its way to New York. More importantly, he had escaped from a Confederate gallows that would have been certain had General Magruder convicted him of treason. Hoyt not only was lucky to be alive, he was returning to the North a wealthy man. On the negative side of the ledger, he had experienced a number of setbacks and delays. Fortunately for him, the Harris Hoyt ledger had two sides. One side showed the profits that accrued to his account, and the other showed the losses that were all debited to his Providence partners.

8

Deceived and Swindled from New York to Matamoros

After the SS *George Washington* departed New Orleans on January 15, 1864, William Reynolds and Charles Prescott received a telegram. It most likely originated from Reynolds' agent in New Orleans. The message alerted the men that Harris Hoyt was on his way to New York. The two men were waiting for Hoyt on the day of his return. They had a contentious reunion at one of New York's most luxurious hotels, the St. Nicholas. On the voyage from New Orleans to New York, Hoyt had time to perfect his explanation about how he had spent all their money and made a profit for himself, but none for them. It was a long, sad story. Hoyt bitterly complained to Reynolds about the treatment he had received at the hands of his partners. He wanted to know why Brastow had sold the *Cora* while he was absent from Matamoros. Reynolds replied frankly that the Providence partners believed that he was "a dishonest man." They thought that the only way they would ever see any of their money was to have somebody they trusted, like Henry Brastow, attend to their business in Matamoros.[1]

To account for his failure to deliver the promised cotton, Hoyt told Reynolds and Prescott that they were the victims of bad luck. He had sent their cotton to the Red River in Arkansas, where General Banks burned it. He pointed out that the USS *William G. Anderson* had stolen another 50 bales of cotton from the schooner *America*, and he blamed General Magruder for burning much of the rest on the road to Matamoros via Laredo. According to Hoyt, he was unable to send out any cotton despite his best efforts. The story was lies and half-truths. He did lose the cotton from the *America*, but not the *Lehman*, and despite his claims, there is no evidence that Generals Banks or Magruder burned any of his cotton. Hoyt continued to ship cotton out of the Rio Grande, but only for his benefit.[2]

Hoyt then chided Reynolds for acting in bad faith. As a result of Reynolds' and Brastow's actions, his "plans were all defeated." If they just had left the entire business to him, "everything would have turned out well." Because Brastow had sold the *Cora*, Hoyt had another excuse for explaining why we was unable to quickly ship cotton to repay William Reynolds and the others for their investment.³

Continuing his bluff, Hoyt intimated that he would just pay the partners for the goods he had sold on the *Cora* and have nothing more to do with them. He had plenty of friends, had made a lot of money in Texas, and had helped both the Confederate and Union governments in the process. He could not repay his partners just then, but he had 36 bales in Tampico that Captain Maynard had probably spirited away on the *Lehman*. Contradicting his claim that General Magruder had burned it all, he said there was another 100 bales on their way from Laredo. The partners would all have a substantial payday if they could just wait until the arrival of this cotton. There was also the possibility of recovering his cotton from the schooner *America* that the *William G. Anderson* had stolen from him. He said that it was only the dishonesty of Lieutenant Hill and U.S. Navy that prevented them from receiving those bales of cotton. He blustered that it was the Department of the Navy doing the stealing, not him.⁴

Hoyt urged Reynolds to accompany him back to Washington, D.C., and help reclaim their cotton from the Navy. Reynolds declined. Far from being conciliatory, Hoyt's offer was a subtle attempt at blackmail. Reynolds knew that Hoyt did not have a permit from the U.S. government to take out cotton from Texas. Reynolds could not publicly admit that he had an interest in cotton that the Navy had seized while sailing from a Texas port to Matamoros. The entire Texas Adventure risked being exposed as an illegal attempt by an American citizen to run the blockade. If he went to Washington with Hoyt, Reynolds would be signing his own arrest warrant.⁵

Instead of going to Washington, William Reynolds insisted that Hoyt go with him to Providence and explain to his Texas Adventure partners why he had not repaid them for their investments. Hoyt agreed, but he first needed to accompany Samuel Bryant back to his home in Clermont, Iowa, and visit his own family there. Hoyt redeemed his wife Marie's diamond jewelry from Reynolds by repaying the $800 he had borrowed prior to leaving for Texas. After visiting his family, Hoyt bought a house in Chicago on Wabash Street for $18,000. He prudently placed their new home in his wife's name, making it harder to trace ownership to himself or have the property seized for repayment of any debts that might come due.⁶

In March, Hoyt retold his story to the other Providence partners, but they were not swayed. At the meeting, General Lyman B. Frieze represented A. & W. Sprague & Co. Like William Reynolds, the 36-year-old

Lyman B. Frieze had served with Governor Sprague at the First Battle of Bull Run as a lieutenant colonel. Upon Sprague's recommendation, Frieze was selected as Quartermaster General of the State of Rhode Island in January 1862. Frieze proudly retained the title of "general" the rest of his life. Less than two weeks after Byron Sprague left his position with A. & W. Sprague, Frieze resigned his appointment with the state. He had accepted Senator Sprague's offer to take Byron's place, effective as of February 1863.[7]

General Frieze departed from the Providence meeting with Harris Hoyt "with the firm conviction that the other parties to the adventure had been deceived and swindled." He and the two other partners had had enough of Hoyt and his empty promises. They wrote off their $25,000 investments and had nothing more to do with any of his Texas adventures.[8]

The gullible Reynolds acknowledged that Harris Hoyt had left New York "poor and with our goods, he came back rich and made only loss for us." Despite evidence to the contrary, he began to think that, perhaps, Hoyt was not a crook after all. Maybe it really was just unforeseen circumstances and extraordinary expenses that had eaten up all of their profits. Whether Hoyt was crooked or not, Reynolds knew that the prospects for recovering his investment were remote. Like a gambling addict, Reynolds seemed to be hoping that the next roll of the dice would be a winner. Perhaps, with patience, everything would turn out all right after all.[9]

When it became clear that he had persuaded Reynolds of his honorable intent, Hoyt became very friendly and anxious to serve. He assured Reynolds that he would return to Matamoros and send back cotton for the amount that he owed. He also promised to help Reynolds collect the money that Labatt & Joseph owed him for the *Citizen*'s cargo.[10]

After Brastow had returned from Matamoros the previous summer, Reynolds had sent another agent named Thomas W. Whitford to Matamoros. Whitford had orders to sell the remainder of the *Citizen*'s goods that were in Labatt & Joseph's warehouse. Instead of getting the expected cotton, all Reynolds got was the bad news that "Labatt had run away into Texas, taken our goods with him, and that we should never get anything from these goods." Reynolds had been victimized by another Texas swindler.[11]

New York merchants like Reynolds were not alone in having to deal with unscrupulous merchants and agents in the Texas cotton trade. Two clever agents named D.T. Bisbie and Samuel J. Redgate managed to scam Confederate officials from Richmond to Texas. Richmond's endorsement helped these men cheat Generals Magruder and Bee along with their quartermasters in Texas. Representing themselves as agents of the house of Bellot, De Miniers of Paris, they claimed to be acting on behalf of the French government. Redgate, a Unionist sympathizer and former member of the Texas legislature, had just returned from England. He had been on the SS *Peterhoff* when the U.S. Navy captured the British-flagged merchantman as it was on its way to Matamoros. He finally arrived at the Rio Grande in June 1863. Like Harris Hoyt, Redgate also had a personal interest in a cotton and wool manufacturing company. It was operating in Columbus just a few miles from Hoyt's carding machines at Prairie Lea. When Redgate and Bisbie were not able to cash some bogus French bank drafts, the Confederates discovered "There was no such house, and in a garret [a dismal top floor attic-room] in Bordeaux, Bellot was found, who protested, of course, the drafts." The Confederate generals in Texas referred to this successful con as the "Bellot contract swindle."[12]

Seeing that Reynolds had grudgingly accepted his explanations for his many failures, Hoyt invited Reynolds to place some freight on the brig *Caracas*. Hoyt had leased the vessel subsequent to their previous meeting using the profits gained from his part in the Texas Adventure. He was planning to send the British brig to Matamoros in the third week of March 1864. Reynolds was understandably hesitant, given his poor luck in the Texas cotton trade in general and with Hoyt in particular. Hoyt went into his best sales pitch, assuring Reynolds that "a small invoice of well-selected goods would pay very handsomely." He was no longer touting humanitarian aid to Texas Unionists.[13]

The plan was for Hoyt's clerk Theodore A. Morris to go out in the *Caracas* on their behalf. Morris was a Southerner whose Confederate brother was a prisoner of war at Camp Chase in Ohio. Hoyt would travel separately, after the *Caracas* departed. He would take a steamer to the Rio Grande via Havana and "probably be in Matamoras [sic] before the brig arrives, and could probably sell … anything which you might ship." Hoping to finally get a small return on his investment and place Hoyt under obligation to him, Reynolds agreed. He would pay Morris and Hoyt 25 percent each of any profits realized from the sale of the cargo.[14]

Reynolds gave Hoyt $5,000 in greenbacks. He also committed to an invoice of about $15,000 worth of goods on the *Caracas*. The commodities included flour, corn, lard, butter, sugar, candles, and an India-rubber boat, the sales of which were to be converted into cotton. Hoyt's only partners in this venture were his clerk Theodore A. Morris, plus William Reynolds and his company's agent James A. Suydam. Each of the four men had a one-quarter interest in the enterprise.[15]

The *Caracas* cleared New York for Matamoros on March 22 but had to divert to Bermuda nine days later. The brig was in distress, and

8. Deceived and Swindled from New York to Matamoros

Bermuda was the nearest safe haven. Three days out of port, the *Caracas* had encountered a storm that washed away all of their provisions with the exception of some crackers and water. She was unseaworthy and had to be repaired. After waiting at Bermuda for over three months, Morris was finally able to transfer the undamaged cargo from the steamer *Caracas* to the British sailing brig *Monarch* that happened to be on its way to Matamoros from Liverpool.[16]

Back in New York, Hoyt delayed his travel to Matamoros, but pressed ahead with his plan to buy and sell Texas cotton. Before departing, he agreed to Charles Prescott's demand to meet in New York City and settle their accounts. Hoyt still owed Prescott 25 percent of the profits he had made on the Texas Adventure, plus the money Prescott had sent to his wife in response to a request from Mrs. Hoyt in January of 1863. Marie Emma Hoyt had requested that Prescott send $150 to her temporary home in Morris, Illinois. She had some unexpected expenses due to an unspecified illness in the family. The only problem for Prescott in meeting with Harris Hoyt was that their rendezvous was set for April 24, 1864. When Prescott showed up, Hoyt had already left the country. He had departed New York for Havana on April 23 aboard the *Corsica*, a "packet steamer" that made a regularly scheduled run from New York to Nassau, and Havana.[17]

In Havana, Hoyt transferred to a Spanish brig and arrived in Matamoros in mid–May. There, he reconnected with the 22-year-old William Compton. He had met Compton at his hotel during his first visit to Matamoros in January 1863. Like many young men in this border town, Compton had fled Texas to avoid the Confederate draft. Since arriving at Matamoros from Brenham in April of 1862, William had been working as a clerk for J.B. Bostock, Freeman & Co., one of the many commission agents doing business at the Rio Grande. Hoyt decided to switch his business to William Compton from his previous agent, Hale & Co. That company's principal partner, John Maloney, had been ill for several weeks and died in the winter of 1863–1864, throwing the affairs of Hale & Co. into disarray.[18]

Hoyt felt that he could rely on William Compton since he was probably acquainted with his parents, Abraham and Rebecca, from his time in Brenham. When the *Monarch* arrived in mid–July, Hoyt hired Compton as his agent for the sale of his cargo. Despite the mishap on the *Caracas*, most of Hoyt's goods, including the corn and flour, made it safely to Matamoros. His only significant loss was an India-rubber boat that the United States government confiscated for their own use on the Rio Grande. Using the returns from the sale of the *Monarch*'s cargo, Hoyt purchased more cotton.[19]

View of Brownsville from Matamoros at the Santa Cruz ferry, from *Frank Leslie's Illustrated News*, Dec 5, 1863 (Library of Congress Prints & Photograph Division).

While Hoyt was in Matamoros, he also organized the shipment of a small lot of wool to New York. The schooner *George* departed on July 20, 1864, and arrived 31 days later with 22 bales of wool that Hoyt consigned to W.H. Reynolds & Co. After sending the *George* on its way, Hoyt had his agent Theodore Morris go into Texas and then crossed the river himself to call on 27-year-old Union General Francis Herron in Brownsville. Hoyt would have known that Herron had been a banker in Dubuque, Iowa, before the war and no doubt hoped to leverage this Iowa connection to his advantage. Neither of the men described the nature of their business, but later events would reveal the reason for Hoyt's visit. It concerned his unsuccessful attempt to recover the India-rubber boat that the Army had taken from him. The reason why the Army confiscated the boat, or how they used it, is unknown, but an inflatable boat would have been handy on the Rio Grande for troops on the move.[20]

The U.S. Treasury agent in Brownsville at the time that Hoyt met with General Herron to contest the seizure of his property was George W. Brackenridge, who was from Corpus Christi, Texas. Early in the war, Brackenridge and his partner had contracted with Charles Stillman to ship cotton from Corpus Christi Bay to the Rio Grande. Most of this early commerce went via the inland waterway. Always a Unionist at heart, Brackenridge was first and foremost an opportunist, as well as an astute businessman. By July of 1863, he had departed Texas and was in Washington, D.C., working as a clerk for the U.S. Treasury Department. He received this appointment thanks to a personal visit with President Lincoln, who recalled a friendly connection with Brackenridge's father who had been an Indiana lawyer.[21]

Brackenridge jumped at the opportunity to accompany the U.S. invasion forces to South Texas. He set up a U.S. Treasury Department office in Brownsville from November 1863 until May 1864. One of his duties was to receive captured Confederate goods including cotton, and other property such as India-rubber boats. Despite his malleable national loyalties, he remained a good friend to Charles Stillman and his partners Richard King and Mifflin Kenedy. Brackenridge's personal loyalty earned him the enmity of Union generals who believed that he was "only here to accomplish his own selfish ends."[22]

Treasury agents were not the only U.S. government officials who were manipulating business affairs along the Rio Grande for their own selfish ends. As the Federal forces prepared to withdraw from Brownsville in July 1864, Colonel Henry Bertram was also cashing in. He ordered soldiers under his command to load captured cow hides onto the King & Kenedy steamboat *James Hale*. They were working for the benefit of a sutler named Charles Mix, a civilian merchant who sold non-military items to soldiers such as tobacco, coffee, and sugar. In return for the use of his Army stevedores to load the hides, Mix gave the colonel a share of the profits. Bertram's improper use of his soldiers and government equipment for personal gain was not his only selfishly illicit act. On July 16, Mifflin Kenedy paid the colonel a bribe of $200. The cryptic entry, "Bribed Col Bertram U.S.A. not to sell," provides little insight into the reason for the transaction, but it may refer to M. Kenedy Co.'s river steamboat, the *James Hale*.[23]

King and Kenedy's former partner, José San Román, had been managing the financial accounts for the firm's Rio Grande steamboats while they were in U.S. custody. He was a good steward of their assets. Shortly after the Federal forces evacuated Brownsville, San Román deposited $159,140.09 into the Kenedy & Co.'s account. Mifflin Kenedy's clerk labeled the payment as "Rec'd as a compensation for the seizure of the Steamboats *Matamoros*; *Mustang*, and *James Hale*." Kenedy may have bribed Bertram to keep the Union colonel from exposing this sham sale and then profiting from it by selling the steamboats himself.[24]

Having failed to recover his inflatable boat, Harris Hoyt cleared from the Rio Grande on August 20, 1864, shortly after the departure of Federal troops from Brownsville. He was bound for Havana on the American-flagged ocean steamer *Mexico* in company with William

Compton. As with most of his business associates and traveling companions who were not relatives, Hoyt ended up owing money to Compton that he never repaid. The *Mexico* also carried a cargo of 303 bales of cotton in individually owned lots of 5, 7, 9, 59, 106, and 117 bales. José San Román owned the largest of these lots. San Román's agents sold all 117 bales of his cotton in Havana for a net gain of almost $28,000. Hoyt said that all of his cotton was still in Matamoros when he departed. However, that claim may have been a lie to prevent Reynolds from laying claim to it. Hoyt may have had some of the cotton that he had hauled to Laredo the previous November on board the *Mexico* under a different name. If he sold the cotton in Havana, it would have been difficult for Reynolds to discover his fraud.[25]

Hoyt changed ships in Havana and returned to New York in the steamer *Roanoke* on September 13, 1864. He reported to Reynolds & Co. that he had not sent out any cotton at all. Hoyt dodged Reynolds' demands for payment by saying that he was very busy with other business matters. Hoyt told him not to worry; he had settled all business affairs with the Providence partners through his agent, Theodore Morris, who was still at the Rio Grande. Hoyt also assured Reynolds that he had 100 bales of cotton on its way to New York. Between 40 and 50 bales of this lot belonged to Reynolds and represented profits from the *Caracas/Monarch* adventure. All of the cotton would arrive soon and it would all be consigned to W.H. Reynolds & Co.[26]

By this time, Hoyt had abandoned his plans to recover the cotton that the U.S. Navy had captured from the schooner *America*. Lieutenant Frederick Hill, the former captain of the *W.G. Anderson*, was back in the good graces of the Navy. After his ignominious forfeiture of command and court martial conviction, Hill had returned to active service on the Mississippi. As of September 1864, Hill was again in command; this time he had a 14-gun sidewheel steamer, the USS *Tyler*, that was operating on the White River in Arkansas. As Hoyt was making his way back to the United States, Hill was sending an armed expedition ashore in hopes of capturing five Confederate officers who had congregated at a known rebel sympathizer's home near the mouth of the White River. When his armed party arrived, the men made their escape, but the mother of two of the fugitive officers remained. Hill was surprised to learn that she had a permit from the local U.S. Treasury agent requiring the USS *Tyler* to escort her cotton to a market. Lieutenant Hill at first refused, but the region's Army general had duly endorsed the order, leaving him no choice but to comply. Hill and his gunboat ironically found themselves having to help transport several bales of Rebel cotton, this time without realizing any personal profit.

Frederick Hill spent the rest of the war in command of the *Tyler* without further scandal or reprimand.[27]

After reporting to Reynolds, Hoyt left New York to visit his family at their new home in Chicago. While he was there, Hoyt wrote Reynolds' agent Suydam and then he penned another letter directly to Reynolds. Both letters requested payment for the wool that had arrived the previous month via the schooner *George*. Reynolds had sold the 22 bales of wool for $2,500. Hoyt brazenly said that this wool belonged to other parties, not to him or Reynolds. Knowing that he had a rightful claim to this money, but worried that Hoyt would take offense and not pay off his other, much larger debts, Reynolds sent Hoyt a bank draft for the full amount.[28]

When Reynolds learned that Hoyt's agent Theodore Morris had returned to New York in early November, he went to the city and confronted him. To his disappointment, Morris had "no bill of lading for any cotton." Morris repeated what Hoyt had said back in September. The only variation in his story was that there were actually 160, not just 100, bales of cotton on their way to New York. This was part of the cotton that Hoyt had crossed into Mexico at Laredo and would soon be arriving on the British sailing brig *Monarch*: 120 bales for Hoyt and 40 bales for the partners. Morris also assured Reynolds that more of his cotton would arrive via the brig *Sybil*, which was loading at the Rio Grande when he left. As Morris would have known, there actually were two "*Sybils*" anchored off Bagdad when he departed. One was a brig (more properly spelled *Sibyl*) and the other was a schooner. The brig did not arrive in New York until March 1865; the schooner would arrive much sooner.[29]

Reynolds asked Morris why he did not remain in Matamoros until the cotton had been shipped. Morris replied that Hoyt had ordered him back to New York to settle the insurance claim for some of the goods from the *Caracas* that had been damaged on its voyage to Bermuda. To make matters worse, Morris had failed to get the proper custom house clearance papers for the cargo. The confusion was understandable. It had been a complex arrangement, since the original bond issued in New York was for the cargo on the *Caracas*. That cargo had to be reshipped on board the *Monarch* in Bermuda and then delivered to Matamoros. As a result of the faulty paperwork, Reynolds could not redeem the bond he had paid for the *Caracas* at the New York custom house.[30]

The primary reason for the disruption of the paper work in Matamoros was the resignation of the conscientious, but hard pressed, U.S. Consul, Leonard Pierce, in August. Tired of the constant threats to his life and limb and disappointed with the Union Army's withdrawal from the Texas coast, Pierce departed for Maine with his family in October. The post remained vacant until late November 1864. Secretary Seward's choice for Consul Pierce's replacement was Emanuel Dorsey Etchison of Baltimore. Etchison had few redeeming qualities and was a sterling example of a consular agent who was primarily motivated by greed.[31]

Etchison had been a dry goods merchant in Washington, D.C. When that business failed, his creditors accused Etchison of fraud. In 1861, he moved to Baltimore where he became the manager of a drug store owned by Thomas Phillips, who was in failing health. Etchison was pocketing the rent for Phillips' store. One night, he suddenly closed the store and secretly moved all the goods to a storage warehouse without the owner's knowledge. Two years elapsed before Etchison appeared at the facility to claim the merchandise, but he failed to prove his ownership of the containers. He then brought suit against the storage company, brazenly justifying his actions by testifying that he had stored the goods to elude his creditors. Etchison then left the country to accept his appointment as U.S. Consul to Matamoros before he could be brought to justice. The prospective consul to Matamoros was rightfully accused of being man of "very dissipated habits, and is a gambler, and of bad reputation, untruthful, and lives by his wits."[32]

There should have been no expectation that Etchison would be honest or efficient in the execution of his duties as the new U.S. Consul. He did not disappoint. When Etchison arrived in Matamoros, he proved himself to be "a humbug, a drunkard, and a fool." According to the general in command of Union forces at the Rio Grande, "He charged our own citizens unwarrantable fees, and … he has in his pockets several thousand dollars in gold not his own. Even his washerwoman was left unpaid." The State Department cashiered him after he enraged the local Mexican authorities who quickly revoked his diplomatic status in January 1865.[33]

Having managed to avoid dealings with Consul Pierce's dishonest replacement, all of the remaining Texas Adventure participants were back in New York City by November 1864. Just a few days after Theodore Morris had met with William Reynolds, Hoyt's former partner, Charles Prescott, had a fortuitous meeting with Morris in the lobby of the Metropolitan Hotel. Located at the corner of Broadway and Prince streets, the Metropolitan was one of the largest and most elegant hotels in the city. When asked about Hoyt, Morris admitted that his boss had done very well in Texas and that he would arrive from Illinois that very day. This time, Hoyt was unable to avoid the persistent Prescott. Hoyt told him that there were 163 bales of his cotton on the *Monarch* and that she would arrive in New York between the 15th and 20th of December.[34]

Hoyt bragged that despite the treachery of Frederick Hill, the U.S.

Navy, and their Providence partners, he had managed to clear $45,000 in profits from the Texas Adventure. Hoyt had used a portion of that windfall to purchase and furnish a home in Chicago the previous February. Having received very little himself, Prescott could not have been pleased with this news. Hoyt was confident that he had fulfilled his part of the bargain by purchasing and running out cotton from Texas. He could not be blamed if none of his partners actually received any of that cotton.[35]

Hoyt echoed Morris' claim that Reynolds' "56 bales of cotton are on the *Sybil*." Naturally, a couple of minor problems arose that were not the fault of Harris Hoyt. The USS *Iosco* had captured the British-flagged schooner *Sybil* on November 20 off the coast of North Carolina. The prize crew from the *Iosco* delivered the schooner and her papers to New York City on December 1, 1864, the same day as the meeting between Reynolds and Hoyt. Although the *Sybil* was loaded with 306 bales of cotton that had cleared from Matamoros, it would be months before Reynolds could obtain any cotton that might belong to him. Even then, the admiralty court would have to rule that the seizure was not justified.[36]

The U.S. government did eventually release both the vessel and its cargo. It would also pay the owners restitution for the inconvenience of their detention. Unfortunately for Reynolds and Prescott, as soon as they saw the *Sybil*'s manifest they knew that none of that money would ever go to them. There was no cotton on board the *Sybil* consigned to Hoyt, Prescott, or Reynolds. Becoming equally as adept at obfuscation as his boss, Morris subsequently explained that his agent in Matamoros had probably shipped all of the cotton on some other vessel. He had no doubt that this unidentified ship had loaded their cotton and "would come along very soon."[37]

Morris also confessed that a man who had known him in Texas was claiming that he owed a $500 or $600 debt. The man had threatened Morris with arrest if he did not pay his debt. Reynolds said that he was willing to cover Morris' bail bond if and when he was arrested. However, "if he had done anything wrong, this was no place for him." Morris evidently decided take that advice and Reynolds never saw Theodore Morris again.[38]

Charles Prescott was aware of the lies that Hoyt and his agent Morris had told about the *Sybil*. Both he and Reynolds also learned that the *Monarch* was not actually on its way to New York after all. The *Monarch* departed the Rio Grande in mid–November and she was fully loaded with cotton. However, she was not destined for New York. The *Monarch* arrived in Liverpool two months later with a cargo of 747 bales. None of that cotton or proceeds from the sale ever made its way into the pockets of any Texas Adventure partner except for Harris Hoyt's. Reynolds had about $20,000 invested in the *Caracas'* invoice. His only return was an $1,800 insurance payment for the goods that were damaged on the voyage to Bermuda.[39]

For Charles Prescott, this was the final straw. On Tuesday, December 6, 1864, he reported the entire Texas Adventure scheme to Major John A. Bolles, the U.S. Army Judge Advocate General (JAG) in New York City. While it is not clear whether Prescott took the initiative in reporting the scheme, he received full immunity. He gave a sworn statement detailing all the individuals involved, with particular emphasis on Theodore Morris, Harris Hoyt and William Reynolds. He testified that "Morris is a rebel, and so is Hoyt, at heart." Prescott also confided to Major Bolles that if the government acted quickly, they could nab two of the most egregious culprits that day, saying, "Colonel Reynolds and Hoyt will be together at the Fifth Avenue or Metropolitan this evening." Like the Metropolitan, the Fifth Avenue Hotel was one of New York City's finest; it occupied the entire frontage between 23rd and 24th streets. Prescott advised the major that he needed to hurry. Harris Hoyt was planning to head west to his new home in Chicago after his meeting with William Reynolds.[40]

9

Aiding the Enemy without Conviction

Charles Prescott was particularly aggrieved with William Reynolds for cutting him out of the deal upon his return from Havana on the last day of 1862. His resentment for Harris Hoyt also ran deep. Hoyt came out of the Texas Adventure a wealthy man, while Prescott had nothing to show for his efforts. He too had a wife and a large family to feed. After almost two years of waiting and hoping, Prescott gave up and turned on his duplicitous partners.

Major John Bolles reported Prescott's accusations to Major General John Adams Dix, who commanded the Department of the East in New York. General Dix, like Secretary of State Seward, was a former senator from New York. Like Seward, he would also become a New York Governor. Dix had preceded Salmon P. Chase as the Secretary of the Treasury in the cabinet of the Democrat, President James Buchanan. The politically astute Dix immediately realized the gravity of Prescott's accusations and the scandalous import of investigating William Sprague, a war-hero senator. The fact that Sprague was the multi-millionaire son-in-law of the man who took his place as Secretary of the Treasury under President Lincoln only added to the sensitivity. From his non-combatant position in New York, Dix fully understood what Sprague, Reynolds, and Hoyt had been doing, and he took action.[1]

General Dix ordered the immediate arrest or questioning of just about everybody associated with the Texas Adventure. His first order of business was to seize all their papers and arrest Harris Hoyt, William H. Reynolds, and Byron Sprague. He even detained John W. Boynton, the man who had sold the wool carding machinery to Hoyt. Dix also ordered the cancelation of Reynolds' bond on the cargo of the *Caracas* (actually the *Monarch*) and ordered the New York Customs House to seize any cotton that might arrive on a vessel named the *Warrior*. The people were real, but the vessels were ghosts. Neither of these merchant ships ever arrived in New York in 1864 or 1865, and no vessel by the name of *Warrior* had even made a port call at the Rio Grande.²

General Dix was no stranger to the subject of interstate commerce, including illicit trade with the South. In addition to being a railroad president before and after the war, he had commanded the Union occupied area of Virginia earlier in the War. This position gave him the opportunity to profit from trade in Norfolk when Union forces occupied the city. Dix sought to personally control all import and export permits for that part of Virginia without having to certify that the shipments were a "military necessity." At the time, it seemed that he was in favor of a strict naval blockade for every port except Norfolk, the one he controlled.³

Major General John Adams Dix, 1861, portrait by Mathew Brady (Library of Congress Prints & Photograph Division).

Although Dix was not able to capture Reynolds and Hoyt at their meeting in the Metropolitan Hotel, he did corral Hoyt that evening, probably at his hotel room. On the morning of December 8, 1864, the provost marshals burst into William Reynolds & Co.'s New York City office at 45 William Street and found that Reynolds was not there. He had already departed for Providence, Rhode Island. As soon as Dix's men left the office, the company's chief clerk fired off a telegram that must have sent chills up Reynolds' spine. It said, "The provost marshal has orders for your arrest and Byron Sprague's, for furnishing aid and comfort to the enemy."⁴

Over the next several days, Dix issued subpoenas for the sworn statements of Robert Knight, Edward P. Taft, General Lyman B. Frieze, and William Compton. Knight and Taft were the two silent investors in the Texas Adventure. They had disassociated themselves from the scheme after Hoyt returned in January 1864 and were cleared of any wrongdoing. Lyman B. Frieze had taken over the management of A. & W. Sprague &

Co.'s financial affairs from Byron Sprague in December 1862. Frieze had concurred with Taft and Knight's assessment of Harris Hoyt and had withdrawn Senator William Sprague's overt support of the Texas Adventure as of March 1864. After giving an initial statement, the Texan William Compton returned to Matamoros in February 1865 to avoid further prosecution. Two other suspects, Reynolds' agents Thomas Whitford and Henry Brastow, had gone to Colorado and could not be reached. Similarly, Harris Hoyt's agent, Theodore Morris, was nowhere to be found.[5]

The most important name that was missing from the list of accused and witnesses was Senator William H. Sprague of Rhode Island. As an unindicted co-conspirator, Sprague was clearly worried. He had married Kate Chase in November 1863 and won election to the U.S. Senate that same year. He was desperate to keep his name out of the papers and his person out of jail. He quickly penned a series of unsolicited appeals and explanations to General Dix. He was working hard to distance himself from the inherently illegal aspects of the Texas Adventure.[6]

Sprague's first message to General Dix was on December 10. It was an urgent, but futile, telegraph that asked the general to suspend any further arrests until the senator had a chance to explain. Sprague pointed to the swindler Hoyt as the culpable party. The senator opined that Hoyt may have used his high level endorsements from John Hay and himself "for treasonable purposes."[7]

Senator Sprague vouched for the loyalty and honesty of everyone except for his cousin and former partner, Byron Sprague and, of course, Harris Hoyt. Byron had supervised the management of the Texas Adventure and had left the firm "with hostile intentions." The senator pointed out that his other close associates had served their country in the field and diligently contributed to the prosecution of the war. He omitted the fact that, just like his cousin Byron, their honorable service was as subordinate officers in his Rhode Island regiment. Sprague feared that his political opponents would use these arrests and accusations against him. If compelled to move forward, he asked Dix to prosecute the case "with as little publicity as possible."[8]

Senator Sprague later explained to General Dix that he and his partners "never realized a dollar from Hoyt's Texas adventure." Instead, they had suffered heavy losses. He admitted that his company needed cotton to keep their cotton mills in operation, but his motives were purely altruistic. His firm only acted on behalf his stake-holders and not for any personal gain. Those stake-holders were the industrious women and children who were toiling away in mills. He had to have cotton to protect the jobs of these poor, hardworking people.[9]

Byron Sprague feigned ignorance about any and all illegal activities. He had, after all, parted ways with his cousin William and the firm of A. & W. Sprague & Co. on November 7, 1862. Byron said that he knew nothing of what had taken place since then. He also subtly yielded to the temptation of pointing a guilty finger at William Sprague, happily suggesting that the then-governor was fully aware of and engaged in the Texas Adventure. General Dix did not immediately absolve Byron Sprague of wrongdoing, but he did give him a parole of honor on December 9, 1864.[10]

William H. Reynolds also tried to distance himself from Hoyt's felonious and treasonous acts by saying that he had "carefully instructed Hoyt and Prescott that nothing should be done that could compromise us with the Government." He said that he was removed from the details of the enterprise since "most of the business was done by my agent and clerks." He too pointed the finger at William Sprague, saying that the senator was the culprit who influenced him to trust Harris Hoyt.[11]

As for himself, Reynolds admitted that he was only guilty of trusting "Mr. Hoyt further than was prudent." He also may have given too much credence to an endorsement from "the highest official authority in Washington." It was another subtle suggestion that if he went down, so would John Hay and President Lincoln. Given his active military service in fighting against the rebellion at the First Battle of Bull Run, the former lieutenant colonel reasoned that it was not possible for him to "willingly engage in a transaction contrary to the wishes of my Government."[12]

Harris Hoyt was the most obvious and the most vulnerable suspect. When he was arrested, his residence was in Chicago, but he maintained an office in New York City. Even though it was Charles Prescott who initially reported the scheme to military officials, Prescott also was under suspicion and had to make several lengthy statements. General Dix released Charles Prescott on parole on December 17, 1864.[13]

The day after his arrest, Hoyt swore that, but for 10 or 20 bales, he never shipped any cotton out of Texas by land or sea. He was probably referring to the cotton he ran through the blockade on the *Elizabeth* in 1862. He seemed to have forgotten about his cotton on the *America* and *Lehman*. Even 10–20 bales would have sold for between $2,500 and $10,000, the equivalent to about $40,000 to $170,000 in 2019. Hoyt blatantly denied ever having any interest in a blockade runner. He also claimed that had he never sold any goods in Texas with the exception of the carding machinery and some personal items.[14]

He specifically denied supplying arms or "munitions of war to any rebel, or in any other way aided the rebel cause either directly or indirectly." As for the *Ella Warley*, he feigned ignorance that the steamer had played any part in his Texas Adventure. Continuing his series of lies and half-truths, Hoyt conveniently forgot that Charles Prescott had delivered the weapons and other cargo to Havana on the *Ella Warley*. Hoyt had then transferred some of that cargo to *Cora* and sold the rest to Confederate Colonel Luckett, adding to his supply of cash that Hoyt took with him into Texas from Matamoros.[15]

When recalled to testify again on December 12 and after several other witnesses had made damning statements, Hoyt decided to clarify some of his earlier claims. William Sprague may have helped inspire his revised recollections. Hoyt's moral compass was firmly fixed on outcomes that were to his own benefit. Financial incentives from the millionaire Sprague could have motivated Hoyt's diversion of blame to the other partners in his second statement.[16]

Hoyt revised his story to say that his plan all along was to "take the *Cora* out in ballast, and be ready at some point to go into any port in Texas that might be opened by the Federal gunboats." This was another one of Hoyt's retrospective explanations. This one capitalized on President Lincoln's Proclamation of February 18, 1864, that raised the blockade of Brownsville. The proclamation technically opened Brazos Santiago to U.S.-flagged merchant ships until April 11, 1865, but it had no practical effect on the *Cora*'s movements. The Union occupation of the coast of Texas south of Caney Creek only occurred after Hoyt had already set out for Mexico from Brenham. When President Lincoln lifted the blockade of Brownsville, Hoyt had already returned to the North. Neither event would have factored into Hoyt's actual activities or plans.[17]

Hoyt again shaded the truth when he told investigators that he had "never received any pecuniary aid" from William Sprague. It was true that he had only received money directly from Byron Sprague and William Reynolds. It was, however, William Sprague's company that contributed $25,000 to the Texas Adventure along with another $75,000 from other investors, primarily as a result of Sprague and Reynolds' encouragement. With complete sincerity, Hoyt melodramatically swore that, he was "not aware of having done anything wrong. I may have committed an error, but if I have, it is an error of the head, and not of the heart."[18]

Harris Hoyt's court-martial commenced on January 23, 1865, at Fort Lafayette. Located in the lower bay of New York Harbor, Fort Lafayette was the favored military prison for political prisoners, Confederate officers, and U.S. citizens suspected of treason. Hoyt was charged with "Violation of the law of war." He had six separate, but related, specifications leveled against him. They included taking wool carding machinery, arms, and munitions into Texas and running cotton overland and through the blockade out of Texas. As the historical record shows, all of these allegations were true. Harris Hoyt was clearly guilty on all counts, but justice does not always prevail when high level political equities are at stake.[19]

Through his counsel, John D. Townsend, Hoyt pleaded not guilty to the charge and every specification except for two: importing machinery and running the blockade. Townsend was a Harvard-educated criminal defense lawyer who had spent several months as a merchant sailor. He abandoned that profession by deserting from his ship in Chile. He made his way back to Cambridge, Massachusetts, and entered law school there. He was uniquely qualified to defend his devious client. For the first charge, Townsend said that the alleged offense occurred beyond the two-year limitation imposed by the articles of war. For the second, he simply asked for more time to prepare his defense for running the blockade. After Dix denied both requests, Hoyt then entered a plea of "not guilty" to all specifications.[20]

In response to a request from General Dix, the War Department was able to confirm that Harris Hoyt wrote to Secretary Edwin Stanton in September of 1862. The Secretary's correspondence log indicated that the accused had asked Stanton to issue a pass that would give him permission to go to Texas. The stated purpose of Hoyt's proposed excursion into enemy territory was to make arrangements for the removal of Union families to the North. Unfortunately, the department had "accidentally mislaid" the actual letter, which prevented the prosecutor from entering the document into evidence. There also was no record of Secretary Stanton's response, leaving open the possibility that somebody in the War Department had given Hoyt a permit to trade across enemy lines.[21]

On March 22, 1865, the Army judge advocate completed his review of all the evidence and testimony. He concluded that Harris Hoyt was a subordinate agent employed by Senator William Sprague and his partners. The partners "furnished the capital, vessels, and cargoes, and were the principals in a vast scheme of bringing cotton from Texas." Both Harris Hoyt and Charles L. Prescott were willing to testify against William Sprague and William Reynolds in return for immunity from prosecution.[22]

Although not called to testify, Senator Sprague claimed complete innocence. He parroted Hoyt's bogus claim that the object of the Texas Adventure always had been "to aid Union citizens in Texas, and obtain information for the Government." The judge advocate general (JAG) investigator came to a different conclusion. Major Bolles observed that nobody else connected with the scheme "seems to have viewed it in that light."[23]

Hoyt had testified that both as Governor and as Senator, William

9. Aiding the Enemy without Conviction

Sprague was fully aware of the progress of the business. Sprague had "advised and aided it to the utmost of his power." Sprague's cousin and former partner Byron also confirmed that William knew that the plan always was to obtain cotton from Texas, with or without permits. Given the evidence at hand and William Sprague's tendency to prioritize his business affairs ahead of political and even personal matters, it is almost certain that these allegations were true.[24]

In his summary, the JAG investigator admitted that the evidence did not "give an entirely clear account" of the affair. He suggested that, perhaps, Senator Sprague and the others should be tried in a civil court. From his legal perspective, the actions of the accused were either a "violation of the laws of war, or a higher crime under the Constitution of the United States." He was referring to Section III, Article 3, of the U.S. Constitution, "Treason against the United States." Despite his doubts, Major Bolles recommended that all of the accused men should at least be brought before a general military court-martial under the Articles of War and charged with trading with the enemy.[25]

This senior JAG officer recognized that going after "American citizens of wealth and high social and political" position was a matter of "delicacy." It seemed "unjust that the subordinate Hoyt should be selected as the sole offender for prosecution and punishment." General Dix also was convinced that Senator William Sprague, his partner Byron Sprague, and William H. Reynolds were all well aware of what Harris Hoyt was doing. Dix had rejected Hoyt's plea for dismissal, but he was unsure whether his military commission really did have jurisdiction over these civilians. In a letter to Secretary of War Edwin Stanton on March 22nd, he confessed that his decision might not hold up against men of "high social standing."[26]

Being the astute political general that he was, Dix passed the buck to Secretary of War Stanton the next day. Three weeks later, the proceedings came to a complete halt. The nation had been rocked by the news that John Wilkes Booth had assassinated President Lincoln. The tragedy disrupted all normal government operations, including the prosecution of the Texas Adventure conspirators. Secretary Stanton waited until June 9, 1865, to order the parole of Harris Hoyt, who had been confined at a house of detention for witnesses in New York City.[27]

By August 13, 1865, Hoyt remained free on parole and was living in Rochester, New York, while his wife remained in Chicago. Five days later, military officials extended Harris Hoyt's parole and permitted him to travel from New York City to visit his family in Chicago through the month of September.[28]

With the conclusion of the Civil War, Edwin Stanton had other, more important, political problems on his hands. As a radical Republican, he and most of the U.S. Congress opposed President Andrew Johnson's lenient policy toward the South. To keep his job and advance his own political agenda, Stanton would need all the allies he could get in the U.S. Congress. He realized that it would be to his advantage for Senator William Sprague to owe him a favor, and a big one at that. Secretary Stanton subsequently promoted restrictive legislation that limited President Johnson's ability to remove a cabinet member from office who had been approved by Congress. Johnson's attempt to circumvent that restriction by removing Stanton from office while Congress was on recess eventually led to his impeachment trial. Since only the Senate can try and convict a sitting present and there were only 54 senators at the time, Stanton wanted every vote he could get.[29]

The impeachment trial was held in the Capitol Building, where Senator William Sprague stoically went against his father-in-law Salmon Chase and wife Kate's wishes by voting for impeachment. The Senate failed to obtain a two-thirds majority conviction by just one vote. Even though Sprague did not cast the decisive vote, his action earned him the enmity of his wife and of Chief Justice Salmon Chase. Chase had stepped down as Secretary of the Treasury before the president's impeachment to accept the higher paying and more secure position of chief justice of the Supreme Court. It was in this new position that Chase had presided over the impeachment trial in the U.S. Senate. Chase had his own ambitions to become the next president, and his daughter Kate was his chief supporter. They needed her husband's money to finance the election effort and they literally could not afford a split. Professionally, Sprague's vote kept him in the good graces of his fellow Republicans and of Secretary Stanton, both of whom would help Sprague stay out of jail.[30]

In the end, Congress had exceeded their authority regarding appointments and the impeachment proceedings were much ado about nothing. The episode served as an unheeded warning to future generations. Nobody was fired, but feelings were hurt and positions hardened. Harris Hoyt was never convicted for his crimes and neither were any of his other co-conspirators in the Texas Adventure. The lack of jail time for the scoundrels of the Texas cotton trade, however, did not mean that their actions were without consequences. The post-war effects of their swindling activities during the civil war continued to ripple through the succeeding decades.

10

Post-War Scoundrels Reconstructed and Resurrected

Union forces raised the Stars and Stripes over the Galveston Customs House on June 5, 1865, as an unambiguous sign that the Civil War was over in Texas. Two weeks later, on June 19, General Gordon Granger issued General Order No. 3 that affirmed President Lincoln's proclamation that all slaves were free within Texas. President Andrew Johnson officially lifted the blockade of Galveston and the rest of Texas four days later permitting trade to return to normal along the Texas Gulf Coast.[1]

Despite the cessation of hostilities and the reopening of all Southern ports, the logistic pipeline to Mexico was a long one and could not be shut off quickly. Texas cotton continued to flow out of Matamoros and the Rio Grande for several months. The astute merchant José San Román reported in May of 1865 that there were 10,000 bales in transit to a poor market in Matamoros. San Román accurately predicted that it would take another six months before there would be no more cotton shipments from the Texas-Mexico border. While the flow of cotton to Liverpool continued unabated, many vessels had to return to New York in ballast (i.e., with no inbound cargo except for additional lead ballast weights for stability at sea). Upon the surrender of the South, the North had access to all Southern cotton and could both use it in its domestic mills and export the excess bales to foreign markets. After four years of deprivation, the U.S. market became oversupplied with cotton. The lack of demand in New York led to a dramatic reduction of trade from the Rio Grande to the North. This sudden drop-off has led some historians to surmise that Texas cotton exports out of Matamoros ended immediately, coinciding with the conclusion of the war.[2]

However, contemporary records conclusively show that cotton shipments from Matamoros to Liverpool continued unabated for several months. Between June and the last shipment exported out of the Rio

U.S. Custom House, Galveston, TX, opened March 1861 (Library of Congress, Prints & Photograph Division).

Grande on December 7, 1865, over 22,000 bales of cotton cleared from Matamoros. Despite the high number of vessels bound for New York that sailed in ballast during that period, a total of fifty-two different vessels that cleared from Matamoros carried Texas cotton in their holds. Over ninety percent of those bales and two-thirds of the vessels were bound for Liverpool, where the market for cotton remained relatively strong.[3]

Additional anecdotal evidence abounds. Captain Sewell of the British ship *Rimac* reported that when he left Matamoros on July 16, 1865, with 960 bales of cotton, "The stock of cotton in and about Matamoras [sic] is described as amounting to something enormous, and all the vessels in port were taken up with cotton freights." In September 1865, one Liverpool newspaper even ran a headline, "Enormous Cotton Shipments from Matamoras [sic]."[4]

While the Matamoros trade took several months to revert to its pre-war norms, the cotton trade did eventually dry up at the Rio Grande. Export trade out of Texas again shifted farther north to Galveston, and for a few years, at Indianola in Matagorda Bay. Despite minor wartime damage inflicted upon Galveston, Port Lavaca, and Brownsville, the state's major cities were ready for business and its citizens were relatively prosperous and well fed. Overall, and especially in comparison to other Southern states, Texas emerged from the ashes of the Confederacy relatively unscarred both physically and emotionally. Texas had not experienced an invasion equivalent to Sherman's destructive march to, or from, the sea.

As a mostly undeveloped frontier, Texas simply presented relatively little for Union forces to destroy. The primary antebellum natural resource that the State still had after war remained intact: land, and plenty of it. The people of these vast spaces that nurtured the Texas cotton trade would use the lessons and profits from this exciting, but risky business to produce a sea-change in attitudes. Texans began to envision a state that could be a prominent player on the national and world stage. Wise decisions in this arena would determine their economic future. The state's business and political leaders began working to address the infrastructure shortfalls that the Civil War had so dramatically exposed. Development of railroads, canals, and ports soon became major themes throughout Texas.

Post-war Texans did not have to rebuild so much as they had to decide where and what to build. Some of the men in the Texas cotton trade, such as Mifflin Kenedy, Richard King, Charles Stillman, and George Brackenridge accumulated wartime profits that formed or added to the foundation of their fortunes. There were others such as the Mills Brothers of Galveston, who soon dissipated their wealth when they failed to anticipate the rapidly changing economic landscape.

At the end of the war, Richard King and Mifflin Kenedy immediately made plans to expand their steamboat business on the Rio Grande. Despite the apparent loss of their steamers to Union and Mexican control, the M. Kenedy & Co. business ledgers show a healthy return on their wartime maritime operations. In addition to the $159,140.09 they received as compensation for the seizure of their three river steamboats in January 1865, there are several other similar entries. These accounts and journals record their profits for the steamer *Alamo* after it arrived at the Rio Grande in October of 1863. After the departure of the Union Army from Brownsville in the summer of 1864, they no longer needed their trusted associate, José San Román, to act as the nominal owner of their steamers. When U.S. President Johnson lifted the blockade, they reinvested their wartime profits from their steamers and bought four expensive new river steamboats that they had on the Rio Grande by the summer of 1865.[5]

Richard King and Mifflin Kenedy were skilled at developing deep personal friendships and lasting business relationships. During the Civil War they had leveraged those relationships and business skills in preserving their steamboats and negotiating favorable government contracts. They did have occasional setbacks like the loss of the SS *Cora* that they had purchased with the intent of adding it to their Rio Grande fleet of steamers. Despite these and other unpleasant difficulties, King and Kenedy were well positioned financially at the end of the war. Just as they had done before and during the war, they then negotiated profitable contracts with the military and sold off surplus vessels.[6]

Both men had the foresight to anticipate the huge demand for beef beyond the borders of Texas. Prior to the war, beef steak had been a local staple. Cattle ranchers were shipping hides and tallow and not the actual cattle. Even during the first year of the war, it was hides and not cotton that was the primary commodity exported out of the Rio Grande. In the years after the war, the former steamboat captains realized that the expansion of the railroads and the demand for fresh beef on the hoof soon would change that economic dynamic. King and Kenedy began to divest themselves of their steamboats. They used their wartime cotton profits to expand and sustain their cattle herds and vast pasture lands throughout South Texas.[7]

By 1865, King & Kenedy's former partner Charles Stillman was one of the richest men in America. In January of that year, Stillman perceived that the Confederacy was on the verge of collapse and was anxious to return to New York. He had not seen his wife and family or his New York partners since the war had begun. Despite having signed the oath of allegiance to the United States on December 2, 1863, he was concerned that he might be arrested if he sailed directly to New York from Matamoros. Stillman decided to take passage on the full-rigged sailing ship *Roger A. Heirn*. He had a one-eighth ownership interest in the ship, making it easy for him to sign on as the vessel's supercargo. As a member of the crew, Stillman could avoid having his name appear on the manifest. He planned to return to New York from Liverpool via Halifax so "the hounds here, would not be able to track me."[8]

Stillman returned to Brownsville after the war was over, but suffered a debilitating stroke in 1866 that paralyzed his left arm. Stillman left the Rio Grande permanently that year and rejoined his partners in New York City. While there, he remained in close contact with Jerry Galvan, his friend and associate who had relocated from Matamoros to Brownsville. Galvan's unusual surname has caused some writers to assume that the Irishman was Hispanic, but his name is an Anglicized spelling of the Gaelic "Ó Gealbháin." More than just a "straw man" for Stillman who facilitated the cotton trade between Texas and New York, Jerry Galvan had his own steamboat interests and ran a successful mercantile business. He also became the Cameron County Judge (chief elected official) and a state legislator. A life-long bachelor, in his later years he suffered from "softening of the brain" (dementia or perhaps malaria) and traveled to New Orleans for treatment in the spring of 1879. Believing that he had recovered, Galvan joined his friend and Richard King's son-in-law, Robert Dalzell, on a steamboat tour of the west. Three days out, Galvan either fell or jumped overboard. His lifeless body was discovered the next day on the banks of the Mississippi.[9]

In New York, Stillman never fully recovered from his stroke, but continued to conduct business until his death in 1875 at the age of 65. By then, he had concentrated his investments in the National City Bank of New York, which his son James later controlled. At the time, this bank was one of the largest in the United States. It has retained that status as it evolved through the years into Citibank.[10]

While Stillman returned to his former home in the North, his friend, the former Confederate cotton trader and Union Treasury agent George W. Brackenridge, returned to Texas after the war. Despite being known as one of the more honest U.S. Treasury agents, Brackenridge's personal assets grew from nothing in 1862 to $100,000 in 1866. It was quite an accomplishment for a mid-level employee who was solely dependent upon a government paycheck. He continued to prosper in Texas, thanks in large part to his continuing friendship with Charles Stillman.[11]

During the Union occupation of Brownsville, it was George Brackenridge who managed Stillman's abandoned property. Stillman had signed the oath of allegiance shortly after Union troops occupied the Rio Grande in November 1863, but his loyalties remained suspect. Despite this official certification of allegiance to the United States, Stillman did not regain his personal property until after the Federal Army abandoned Brownsville in July 1864. In the interim, he was pleased with Brackenridge's stewardship. After the war, Brackenridge also assisted Stillman with his successful claim for $30,000 in compensation for cattle that the Union Army had confiscated from his ranch.[12]

The benefits of their relationship, however, were mutual. While Stillman was in semi-retirement in New York, Brackenridge was a regular visitor. Stillman supplied him with $200,000 in cash to help establish and sustain the San Antonio National Bank. Thanks in large part to Stillman's support, Brackenridge soon became one of the wealthiest and most civic-minded men in Texas. In addition to being a principal in his bank, he was president of the San Antonio Water Works Company from 1883 to 1906. He was a director of the Express Publishing Company and president of the San Antonio school board. He was also a regent of the University of Texas at Austin from 1886 until 1911 and again from 1917 to January 1919.[13]

George Brackenridge was a very effective manager and a steadfast friend even to those who had served the cause of the Confederacy. Because of his seemingly economically motivated and fungible national loyalties, many Texans continued to view him as a carpet-bagging profiteer. But his personal loyalty and philanthropy were undeniable. Thirty years after Stillman's death, Brackenridge made an unsolicited transfer of over $87,000 in bank stock to Stillman's heirs. He also donated school buildings in San Antonio and Seguin, at the University of Texas at Austin, and another in Galveston for the benefit of female medical students.[14]

As an advocate for women's education, Brackenridge financed the founding of the school of home economics at the University of Texas, and created a loan fund for women students in architecture, law, and medicine. He also donated 500 acres on the Colorado River to the University of Texas and supported the employment of women as instructors in the university system. While he was still living, he donated 343 acres to the city of San Antonio, now known as Brackenridge Park. It is home to the city zoo, a golf course, the Witte Museum, and many other public venues.[15]

Another one of Stillman's associates and a former partner, José San Román, also continued to prosper after the war. The Spanish-born shipping agent moved his operations back to Brownsville from Matamoros to escape the continuing strife of the Mexican Civil War. Thanks in large part to the Civil War on the American side of the river, San Román was one of the richest men in South Texas. He entrusted the management of his large mercantile firm to his cousin and wartime clerk Simón Celaya. In competition with King and Kenedy's steamboats, San Román helped to secure a new charter for the Rio Grande Railroad Company. With Simón Celaya as president of the narrow gage railroad, they laid twenty-two and a half miles of track from the dock at Point Isabel (now Port Isabel) to Brownsville. San Román returned to Spain in 1878, leaving his major Texas interests in the hands of Celaya and his relatives Feliciano and Justo San Román.[16]

Other Civil War cotton traders in Texas were not so fortunate. In Galveston, Robert and David Mills of R. & D.G. Mills had been a formidable, if somewhat opportunistic, team before and during the war. Robert managed the cotton brokerage and business end of the company while David took care of the plantations and the 800 slaves working on them. After the war, however, they lost their labor force and in the general downturn in business, their customers were unable to pay their bills. The Mills brothers were forced to dig into their cash reserves to cover their own obligations. Their $3 to $5 million fortune completely evaporated when the post-war cotton market collapsed. R. & D.G. Mills declared bankruptcy in 1873.[17]

Charles Russell, the quartermaster for General Bee, who had managed

10. Post-War Scoundrels Reconstructed and Resurrected   139

much of the cotton trade at the Rio Grande, returned to his law practice in Karnes County after the war. In 1866 the voters chose him as their County Judge, the chief political officer in the county, but his term was short-lived. The reconstruction government of Texas abolished the County Judge position in 1869 primarily due to the predominance of former Confederates, like Major Russell, in the position. Judge Russell then returned to his law practice, where he was known for having a fine law library. He also had an excellent grasp of real estate law, due in part to his pre-war experience as a surveyor. In one property dispute case, he noticed that the official survey had a significant recording error. The transcribing clerk had forgotten to include a decimal point and listed the width of the neighboring property as 1055 varas (977 yards) instead of 105.5 (97.7 yards) as documented in the original field notes. As a result, the court awarded Russell's client the neighbor's fine, three-story Victorian-style home as well as the land beneath it. Charles Russell was obviously a good advocate to have on your side, but to some in the county, he became known as "a damned rascal."[18]

The impact of the Civil War Texas cotton trade was felt far beyond the borders of the state. In 1868, the United States and Mexican governments agreed to form a joint commission to adjudicate all the American claims that had been filed against Mexico in the twenty years since the signing of the Treaty of Guadalupe Hidalgo. There were a total of 1017 claims for over $470 million in damages. By mutual agreement, the great majority of the cases were dismissed as being without merit, but 186 cases received awards that totaled over $4 million. With a payout success rate of less than 1 percent, most of the fraudsters' claims failed to extort any money from Mexico. However, one of those who did receive a favorable judgment was Benjamin Weil. Weil and Samuel Loeb had partnered with Harris Hoyt in the blockade running schooner *Lehman*. Weil's award from the joint commission was for $334,950.[19]

Weil had filed his claim against the Mexican government for 1,914 bales of lost cotton. He said that the conniving Mexican bandit-general Juan Cortina had robbed him of the cotton in September 1864 after he had crossed the cotton into Mexico from Texas on carts. Predictably, Benjamin Weil proved to be a scoundrel as well. An initial arbiter awarded Weil restitution, but on second look, the U.S. Congress and the courts proved that Weil actually had owned none of that cotton. He concocted the entire story to collect a perceived debt that originated with the now-defunct Confederate government.[20]

Having discovered Weil's perjury in the first case, the secretary of state and Congress also decided to take a look at his second claim that was for the "respectable sum of $3,962,000." This case alleged that Mexico had illicitly seized the La Abra Silver Mine after the conclusion of the American Civil War. Despite scant evidence to prove the legitimacy of the claim, the arbiter had awarded the claimants over $683,000 including about $480,000 for Weil. Recognizing Weil's obvious perjury, Mexico appealed. Despite additional compelling evidence that once again proved that the entire claim was bogus, Weil received five payments totaling $171,000. The reason Benjamin Weil only received a partial payment was that he died before he was able to collect the full amount. Perhaps it was the guilt borne out of his public disgrace, but shortly after the commission's initial favorable ruling in 1875, he was committed to an insane asylum in his home country of France. He died there two years later. Weil's partner in Galveston, Samuel Loeb also had a small share in the claim. Like Weil, he died before he could collect the full amount. In 1897, the U.S. Court of Claims finally decided that despite the arbiter's ruling of 1875, the award was unjustly based on perjured testimony, and the United States returned the money to Mexico.[21]

Another post-war international repercussion of the Texas cotton trade involved John L. Macaulay, the owner of the illegally acquired blockade runner, *Blanche*. The persistent, but deceitful, Macaulay had sailed from Cuba to the United Kingdom. He had hopes of claiming any indemnity that Spain or the United Kingdom might receive as a result of the U.S. Navy's wanton destruction of the British-flagged steamer and its cotton in Cuban territorial waters. With the refusal of the U.S. to honor any part of those claims, he was unable to collect the money that might have gone to the Confederate government. Although Macaulay was unsuccessful in those efforts, his presence in Europe inspired the litigious and equally deceitful British citizen, Nelson Clements, to take action. Clements sued his former partner for a share of the profits that John Macaulay and his brother James had realized from the *Blanche*'s two successful runs through the blockade.[22]

Clements had to seek justice in Scotland because neither the courts of Texas nor the U.S. Supreme Court would hear his case. The American judicial system would not countenance any claim based on an invalid Confederate contract that they considered inherently illegal. Undeterred, Clements claimed that John Macaulay, as the principal, beneficial owner of the *Blanche*, owed him $12,000 for his 20 percent share in its profits. The case set a legal precedent regarding the proper jurisdiction for cases in which a party to a contract could not get justice at a logical and convenient venue; i.e., the United States. The verdict was a moral victory for Nelson Clements, but it did not, however, gain him any monetary reward.[23]

Since the *Blanche* was technically a British-flagged vessel, Her Majesty's government had also submitted a claim. The U.S. rejected that claim with the same élan as it had the Spanish petition. Secretary Edwin Seward's dubious rationale was that the Confederates had illegally seized the vessel from Charles Morgan's Southern Steamship Company at the outset of the war. He also reasoned that since the *Blanche* was owned by either the defunct Confederate government or some of its citizens, the loss was theirs alone. Because the Confederate States had ceased to exist, there could be no claim. Seward's ethics on this matter were entirely situational. He happily claimed and accepted all former Confederate-owned assets on behalf of the U.S. government, such as the CSS *Shenandoah*, but he would not recognize any of its debts. With other post-war issues to deal with, the United Kingdom was content to let the incident disappear from the international diplomatic scene after 1866. Not even the nominal British owner of the cargo was able to receive any compensation for his loss. Despite his failure to collect reparations from the government, John Macaulay became a successful Wall Street capitalist and speculator.[24]

Back in the United States, Lieutenant Frederick Hill, the former captain of the USS *William G. Anderson* who had confiscated Hoyt's cotton on the schooner *America* for his own profit, was more successful in pursuing a less dangerous, but equally deceitful livelihood as a writer and newspaperman. After his release from the Navy, he returned to the Boston area and his former literary career. In 1886, he bought the *Cambridge Chronicle* and then became editor of the *Cambridge Tribune*. He also penned four books on nautical themes using his full name, Frederick Stanhope Hill. These books included his memoirs titled *Twenty Years at Sea; or, Leaves from My Old Log Book*. Like most, his autobiographical recollections of the war were illuminating, but self-serving when it came to his own conduct. He also wrote poetry, a play, and a history of the Anglican Church.[25]

As the American cotton trade adjusted to peacetime conditions, post-war retribution activities began in earnest in the United States. Union efforts to exact revenge were not exclusively focused on the Reconstruction South. Over the next seven years, American diplomats blamed the United Kingdom for allowing the Confederacy's commerce raiders, primarily the CSS *Alabama*, *Florida*, and *Shenandoah*, to destroy much of the U.S. merchant fleet. An international tribunal eventually ruled that the United Kingdom failed to exercise due diligence against the raiders and owed the United States $15 million in compensation. Payment in gold was due within one year.[26]

The British, Mexicans, and former Southern Rebels were not the only targets for Northern retribution. Popular sentiment strongly favored payback against those Americans who, in their view, had profited from their suffering. Attacks against profiteering individuals and companies within the Union states were common, particularly if they also happened to be a political opponent or competitor. The Rhode Island legislature, for example, initiated an investigation of General Lyman Frieze for his actions during his tenure as Quartermaster General of the State.[27]

General Frieze had managed to escape prosecution for his role with A. & W. Sprague & Co. and the Texas Adventure scandal. There were, however, some accounting irregularities that pointed to his culpability while he was an official with the State of Rhode Island. The investigators questioned his actions regarding the purchase of 1,935 horses from A. & W. Sprague & Co. for Rhode Island's state troops. Multiple discrepancies were evident among the receipts and invoices that he had variously entered into state, company, and private accounts. Frieze and his assistant tried to explain away the issue as a "clerical error." The investigators were not convinced, and the politicians sensed an opportunity to undermine one of Senator Sprague's protégés. At best, the general was guilty of "the want of precision and care" when it came to maintaining his accounts, invoices, and receipts.[28]

William Sprague had obviously used his influence with Lyman Frieze to the advantage of A. & W. Sprague & Co., but it also appeared that General Frieze was padding his own pockets as well. Rampant wartime fraud among contractors and corrupt government officials made it easy for the public to believe accusations of misconduct. The Union Army often had received out-of-date, rancid provisions as well as artillery shells that contractors had packed with sawdust instead of gunpowder. At President Lincoln's urging, Congress had passed the "False Claims Act" in 1863. The legislation was intended to combat these kinds of corrupt practices that companies committed against the government.[29]

Rhode Island Governor James Y. Smith, who had succeeded Sprague in office, publicly accused Frieze of fraud, embezzlement, and wrongful conversion of money. At Governor Smith's request, the state's General Assembly spent several days in public hearings that received full verbatim coverage in the newspapers. The investigation had all the crude trappings of character assassination perfected in the political theater of more modern times. A motion for censure failed after a more careful auditing of Frieze's poorly rendered ledgers pointed toward carelessness rather than thievery.[30]

The net result of the investigation was a political defeat and embarrassment for Governor Smith. General Frieze received a full vindication and, by extension, so did Senator William Sprague. Later, Frieze was Rhode Island's Collector of Internal Revenue and earned the reputation as a "strong, clear-headed, courteous man." He then returned to the textile industry where he worked until the month before his death in 1917 at the age of 82.[31]

Another of the Texas Adventure conspirators, Colonel William Henry Reynolds remained involved in a number of speculative business ventures throughout the remainder of his life. He had mixed results. At the end of the war, and for a few years afterwards, he was a principal owner of two cotton mills in Rhode Island. He was president of the short-lived Warwick Railroad Company of Rhode Island, and then a business partner with the inventor of the telephone, Alexander Graham Bell.[32]

Reynolds purchased a majority interest in Bell's British patent and half the rights to his patents in several other European countries. He then moved to London to help promote investment and manufacture of Bell's telephone. In 1877, Reynolds and Bell succeeded in gaining an audience with Queen Victoria to demonstrate the tantalizing new invention. After their meeting, Bell wrote that he found the "Queen was humpy, stumpy, [and] dumpy," but she was favorably impressed with his telephone. Despite the Queen's endorsement, the European telephone business was slow to develop. Reynolds did not prosper in Europe due to patent infringement, competition from Thomas Edison, and his own inability to attract investors.[33]

True to form, Reynolds continued to chase his dreams of high risk, get-rich schemes. He was an unwitting pawn in an Arizona copper mine swindle and ended up on the wrong end of a lawsuit in which he was the only plaintiff. Another of his failed investments was a railroad construction project and river steamboat operation in Bolivia. Although he continued to dabble in such risky investments, Reynolds appears to have learned his lesson from his near-disastrous involvement with Harris Hoyt's Texas Adventure. His high-living son had to learn that lesson on his own. The 32-year-old Charles Reynolds was arrested for forgery in 1890, while William Reynolds was living in London. His son's fraudulent activities aside, the elder Reynolds managed to steer clear of any further scandals. In his personal life, he remained a respected member of the community and was an active participant in Civil War veterans' groups. He died at the age of 78 in New York City and is buried in Providence at Swan Point Cemetery.[34]

William Reynolds had been a gullible participant in the Texas Adventure, but he was not the reason the scheme became a public scandal. His former boss, Senator William Sprague, through his cooperation with Secretary William Stanton, had managed to keep the affair out of the newspapers for over five years. The Texas Adventure and court martial of Harris Hoyt lay dormant and forgotten until the late fall of 1870. It became a public spectacle when one of William Sprague's political antagonists exposed the Senator's involvement.[35]

Sprague's role in the Texas Adventure scheme might never have come to light at all, had it not been for Harris Hoyt's self-righteous arrogance. Hoyt had filed a claim with the U.S. Congress for the India-rubber boat that the U.S. Army had confiscated on his second voyage to Matamoros and Brownsville. As the investigation dragged into the fall of 1870, Hoyt forwarded additional documents to be entered into evidence for a government auditor. Among the items were copies of his endorsements from John Hay and William Sprague and some letters that had been "missing" from the War Department's files during Hoyt's original court martial.[36]

All this came to the attention of the Rhode Island Republican Congressman Thomas Jenckes. Citing the War Department's Judge Advocate General Report of the Harris Hoyt court martial, Jenckes launched an attack against Senator Sprague. The congressman accused Sprague of trading with the enemy and "aiding them with money and munitions of war." Unfortunately for the Rhode Island representative, he was unpopular with his fellow politicians for advocating U.S. Civil Service reform. Civil Service appointments were an important source of political influence, finances, and a prime factor fueling public corruption. As a result, Jenckes had little political clout among his peers. Sprague countered by financing Jenckes' opponent who successfully ousted him from office in the 1870 election. Sprague also went on the offensive by demanding a public Senate investigation of his role in the Texas Adventure. The senator knew that his colleagues would fully vindicate his actions.[37]

The Senate quickly opened an investigation and on December 14, 1870, requested the old case file from the War Department. The new Secretary of War, William W. Belknap, forwarded the Texas Adventure documents to the Senate committee on February 27, 1871. Their hastily convened hearings addressed the alleged complicity of Senator William Sprague and his Providence, Rhode Island, business partners in the "so-called Texas Adventure." This kind of adventure was also known as unlawful trade with the enemy during the Civil War. The committee received cursory statements from available witnesses and reviewed all the documents from General Dix's investigation and court martial proceedings. Predictably, the Senate soon concluded that the there was "nothing in the papers implicating Senator Sprague."[38]

William Sprague's vindication in the Texas Adventure scandal did not mean he was free from public ridicule. He continued to serve in the U.S. Senate until 1875, but like the Mills brothers of Texas, his business had failed during the Panic of 1873. As the international economic recession stretched on for several long years, Sprague declined to run for a third term. He and Kate Chase finally divorced in 1882 after a lengthy, contentious, and very public trial that provided scandalous grist for the newspapers of the day. The split was due to the cumulative effects of the ruination of Sprague's milling business, his drinking, and their mutual infidelity. Kate had been conducting an unconcealed affair with the notorious, but handsome and charming presidential hopeful, Senator Roscoe Conkling. In addition to being a philanderer, Conkling was the epitome of a corrupt politician. Among his many transgressions, he had conspired with Major General Napoleon Dana during the Civil War to buy Texas cotton on the Rio Grande at bargain rates.[39]

Harris Hoyt's career as a swindler would outlive William Sprague's reign as a business owner and senator. After his final parole and misguided 1870 claim for a confiscated India-rubber boat, Hoyt disappeared from the public view for five years. He briefly reappeared in the historical record in a short New York newspaper article of February 1875. It was an announcement of the marriage of Clarence R. Bartlett to Cora L. Hoyt. Cora Louise was the 19-year-old daughter of Harris Hoyt and namesake of his former Civil War schooner. Bartlett was a Canadian who worked as a cashier for the Inman Steamship Company, one of the United Kingdom's largest passenger liner companies. Cora's husband died less than two years later after moving to Florida in an unsuccessful attempt to improve his health.[40]

Harris Hoyt's name returned to the headlines in April of 1879. This time it was in association with another well known swindler. George N. Townsend had been arrested in West Virginia for passing fraudulent bank drafts and as the headline announced, "He Deceived the 'Simple-Minded Mountaineers.'" Townsend claimed to be acting for the "Honorable Harris Hoyt" of Brooklyn, a partner in Hoyt & Lansing. Hoyt's partner was Z.D. Lansing, another promoter, real estate speculator "and manipulator of schemes."[41]

It seems that Hoyt could not overcome his swindling past. In 1889, both he and his wife, Marie Emma Hoyt, were indicted for false representation and perjury in a New York court. The "elderly, gray-haired couple" had both posted bogus "straw" bonds. They had fraudulently valued the bonds at $30,000 each and deposited them as collateral for a substantial interest in a West Virginia company that was speculating in real estate. Upon investigation, the Hoyts had no property or any other assets to make good on those bonds. The newspapers described Mr. Hoyt as "a very small man, and looks as if he had a wholesome respect for his wife, who is considerable larger." During the hearing a haughty, but dignified, "Mrs. Hoyt did most of the talking."[42]

In 1893, Harris Hoyt's role in another complex swindle came to light. This one also involved land in West Virginia. A front page headline screamed, "A HUGE FRAUD! Bankers and Capitalists Duped by a Swindle Built on Forgery. Bonds for $1,000,000 That Are Valuable Only as Waste Paper." Hoyt's con this time involved a forged deed for a large tract of land in West Virginia. The forger was paid $2 in a barroom for creating the deed. He passed it to a man using an alias, who passed it to Harris Hoyt, who passed it to his partner Z.D. Lansing, who passed it to two other people. The original forgery occurred in 1875, but the forger back-dated the documents to 1866. Virginia authorities had identified the documents as forgeries in 1879, but years later, Hoyt and his partners managed to convince unwitting victims that the deed was genuine.[43]

By the time this scandal hit the papers in 1893, it was of no concern to Harris and Marie Hoyt. They had departed New York for Liverpool in April of the previous year. They enjoyed a first class cabin on board the Inman Steamship Company's passenger liner, the SS *City of New York*. Predictably, Harris Hoyt left New York owing $3,000 in back rent. Newspapers reported that the elderly couple were living in a London flat at the Imperial Mansion on Charing Cross Road.[44]

Hoyt's daughter, the 36-year-old widow Cora Louise Bartlett, did not travel with them. She was, however, already in London. She married the publisher Franklin H. Parkes there in July 1893. The witnesses to the nuptials were her parents, Harris and Marie E. Hoyt. By 1901, Cora had apparently divorced her second husband and was living in London with her mother. Her father, the 88-year-old Harris Hoyt, died sometime in 1899, little known and barely mourned.[45]

11

Conclusion

Except for Harris Hoyt, the principals in the Texas Adventure enjoyed little success as a result of their involvement in the Texas cotton trade. None of them were able to sustain their post-war financial success. Dishonesty had a way of catching up to them. Although many men who engaged in the Texas cotton trade emerged from the conflict as wealthy men, only a few were able to build upon that success. Those men were able to wisely invest the wealth gained through that trade and move on to other pursuits. They relied on sound business practices, reliable relationships, and an ability to adapt to evolving economic realities.

In contrast to the men who achieved long term success stand the swindler Harris Hoyt and those like him. Hoyt met with many of the most powerful Americans of his era, but was truthful with none of them. They rushed into his web of deceit as willing participants. In the pursuit of quick profits during the economic upheaval of the American Civil War, these men dressed up their illicit schemes as altruistic appeals for charity and compassion. Perhaps it was Hoyt's unassuming and humble appearance, but in addition to his ability to separate men from their money, he managed to stay out of jail. He was not alone. Of the many scoundrels who participated in the Texas Cotton trade, none of them served any time in jail for their swindling schemes. Similar to their counterparts in subsequent eras, these nineteenth century white-collar criminals succeeded for a while, but could not maintain their success with an enterprise that was built on lies.[1]

A less satisfactory demonstration of how justice is supposed to overcome corruption and love will conquer all is the personal story of Marie and her beau Harris Hoyt. The final chapter in their real life story has little in common with the triumphant final scenes of Meredith Willson's *The Music Man*. The fictional Professor Harold Hill's boys' band scam ended up benefiting everyone in River City, Iowa. Professor Hill's love interest, Marian, set the professor on the path to decency and honest living. Harris

Hoyt's influence on his love interest was quite the opposite. His third (and last) wife, Marie Emma Bryant, had grown up in Clermont, Iowa, a small town on the Turkey River, a small tributary that flowed into the Mississippi. Instead of leading her husband to an honest profession, Marie was swept into the vortex of Harris Hoyt's swindling post-war schemes. She eventually fled to England with Harris and her daughter Cora and did not return to Iowa.

Almost all of the scheming participants in the Texas Adventure came away with empty pockets, except for Harris Hoyt. However, his long-term success could not be built on dishonesty. When he had exhausted his Texas Adventure windfall, Hoyt had to resort to new scams. Although some may have been successful, these risky cons inevitably led to his exposure and kept him on the move to stay one step ahead of the law and his creditors. Even Hoyt's victims were often conniving culprits in their own right. Most were complicit at some level in his dishonest dealings and many continued to live a life of deceit in other business ventures. In a bit of poetic justice, Harris Hoyt eventually was betrayed by the victims that he had trusted in both New York and Texas.

APPENDIX 1

Scoundrels and a Few Others

The following biographical sketches provide additional information for many of the major characters who appear in the preceding chapters. Appropriate citations for the information listed here, some of which has never been published, can be found within the text.

Alden, Commander James (1810–1877). Commanding officer of the USS *South Carolina* who initiated the blockade of Texas; retired as a Rear Admiral.
Ashby (aka "Ashbey"), James Henry (1827–1874). Originally from New York, he was master of the Louisiana schooner *West Florida* (aka *Cephise* & *Hanover*). He used a Butler pass to run the blockade; also owned and commanded the blockade runner *Andromeda*.
Banks, Major General Nathaniel Prentice (1816–1894). Appointed as a Civil War major general due to his political influence as a former Massachusetts congressman and governor. He relieved Ben Butler at New Orleans in Dec. 1862, occupied the Texas Gulf Coast Nov. 1863–July 1864 from Brownsville up to Matagorda Bay, commanded the ill-fated Red River Campaign.
Barney, Hiram (1811–1895). Appointed by President Lincoln as head customs collector for the Port of New York from 1861 to 1864, he also practiced law in partnership with Benjamin F. Butler and his son.
Barrett, Joseph Hartwell (1824–1910). U.S. Pension Office Commissioner appointed by President Lincoln, he gave Harris Hoyt an introduction to John Hay. To boost Lincoln's reelection campaign, Barrett published a biography of the president in 1864.
Bartlett, Clarence Russell (1841–1877). First Husband of Harris Hoyt's daughter Cora Louise, he was a cashier for the Inman Steamship Co. in New York, but died after less than two years of marriage.
Bartlett, Cora Louise (See: Hoyt, Cora Louise).
Bee, Brigadier General Hamilton Prioleau (1822–1897). A veteran of the

Mexican War and former Texas state legislator (1849–1859), he was speaker of the house (1855–1857) from Laredo. Nicknamed "General Wasp," he was the Confederate general in command of the lower Rio Grande district. The City of Beeville is named in his father's honor. Bee was an effective political general but failed as a combat leader during the Red River campaign. After the war, he briefly worked in Havana but remained in Mexico until he returned to Texas in 1876. He managed a farm for what is now Texas A&M University, practiced law in San Antonio, and was a state agency commissioner in Austin.

Belknap, William Worth (1829–1890). Secretary of War during the Senate's investigation of William Sprague. A former Iowa legislator and brigadier general during the Civil War; he was impeached for accepting kickbacks, but acquitted.

Bell, Alexander Graham (1847–1922). Inventor of the telephone and partner of William H. Reynolds.

Benjamin, Judah Phillip (1811–1884). A former Louisiana Senator who served as Confederate attorney general (1861), Secretary of War (1861–62), and Secretary of State (1862–65), he was the only Civil War cabinet member on either side who was Jewish.

Bertram, Colonel Henry (1825–1878). Prussian immigrant who was born Emil Gustave Victor Beeger, he fought in the Mexican-American War as Sergeant Henry Beeger, but deserted and changed his name again to Bertram. While commanding the Union Army's 1st Brigade within General Herron's Division during the evacuation of Brownsville in July 1864, he received a bribe from M. Kenedy & Co.

Bisbie, D.T. (aka Bisbee) (dates unknown). He traveled to Europe during the war and claimed to be an agent of the Paris firm of Bellot, De Miniers & Co. of Paris. He was a former Norfolk newspaper editor and member of the Virginia House of Delegates.

Blacker, Charles Louis Adolphus (1827–1886). The British vice-consul to Matamoros (1861–1863).

Boynton, John Watson (1811–1878). Agent for the Boynton Machinery Company, Hartford, Connecticut, who sold wool carding machines to Harris Hoyt.

Brackenridge, George Washington (1832–1920). Civil War cotton trader in Texas who joined the Union cause as a Treasury Agent in Brownsville. He returned to Texas and became a prominent businessman, public servant, and philanthropist.

Brastow, Henry Billings (1828–1904). Agent and supercargo for William H. Reynolds on the *Snow Drift* and the ill-fated *Ella Warley*. He

Appendix 1. Scoundrels and a Few Others

moved to Colorado Territory at the end of the Civil War and then to California.

Broadwell, William A. (1823–1869). During the war, he was a brigade quartermaster for Missouri and Arkansas troops. He was promoted to Lt. Col. in August 1863 and became Chief of the Cotton Bureau for the Trans-Mississippi Department. After the war, he fled to Mexico, but returned to New Orleans as a cotton broker. He was one of many casualties on board the Red River steamer *Mittie Stephens* that caught fire and sank in Caddo Lake on its way from Shreveport, Louisiana, to Jefferson, Texas.

Bryant, Samuel Stephen (1802–1888). Father of Harris Hoyt's third wife Marie, he participated in the Texas Adventure. Originally from Vermont, he settled in Iowa.

Burkhardt, James T. (1833–after 1873). Originally from Switzerland, he was the owner and captain of the sloop *Little Carrie* that ran cotton from Galveston to Havana via Tampico.

Butler, Andrew Jackson (1815–1864). He served as an unofficial aide and profiteering front-man for his younger brother in Louisiana with the honorific title of "colonel." He died in a New York City hotel of tuberculosis shortly after his return from the South.

Butler, Benjamin Franklin (1818–1893). A political major general who commanded Union forces in New Orleans (May–Dec. 1862), he became known as "Beast Butler" for his harsh treatment of local citizens, corruption and petty looting. He led the failed attack on Fort Fisher in North Carolina in Dec 1864. After the war, he was elected to the House of Representatives where he took a leadership role in the impeachment of President Andrew Johnson.

Cammack, Addison J. (1827–1901). Nicknamed "Ursa Major," he was a gruff and burly Havana-based agent for Southern blockade runners and a partner with New Orleans–based swindlers. After the war, he became a New York Stock Exchange broker known for his insider trading and manipulation of the markets to exploit enthusiastic "Bulls."

Celaya, Simón (1828–1908). Assistant and partner of his cousin José San Román in Matamoros and Brownsville, he had been the Spanish vice-consul. After the war, he became a wealthy Texas merchant.

Chase, Katherine "Kate" Jane (Mrs. Kate Sprague) (1840–1899). Ambitious daughter of the Secretary of Treasury Salmon Chase, she married Senator William Sprague in 1863 with President Lincoln in attendance. Divorced in 1882, she had a public affair with the notorious and corrupt Senator Roscoe Conkling.

Appendix 1. Scoundrels and a Few Others

Chase, Salmon Portland (1808–1873). U.S. Secretary of the Treasury (1861–1864) and Chief Justice of the Supreme Court (1864–1873) who had ambitions to be president. His daughter Kate married Senator William Sprague.

Chubb, Thomas Beaverstock (1811–1890). He came to Texas during its war for independence as master of a sailing vessel. A lifelong mariner, he served as commodore of the Galveston Harbor Police during the Civil War, was captured in November 1861 but exchanged and returned to duty in March 1862. He served as harbormaster in Galveston from 1882 until his death at his summer home in Vermont. His 1859 Greek revival home still stands in Galveston where he is buried at the Evergreen Cemetery.

Clements, Nelson (dates unknown). A British citizen living in Galveston, he traveled to Europe in 1862 as a profiteering purchasing agent for the State. He was a partner with the New Orleans swindlers who obtained the *General Rusk/Blanche* from the Army and used it as a private blockade runner.

Compton, William Young (1842–1919). Shipping agent from Brenham. Texas who worked in Matamoros to avoid the Confederate draft. Traveled to New York with Harris Hoyt, but returned to Texas after the war and became a cattle rancher in Milam.

Conkling, Roscoe (1829–1888). Flamboyant and handsome New York Senator (1867–1881) and political boss who conducted a public affair with Kate Chase Sprague. Deftly used political appointments and influence for his personal and professional advantage.

Crawford, John Vincent (1829–1899). Acting British Vice Consul in Havana under his father Joseph; assisted Charles Stillman with his trading activities. A career diplomat who was born in France and died in Germany.

Crocker, Frederick (1821–1911) As captain of the USS *Kensington*, he discovered General Butler's illicit scheme to issue passes to blockade runners. In 1863, he was captured during the Battle of Sabine Pass aboard the USS *Clifton*. After the war, he moved to Uruguay and served as U.S. Consul at Montevideo (1876–79).

Dana, Major General Napoleon Jackson Tecumsah (1822–1905). A West Point graduate and veteran of the Mexican War, he commanded the Department of the Gulf from September 1863 to January 1864. After the war, he was a mining and railroad executive in the West and a Pension Department officer in Washington, D.C.

Devine, Thomas Jefferson (1820–1890). Confederate judge for the Western District of Texas (1861–1864) who helped arrange the nominal transfer of Rio Grande river steamers to Mexican owners. He returned to his home in San Antonio via Mexico after the war, and like George Brackenridge, was a University of Texas regent. The city of Devine, Texas was named in his honor.

Dix, Major General John Adams (1798–1879). Democratic senator from NY (1845–1849), briefly Secretary of the Treasury under President Buchanan (1861). The most senior of the Union's three political Major Generals (over Banks and Butler), he was considered too old for field command. He commanded administrative forces in Pennsylvania, Maryland, Virginia, and the Department of the East in New York. After the war he was Minister to France (1866–1869) and governor of New York (1873–1875).

Donahue, John H. (1835–1874). Charles Stillman's alcoholic agent in New York who conveniently could not be located during a congressional investigation.

Etchison, Emanuel Dorsey (1808–about 1879). Dishonest U.S. consular agent in Matamoros from late Nov 1864 to Mar 1865. After the war, he lived in Canada, but returned to Baltimore in 1869 and attempted to kill a man he accused of seducing his wife.

Evans, William Richardson (1834–1885). A merchant and blockade running captain of the schooner *America*, and SS *Cora*. He moved his family to Matamoros, but lost two children during the war and returned to his business in Galveston afterwards. He remained an active supporter of the Y.M.C.A that he helped establish on the island.

Farragut, David Glasgow (1801–1870). The first U.S. admiral, he was known for capturing New Orleans and Mobile. He commanded the blockading fleet in the Western Gulf (1862–1864).

Ford, John Salmon "Rip" (1815–1897). Colonel in command of Confederate operational forces at the Rio Grande (1861–1862 & 1864–1865). A former newspaper editor, state senator, and Texas Ranger. During the Mexican-American War, he closed his many condolence letters with "Rest in Peace, Ford," that he later abbreviated to "R.I.P."

Fremantle, Sir Arthur James Lyon (1835–1901). British Army observer who first entered the Confederacy at the Rio Grande and later witnessed the Battle of Gettysburg and the New York City draft riots. He fought in the Afghan wars, was Governor of Malta, and retired as a Lieutenant General.

Frieze, Lyman Bowers (1825–1917). Trusted associate of William Sprague who served as a Union lieutenant colonel at the First Battle of Bull Run. He joined A. & W. Sprague and Co. in 1863, and was investigated for his role in the Texas Adventure and accounting irregularities while Quartermaster General of Rhode Island.

Galvan, Jerry (aka Jeremiah O Gealbhain), (ca 1824–1879). He emigrated from Ireland in 1846 via New Orleans; became a successful merchant, rancher, and associate of Charles Stillman in Matamoros and Brownsville. A lifetime bachelor, he was the Judge of Cameron County and a Texas state legislator (1874–1876), but drowned in the Mississippi River after a visit to New Orleans for his health.

Gilmer, Alexander (1829–1906). Irish immigrant operating out of the Sabine River as a lumberman, store owner, ship builder, and blockade runner. Captured on his schooner *Elizabeth* in 1863, he continued to run the blockade and participated in the capture of U.S. Navy gunboats. After the war, he continued his successful mercantile business, operated numerous sawmills, and founded a bank.

Greer, Brigadier General Elkanah Bracken (Brackin) (1825–1877). A merchant, planter, and lawyer from Marshall, Texas, he was Commandant of Conscripts for the Trans-Mississippi Department.

Hart, Simeon (1816–1874). Flour merchant from El Paso, who was a Confederate major and chief purchasing agent for the Trans-Mississippi Department in Texas. Frequently in conflict with Major Russell regarding cotton on the border, he proved himself honest, but overwhelmed by his duties. After the war, he was a newspaper editor and had to contend with Unionists to regain ownership of his flour mill and other property near his home in El Paso.

Hay, John Milton (1838–1905). Private Secretary to President Lincoln who traveled with him from Illinois. After a series of diplomatic positions, he became Secretary of State under Presidents McKinley and Theodore Roosevelt.

Hays, John Coffee (1817–1883). Surveyor, Texas Ranger, and Mexican War officer who was a cohort of Rip Ford, Ben McCulloch, and Samuel H. Walker. He lived in Texas for 13 years (1836 to 1849), but by 1853 was the Surveyor General of California.

Hébert, Brigadier General Paul Octave (1818–1880). West Point graduate and former governor of Louisiana (1853–1856), he commanded Confederate troops in Texas (1861–1862), until he was relieved by General Magruder. After the war, he returned to Louisiana and served as the State's engineer.

Helm, Major Charles John (1817–1868). U.S. Consul (1858–1861) and then Confederate agent in Havana throughout the war. He served in the Mexican war and as Kentucky State congressman from (1851–1853). After the war, he lived in Canada.

Appendix 1. Scoundrels and a Few Others

Herron, Francis Jay (1837–1902). A banker from Iowa, he was the Civil War's youngest major general and commanded the Union's 13th Regiment on the Rio Grande (1863–1864) and the District of Northern Louisiana. He remained in Louisiana as a tax collector, U.S. Marshal (1867–1869), and secretary of state. He moved to New York in 1877 as a lawyer and banker, but died a pauper in a tenement.

Hill, Frederic Stanhope (1829–1913). A former merchant mariner, U.S. Customs agent, and newspaperman from Boston, he commanded the USS *William G. Anderson* and *Tyler* during the war. He captured several blockade runners and the cotton from Hoyt's sunken schooner *America*. After the war, he was a successful writer and newspaper editor and owner.

Hill, Professor Harold (fictional character). The swindling boys' band organizer and instrument and uniform salesman in Meredith Willson's hit Broadway musical (1957), Hollywood movie (1962), and television production (2003), *The Music Man*.

House, Thomas William (1814–1880). Originally from England, House moved to Houston in 1838 as a baker and confectioner. He then became a successful dry goods and grocery merchant and worked to improve river transportation. His position led to his ownership of several blockade runners (including the *Velocity*, *Mary Sorley*, SS *Cora*, and the former U.S. warships *Sachem/Clarinda*, *Clifton*, and *Harriet Lane*) during the Civil War. He was a Houston mayor, banker, railroad owner, and a major investor in the city's utility and transportation infrastructure.

Houston, Sam (1793–1863). A former governor of Tennessee, he served as the Texas revolutionary Army's general, president of the republic, governor, and U.S. senator. Forced to resign as governor when he refused to sign the Confederate loyalty oath, he offered encouragement but no support to Union sympathizers like Harris Hoyt.

Hoyt, Ann Elizabeth (Sayre) (1811–1842). Originally from New York, she was the first wife of Harris Hoyt at the age of 18. She died in Clinton County, New York, a week after giving birth to twins. Of her seven children, five lived into adulthood and only three were still alive when Harris Hoyt moved to Texas in 1859. The only boy, one of the twins, died shortly after his mother.

Hoyt, Charlotte Elizabeth (Winchell) (1816–1852). Originally from Clinton County NY, married Harris Hoyt less than one year after the death of his first wife. Her first son, Horace Washington, died as an infant. She died in Batavia, Illinois, six weeks after giving birth to her second son Harris George.

Hoyt, Cora Louise (1856–ca 1905). Only child of Harris and Marie Emma Hoyt and youngest of Harris Hoyt's seven surviving children. Born in Batavia, Illinois, she married and had her only child (Ethel Agnes) by the Canadian Clarence R. Bartlett who died shortly thereafter. She then moved to London and married the Englishman Franklin H. Parkes.

Hoyt, Harriet Cornelia (1838–1925). Harris Hoyt's fifth child with his first wife Ann. Born in Vermont, she was named after their fourth child who died at the age of 13 months in 1837.

Hoyt, Harris (1811–1899). Career swindler from New York, who also lived in Vermont, Illinois, and Texas, and stayed with family members in Indiana and Iowa. His three wives bore him ten children, only three of whom outlived their father. Believed to have died in London, while living there with his wife and their daughter Cora Louise.

Hoyt, Harris George (1852–1931). Second son of Harris Hoyt's second wife, he traveled with his father to Texas and back to the mid-west via Mexico and New York.

Hoyt, Horace (1811–1880). Twin brother of Harris Hoyt, who like his brother moved from New York to Illinois. He was in Texas and Mexico with his sons Harris and Thomas. Like his brother, he had three wives: Margaret Morse (1835), Elmira Smith (1861), and Susan Langdon (1875), but quietly lived out his years as an Illinois farmer.

Hoyt, Marie Emma Bryant (Carpenter) (1831–1919). The third wife of Harris Hoyt who had one son, William, from a previous marriage. Her only child with Hoyt was Cora Louise, the namesake of the schooner *Cora*. A large woman who intimidated her husband, she was indicted with him for false representation and perjury in New York. She later moved to London and remained there with her daughter.

Hoyt, Thomas C. (1844–1879). Youngest son of Horace Hoyt who worked and traveled with his father in Matamoros.

Hunter, Commander Charles (1813–1873). Captain of the USS *Montgomery* who was court martialed and dismissed from the Navy for destroying the Confederate blockade runner *General Rusk/Blanche* in Cuban waters. Hunter, his wife Mary, and two of his four daughters died as passengers when the steamship *Ville du Havre* was struck amidships and sank off the coast of France in November 1873.

Hutchins, William J. (1813–1884). A merchant, banker, steamboat owner, and railroad developer who came to Houston, Texas, in 1838 via New York and Florida. During the War, he was mayor of Houston and owner of a cotton compress company. Lt. Gen. E. Kirby Smith

Appendix 1. Scoundrels and a Few Others   157

appointed him chief of the Texas Cotton Bureau in December 1863 with the rank of Lt. Col. The war reduced his fortune, but he retained extensive real estate holdings.

Jenckes, Thomas Allen (1818–1875). Republican Representative from Rhode Island (1863–1871) who attempted to expose Senator William Sprague's Texas Adventure. He was defeated in his bid for reelection due in part to Sprague's support for his opponent.

Jockusch, John William (1819–1898). Prussian consul in Galveston from 1848, he became a naturalized citizen in 1850 and partner with R. & D.G. Mills. During the war, he moved to Brownsville and worked as a commission agent. Afterwards, he returned to Galveston and again served as Prussian consul through 1873 until his banking business failed. He also was a Galveston city alderman and purchasing agent.

Johnson, Andrew (1808–1875). 17th U.S. President (1865–1869) who was impeached for attempting to replace Secretary of War Stanton and his lenient policies toward the South. He was acquitted at his Senate impeachment trial by one vote.

Kenedy, Mifflin (1818–1895). Rio Grande steamboat captain, entrepreneur, and senior partner in the firm of M. Kenedy & Co. with Richard King and Charles Stillman. As he had during the Mexican War, he was adept at gaining government contracts and investing in land and cattle during the Civil War and afterwards.

Kennedy, John Alexander (1803–1873). New York City Superintendent of police from Baltimore who detected Harris Hoyt's attempt to export armament to Texas. He was severely beaten while unsuccessfully attempting to quell the City's draft riots (no relation to the 35th president).

King, Richard (1825–1885). Steamboat captain and entrepreneur, land holder, and founder of the King Ranch who came to the Rio Grande at Mifflin Kenedy's invitation. His rancho at Santa Gertrudis became a staging depot for the cotton trade. He and his M. Kenedy & Co. partners greatly enlarged their fortunes during the war.

Kittredge, John W. (1818–1899). A former merchant ship captain, Kittredge commanded the USS *Arthur* and terrorized the central Texas coast, but was ambushed and captured on a shore expedition. After he was exchanged and returned to command, the U.S. Navy court martialed and dismissed him for pistol-whipping a sailor. After the war, he was a coal merchant in New York.

Knight, Robert (1826–1912). A principal with his brother Benjamin in B.B. & R. Knight & Co. of Providence, Rhode Island, he was a silent investor with Sprague and Reynolds in Harris Hoyt's Texas adventure. Co-founder of the clothing brand "Fruit of the Loom."

Laverty, Henry (1818–1865). Irish immigrant out of New Orleans who was captain of the schooners *C.P. Knapp* (May 1861–Oct 1862) and *Francis Marguez, Jr.* (aka *Rob Roy*) (Jan–Jul 1863), he sailed the *Francis Marguez, Jr.*, to the Rio Grande (Jan–Mar 1863) and remained as captain when William Watson purchased and renamed the schooner the *Rob Roy*. Sailed to Belize and Matamoros, but did not want to risk running the blockade into Texas. He continued as captain of several different schooners until his death in Nov 1865.

Lea, Tom Calloway III (1907–2001). Accomplished artist, correspondent, novelist, and historian from El Paso who wrote the acclaimed two volume history about the King Ranch.

Levy, Marx (1847–1924). A Texan of Polish Jewish ancestry who was a young partner of Benjamin Weil and Samuel Loeb as they transported Harris Hoyt's cotton to Mexico.

Lincoln, Abraham (1809–1865). 16th President of the United States, whose assassination shocked the nation and delayed Harris Hoyt's court martial.

Lockwood, Samuel Drake (1789–1874). A prominent Illinois official who lived in Batavia, Kane County, he helped form the Republican Party and gave Harris Hoyt a letter of introduction. His wife, Mary Nash, was Abraham Lincoln's aunt.

Loeb, Samuel E. (1833–1905). French born Jewish merchant from New Orleans who was a partner with Benjamin Weil during the Civil War. Working in Texas and Matamoros, he ran cotton from Galveston to the Rio Grande on the schooner *Lehman*.

Lubbock, Francis Richard (1815–1905). Arrived in Texas in 1836 via South Carolina and New Orleans, he owned a general store, was a rancher, and served as comptroller for the Republic of Texas and clerk of Harris County. As Governor of Texas (Nov 1861–Nov 1863), he tried to control the cotton trade with Mexico and supported state industrial development, including Hoyt's wool carding company. He then served in the Confederate Army as a lieutenant colonel. After the war, he was a tax collector and Texas State Treasurer. One brother, Thomas Saltus Lubbock, was a Texas Ranger and namesake of the city of Lubbock, Texas. Another, Henry Schultz Lubbock, took command of the Texas Marine Department after Leon Smith.

Luckett, Brigadier General Philip Noland (1824–1869). Trained as a physician, he came to Corpus Christi via Virginia and Ohio. He served in the Mexican War as surgeon for Rip Ford's Texas Rangers. During the Civil war, he served as a Confederate infantry officer who rose to command at the Rio Grande, in Galveston, and Arkansas. His health suffered during his post-war imprisonment.

Macaulay, James A. (1823–1884). A New Orleans grocery merchant who came to Texas as a partner of his brother John, Robert Mott, and Nelson Clements in a scheme to obtain the Confederate steamer *General Rusk* (aka *Blanche*) as a blockade runner. He was a banking partner of the Havana-based Addison Cammack.

Macaulay, John Laing (1831–1897). Younger brother and partner of James Macaulay from New Orleans. After the war, he became a prominent cotton merchant and Wall Street capitalist and investor.

Magruder, Major General John Bankhead (1807–1871). West Point graduate who excelled early in the war but was ordered to Texas when he fell into disfavor with General Robert E. Lee. Known as "Prince John" for his fastidiously handsome appearance, he quickly attacked and repelled Union forces from Galveston Bay. Recognizing the importance of the cotton trade, he attempted to regulate and protect it with mixed results. After the war, he made a brief sojourn into Mexico, but returned to Texas where he remained.

Maloney, John P. (unk–1864). A British commission agent and steamboat operator in Matamoros a principal partner of Hale & Co. He was a trusted associate of Richard King and his partners who also handled Harris Hoyt's first shipment into the Rio Grande and Texas in 1863. He died at the Rio Grande after a brief illness.

Mills, David Graham (1811–1885). He formed R. & D.G. Mills & Co., a cotton growing and brokerage company with his brother Robert. He managed the plantations while his brother managed the brokerage business. After the war, the brothers struggled to maintain their cotton business, finally going bankrupt in 1873 when the cotton market collapsed.

Mills, Robert (1809–1888). See: Mills, David Graham.

Milmo, Patricio (Patrick) (1826–1899). Irish-born Matamoros merchant and banker who had resided in Mexico since 1848. The son-in-law of Santiago Vidaurri, the Mexican Governor of Tamaulipas, he colluded with Confederates and Unionists alike to leverage his business interests. His estate was valued at $10 million upon his death.

Moïse, Major Theodore Sydney (1808–1885). A successful portrait and animal artist who worked in South Carolina, Mississippi, and Kentucky before establishing himself in Louisiana in 1842–43. He painted Henry Clay, Andrew Jackson, and his eventual Confederate boss, Governor P.O. Hébert. Although he was Jewish, his second wife was a Catholic. He was frequently in debt, which probably led him into an illicit partnership that allowed civilians to use the CSS *General Rusk* as a blockade runner at no cost. After being dismissed from the Confederate Army, he returned to his portraiture business.

Mooney, Thomas P. (1817–1874). Texas businessman who allowed Harris Hoyt to set up his wool carding machinery at his gristmill and sawmill on the San Marcos River. Eventually purchased the machinery and may have had an interest in the cotton Hoyt ran through the blockade.

Moore, Thomas Cincinnatus (1817–1895). Illinois Lawyer and Kane County Clerk who wrote a letter of introduction for Harris Hoyt.

Morell, Jose (aka Joseph Morrell) (1803–1875). Trusted friend and partner of Charles Stillman and Mifflin Kenedy; mercantile store and textile factory owner in Monterrey, Mexico.

Mott, Robert (1817–1889). A prominent New Orleans lawyer who was a partner with the Macaulay Brothers and Nelson Clements in the illicit scheme to defraud the Confederate government out of their steamer the CSS *General Rusk*.

Murrah, Pendelton (about 1827–1865). He contracted tuberculosis while a lawyer in Alabama and moved to Texas in 1850. He briefly served as a quartermaster officer in 1862, but resigned due to poor health. As Texas governor (1863–1865), he clashed with Generals Magruder and E. Kirby Smith about the conscription of troops and purchasing cotton for the Confederate Army. He reluctantly yielded during the Union Army's Red River offensive in the spring of 1864. Near the end of the war, he joined other Confederate leaders and fled to Mexico, but died of tuberculosis after reaching Monterrey.

Nichols, Ebenezar B. (1815–1872). Arrived in Texas from New York in 1838 and, after battling Indians and Mexicans on the frontier, he became a merchant in Houston. Moving to Galveston in 1850, he became a cotton factor and commission agent. A delegate to the Texas Secession Convention, he raised and disbursed funds for the public safety. He served on Magruder's staff and was a financial agent. After the war, he was president of the National Bank of Texas and was a leader in Galveston's business and civic affairs.

Oetling, George, (unk birth–death). The Prussian vice consul in Matamoros. A partner with William Droege in the banking and commercial firm of Droege, Oetling, & Co. with offices in Matamoros (through 1868), Tampico, Manchester (UK), and Hamburg.

Parkes, Franklin Howard (1852–1919). London publisher and second husband of Cora Louise Hoyt Bartlett.

Appendix 1. Scoundrels and a Few Others

Pierce, Edward Lillie (1829–1897). A Massachusetts lawyer and Republican abolitionist who clashed with Lt. Col. W.H. Reynolds as he promoted the education of former slaves in the Port Royal, South Carolina vicinity.

Pierce, Leonard, Jr. (1828–1872). A former merchant seaman and U.S. Army paymaster, he was U.S. Consul to Matamoros (1862–1864). He left for New York in 1865, but returned to Texas after the war. He lived in Roma and Brownsville and is buried there.

Prescott, Charles Lyman (1821–1869). A business partner with Harris Hoyt in charge of acquiring and outfitting the vessels involved in the Texas Adventure. He traveled to Havana with his wife while he was supercargo of the SS *Ella Warley* and escaped prosecution when he testified against the more prominent conspirators.

Quintero, José Agustín (1829–1885). Cuban-born attorney, journalist, and confidential Confederate agent for President Jefferson Davis in Brownsville, Matamoros, and Monterrey. He was a perceptive and effective agent who assisted the Texas cotton trade through Matamoros. After the war, he moved to New Orleans where he was a lawyer, the consul for Belgium and Costa Rica, and editor of the New Orleans *Times-Picayune*.

Redgate, Samuel Joseph (1800–1893). A former Texas legislator (1846–1847 & 1860–1861) and Unionist sympathizer. During the war, he was a principal in the "Bellot contract swindle," after he returned to Texas from Europe. After the war, he was a banker in Ohio, but returned to Texas two years before his death.

Reynolds, Charles Frederick (1858–1902). Son of William H. Reynolds who was arrested for forgery in 1890.

Reynolds, William Henry (1828–1910). Principal of W.H. Reynolds & Co. and a former employee of A. & W. Sprague & Co., he was a Lieutenant Colonel in Governor Sprague's Rhode Island Regiment. Later appointed as a Treasury agent in South Carolina, he obtained thousands of bales of Cotton for A.W. Sprague and was forced to resign, but formed his own cotton brokerage company. He was arrested, but not prosecuted for his role in Hoyt's Texas Adventure. After the war, he immersed himself in a series of high risk investments with some success, but was the only plaintiff in an Arizona copper mining swindle and his son was arrested for forgery.

Roosevelt, Theodore (1858–1919). 26th President of the United States (1901–1909) whose Secretary of State, John Hay, had been Abraham Lincoln's private secretary and whose father had paid for a substitute to avoid the Civil War draft.

Appendix 1. Scoundrels and a Few Others

Russell, Charles Arden (1822–1878). A stint in the U.S. Army during the Mexican War brought him to Texas where he married and became a surveyor in Karnes County. He was General Bee's Civil War quartermaster at the Rio Grande where he frequently clashed with Major Hart and was accused of engaging in unscrupulous trade with Mexico. After the war, he was briefly the Judge of Karnes County and practiced law in Refugio, Texas.

San Román, José (1822–1895). Arrived in Matamoros from Spain via New Orleans in 1846 and became one of the richest men in South Texas. A shrewd but honest merchant, banker, and shipping agent, he was both a partner and competitor with King, Kenedy, and Stillman in the steamboat and shipping business. After the war, he continued to do business on the Rio Grande, but returned to Spain in 1878.

Santleben, August (1845–1911). An ox team driver between Columbus and Eagle Pass, Texas early in the war. He enlisted in the Union Army and saw limited action in Louisiana. After the war, he established a prairie schooner stage line between San Antonio and Mexico and served as a San Antonio city alderman.

Santleben, Christian (1809–1889). He arrived in Galveston from Hanover with his wife Sophie and infant son, August, in 1845. Like many German immigrants, he opposed secession, but remained in Texas during the war working as a teamster.

Scherffius, George Henry (1838–1894). Arrived in Texas as a child and became a merchant sea captain operating out of Sabine Pass. Probably the most successful blockade running captain in Texas, he commanded several vessels including Harris Hoyt's former schooner, the *Cora*, and the former USS *Sachem* (renamed *Clarinda*) that he successfully ran into Vera Cruz at the end of the war. After the war, he was the Harris County Treasurer for 14 years, and served one term as Houston's mayor (1892–1894). He and two of his children died of food poisoning after eating sardines at a circus.

Scurry, William Reed (1821–1864). Arrived in Texas from Tennessee in 1839 and became a district attorney in 1841. He served in the Texas Congress (1844–1845) and was a Major in the Mexican War. When Harris Hoyt requested the services of W.R. Evans, he was Commander of the Eastern Sub-District of Texas. During the Civil War, he fought in New Mexico, Galveston, and died of his wounds on April 30, 1864, leading his men at the Battle of Jenkins Ferry in Louisiana.

Seward, William Henry (1801–1872). A former New York state senator (1830–1834), governor (1838–1842), U.S. senator (1849–1861), he was secretary of state for Presidents Lincoln and Johnson (1861–1869). While secretary of state, he refused to grant Harris Hoyt blockade running permits. He was seriously wounded as part of the Lincoln assassination plot.

Shufeldt, Robert Wilson (1822–1895). A former Navy officer and merchant captain, James D. Bulloch relieved him as captain of the SS *Black Warrior* in 1853, and he relieved the Confederate agent Charles Helm as U.S. Consul to Havana in 1861. He was energetic in his duties and delayed Harris Hoyt's Texas adventure for several months. Shortly after that experience, he returned to active Navy service in early 1863 and rose to the rank of rear admiral.

Skaggs, Eli Harrison (1818–1890). A well known Louisiana gambler, speculator, plantation and steamboat owner, he obtained a "Butler Pass" for his steamer, the *Indian No. 2*, which was actually in Confederate service at the time.

Smith, Edmund Kirby (1824–1893). A West Point graduate from Florida, he had served over 15 years in the U.S. Army when he accepted a Confederate commission as a Lieutenant Colonel. By October 1862, he was a Lieutenant General in command of the Trans-Mississippi Department which included Texas. After the war, he traveled to Mexico and then Cuba, before being granted amnesty. He was president of an insurance and a telegraph company before leading two academies and then settling down as a mathematics professor.

Smith, James Youngs (1809–1876). Governor of Rhode Island (1863–1866) who won the election after William Sprague resigned to become a U.S. senator. He mounted an indirect attack on Sprague through an unsuccessful investigation of General Frieze.

Smith, Leon (ca. 1820–1889). Steamboat captain that General Magruder appointed as a Confederate Army major in command of the Texas Marine Department with the honorary title of commodore. He commanded most of the Confederate gunboats and logistic vessels in Texas and led several successful operations against U.S. naval forces. After the war, he was the agent for a telegraph company in New Orleans and San Francisco. He then departed for Alaska where he was murdered at his trading post the day after Christmas.

Sorley, James (1820–1895). Born in Scotland and educated at Liverpool, Sorley came to Mobile in 1836 and then Galveston in 1851 where he was a cotton merchant. He became prominent in civic affairs and was the only Confederate Customs collector at Galveston. He was also a member of the Texas Cotton Bureau. After the war, he was president of the Galveston Chamber of Commerce and went into the cotton business with James D. Bulloch, the former Confederate Navy Agent in Liverpool.

Sprague, Byron (1824–1866). The only son of one of the founders of A. & W. Sprague & Co., and partner with his cousin William until he resigned in Nov 1862 under hostile circumstances. He died suddenly in 1866 as a result of "brain congestion," most likely a stroke.

Sprague, Mrs. Kate (See: Chase, Katherine "Kate" Jane).

Sprague, William IV (1830–1915). A principal partner in A. & W. Sprague & Co. and owner of five New England textiles mills with controlling interest in a railroad that connected them until the business collapse during the Panic of 1873. He was Governor (1860–1863) and U.S. Senator (1863–1875) from Rhode Island, and colonel in command of state troops at the First Battle of Bull Run. He was the primary supporter of Harris Hoyt's Texas Adventure. He married and had four children with the former Kate Chase, daughter of Lincoln's secretary of the treasury; they divorced in 1882 alleging mutual infidelity.

Stillman, Charles (1810–1875). Originally from Connecticut, he arrived in Matamoros as a merchant in 1828. He established several lucrative partnerships in cotton brokerage real estate, Mexican silver mines, merchandise outlets, shipping, and warehousing. Those partnerships often evolved into loyal friendships in New York (James and Newton Smith), Monterrey (José Morell), Matamoros (Jeremiah Galvan), and South Texas (Richard King and Mifflin Kenedy), and even included Union loyalists such as George Brackenridge. He reaped great profits from the cotton trade during the war that he and his son sustained after the war by investing in the National City Bank of New York, a predecessor of Citibank.

Taft, Orson "Orray" (1793–1865). A principal with Orray Taft & Co. with his only son Edward Padelford (of six children), he was a silent partner in Harris Hoyt's Texas Adventure with a $25,000 investment and ⅛ share in any profits.

Townsend, John Drake (1833–1886). Prior to the war, he was a merchant seaman and then graduated from Harvard law school. He served as Harris Hoyt's counsel during his court martial. He became a prominent New York City criminal lawyer who defended accused murders and helped prosecute corrupt city officials.

Vanderbilt, Cornelius (1794–1877). Nicknamed "the commodore," he was one of America's wealthiest men through investments in railroads and steamships. He offered to lease the *Ella Warley* from Charles Prescott to use as a transport for General N.P. Banks' Louisiana campaign.

Appendix 1. Scoundrels and a Few Others 165

Vidaurri, Santiago (1809–1867). Mexican Governor of Tamaulipas since 1855, the Juáristas executed him without a trial in 1867.

Watson, William (1826–1911). Blockade running captain and owner of the schooner *Rob Roy* who ran into Matamoros, Havana, the Brazos River, and Galveston during the same timeframe as Harris Hoyt's blockade running adventures.

Weil, Benjamin (1823–1877). Arrived in Louisiana from France in 1846 and established himself as a merchant with Marx Levy. During the Civil War, he and his partner Samuel Loeb set up a brokerage business in Houston and Matamoros and became involved with Harris Hoyt. After the war, he and his partner committed perjury in filing false claims against Mexico. He collected over $170,000, but suffered a mental breakdown and died in 1877.

Welles, Gideon (1802–1878). He was owner of the Hartford *Times* newspaper, a Connecticut state congressman and city post master. Prior to becoming Lincoln's Secretary of the Navy (1861–1869), his only Federal office had been as Chief of the Navy Bureau of Provisions and Clothing (1846–1849). After the war, he wrote a biography, *Lincoln and Seward* (New York: Sheldon & Co., 1874) and a candid three volume diary about his service as Navy Secretary.

Willson, Robert Reiniger Meredith (1902–1984). Musician, composer, author, and radio personality from Iowa who also served in the Army. He wrote the script, lyrics and music for the hit Broadway musical and the movie titled *The Music Man* that featured the reclamation of the swindler Professor Harold Hill. Willson also wrote several hit songs and two other successful musicals.

Witham, Joseph C. (1832–1897). Left a career as a jeweler's apprentice to follow his father's footsteps as a merchant seaman. Captain of the *Snow Drift* from New York to Havana and Matamoros. After his sailing days were over he became marine insurance inspector and died shortly after a serious fall while inspecting a steamship.

Yturria, Santiago (1833–1867). The Matamoros-born younger brother of Francisco, he served as a manager for the family's Matamoros mercantile operation. He was a wartime surrogate for Charles Stillman while he was also the acting British vice-consul. He died in 1867 of tuberculosis.

APPENDIX 2

Sails, Steamers, and the Texas Cotton Trade

This appendix provides brief summaries of prominent vessels mentioned in the text. The listed names of captains and ship's masters (when known) and the warship armament reflect the timeframe that they are mentioned within the text. Appropriate endnote citations are located within the text.

A note about tonnage: There are many different methods of determining tonnage. Tons burden (sometimes spelled burthen) was a nineteenth century measurement of a vessel's carrying capacity, but measuring formulas varied widely. In 1864, a standardized methodology appeared, but it was several years before its use became uniform. Other tonnage measurements include: Deadweight (total weight a vessel can carry); Cargo (total cargo weight); Gross (weight of the vessel alone); Net (gross tonnage minus spaces for crew, engines, fuel, and ship operations); and variations of Displacement (weight of water displaced, loaded and unloaded). Tons displacement is more commonly used in the current era. For comparison, a vessel displacing 1335 tons might have a net tonnage of 400, gross tonnage of 600, and deadweight carrying capacity of 1000 tons. Varying usage of British and American measurements of tons (2,240 and 2,000 pounds) also accounts for variations in reporting of a vessel's tonnage.

A note about naval guns: a 32-pounder was a smooth-bore (unless labeled as "rifled") muzzle loading (unless labeled as "breech" loading) cannon that fired a projectile weighing 32 pounds. Other common projectile weights were 100, 30, 24, 20 and 12 pounds. Some guns were measured by the diameter of the bore in inches. Howitzers were lighter weight guns that could be deployed aboard smaller vessels.

The following listing is organized by vessel name, and (when known): tonnage, flag (if non–U.S.), type (rig/propulsion), armament (warships

Appendix 2. Sails, Steamers, and the Texas Cotton Trade

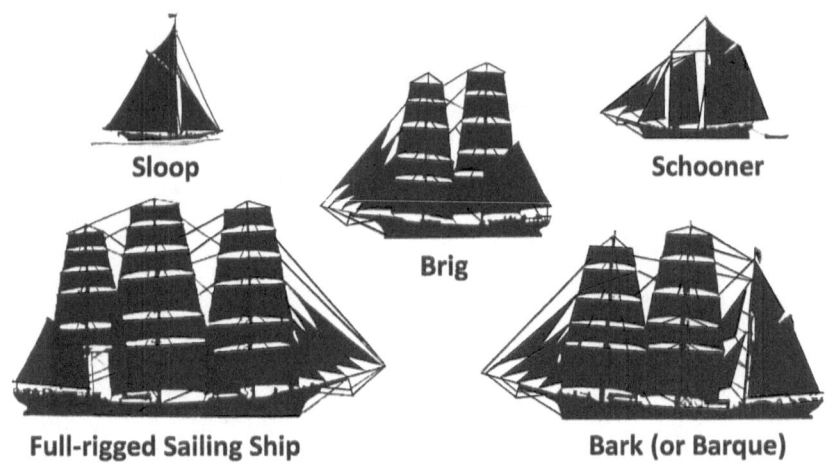

Sailing rig silhouettes (author's illustration).

only), when and where built, captain or ship master's name, and a summary of significant events.

SS *Alamo*: 123-ton side-wheel steamer; built Nov. 1860 at Wheeling, Virginia, Capt. Anderson, Designed for the Trinity River trade in Texas, by March. 1861 it was in Galveston Bay under Capt. N.L. Dorsey. In August 1863, Commodore Leon Smith sailed the *Alamo*, *John F. Carr*, and *Mary Hill*, from Galveston Bay to the Brazos River. Leaving the *Mary Hill*, he took the other two steamers down to Matagorda Bay. By Oct. 31, 1863, the *Alamo* was on the Rio Grande as an upriver steamer, under the ownership of M. Kenedy & Co. where it remained until abandoned in 1867.

SS *Alice*: (See: SS *Matagorda*).

America: Small Confederate coastal schooner, Capt. William R. Evans. The USS *W.G. Anderson* captured her on August 27, 1863 off Corpus Christi with 55 bales of cotton from Galveston; capsized and sank.

Andromeda: 223-ton British schooner, built 1858 at Setauket, New York, Capt. James H. Ashby. She was captured off Havana in May 1863 with 597 bales of cotton from Sabine Pass and condemned for $127,727.96 at Key West. Capt. Ashby regained ownership and made 6 voyages to the Rio Grande.

USS *Arthur*: 554-ton bark, with 6 × 32-pounder smoothbores, built 1855 at Amesbury, Massachusetts, Acting Lieutenant John W. Kittredge. Purchased by the U.S. Navy in 1861, she aggressively operated off the South Texas coast Jan. 1862–March 1863, attacked Corpus Christi;

captured the sloop *Belle Italia*, and schooners *Breaker*, *J.J. McNeil*, *Reindeer*, and *Water Witch*.

Banshee: 489-ton British-flagged sailing ship, built 1850 at Baltimore, Capt. D.N. Moss (Oct. 1862–May 1863), and R. Hayden (July 1863–June 1864). Purchased by Charles Stillman in Oct. 1862, she made three voyages from Matamoros to New York and carried a total of 1,288.5 bales of cotton.

Belle of Lamar: Confederate Coastal sloop. A survey and logistics vessel in Corpus Christi Bay.

Belle Sulphur: 126-ton Confederate side-wheel steamer, built 1856 at Louisville, Kentucky, Capt. John Payne. Owned by Peel-Dumble & Co.; leased to the Confederate Army in April 1862; wrecked returning to Sabine Pass from Berwick Bay in May 1862.

SS *Blanche*: (See: *General Rusk*).

C.P. Knapp: 109-ton British schooner, built 1859 at Pascagoula, Mississippi, Capt. Henry Laverty. (Larger than the *Rob Roy*, its registered dimensions as of Dec. 1860 were: 82'10" × 26'2" × 5'11"). Captured and released on voyage to Havana from Louisiana August 1861; carried 150 bales of cotton from Matamoros to Havana in Jan. 1862.

Caracas: 229-ton British brig, built 1849 at Tenerife, Azores, Capt. Locke. Harris Hoyt leased this brig from New York to Matamoros, but it was damaged in a storm and put into Bermuda for extensive repairs in March 1864.

Carioca: 502-ton Italian ship, built 1851 at Kensington, Pennsylvania, Capt. G.B. Maggio. She carried 905 bales of cotton from Matamoros to Liverpool via New York (Nov. 1863–May 1864). Capt. Maggio left 100 bales of Charles Stillman's cotton at the Rio Grande in exchange for loading another 100 bales at a higher freight rate.

Caroline: 23-ton British schooner, built 1860 at Pass Manchac, Louisiana, Capt. G.D. Harney. She was owned by William R. Evans, and wrecked at the mouth of the Rio Grande on Oct. 10, 1864, returning from New Orleans.

Citizen: 95-ton British schooner, built 1856 Riverhead, New York, Capt. John Lancy (Jan. 1863–April 1863), Capt. S. Osborn (June 1863–Feb. 1864), and Capt. A. Moltzen (April 1864–July 1865). One of the Texas Adventure vessels purchased by William Reynolds, it delivered a total of 130 bales of cotton on two voyages between New York and Matamoros in June 1863 and August 1864.

SS *City of New York*: 10,498-ton British twin-screw steamer, built 1888 at Glasgow, Capt. Watkins. Inman Steamship Company's large passenger liner, running between New York and Liverpool; later sold to the U.S.

USS *Clifton*: 892-ton side-wheel steamship, with 2 × 9" smoothbores, 4 × 32-pounders, built 1861 at Brooklyn, New York, Acting Lieutenant C.H. Baldwin. Designed as a ferryboat. The U.S. Navy purchased the steamer in Dec. 1861. It participated in the capture of New Orleans, attack at Vicksburg, and occupation of Galveston, but Confederate forces captured the warship at Sabine Pass on Sept. 8, 1863, and burned her in March 1864.

Cora: (See: *Snow Drift*).

SS *Cora*: 127-ton stern-wheel steamer, built 1856 at Elizabeth, Pennsylvania, Capt. Charles Gearing (April 1863–Nov. 1863), John Sargent (Dec. 1863–Feb. 1865), and William R. Evans (March 1865). She arrived in Texas from New Orleans in 1859 for service on the Trinity River and Galveston Bay. By April 1863, the steamer was on the Brazos River working under a Confederate government contract. Its owner, Thomas Gripon, then sold one-third shares to Richard King and Charles Gearing and ran the blockade from the Brazos into Matagorda Bay in May 1863. King bought Gearing's share in August 1863 and placed William Evans in command. The USS *Quaker City* captured her on March 24, 1865, attempting to run into the Rio Grande.

SS *Corsica*: 1,042-ton British steamer, built 1863 at Glasgow, Scotland, Capt. Frederick Le Messurier. A Cunard line passenger steamer that ran between New York, Nassau, and Havana during latter half of the Civil War.

USS *DeSoto*: 1675-ton side-wheel steamship, with 8 × 32 pounders, 1 × 30 pounder rifled, built 1859 at Brooklyn, New York, Capt. William M. Walker. The U.S. Navy purchased her in August 1861 and she joined the Gulf Blockading Squadron in December. She captured sixteen blockade runner prizes, including the schooner *William* on July 1, 1862, out of Sabine Pass with 450 bales of cotton.

Elizabeth: 41-ton British sloop, built 1852 at Galveston, Capt. Henry Scherffius. The USS *Hatteras* captured her on the return voyage to Sabine Pass from Kingston, Jamaica, via Havana on July 5, 1862. The seized cargo included rum, coal oil, gin (two barrels consumed during the passage), red wine, castor oil, medicine, and lead.

SS *Ella Warley* (formerly *Isabel*): 1115-ton British side-wheel steamer, built 1848 at Baltimore, Capt. George R. Schenck. She was renamed in 1861 and captured while running blockade from Havana to Charleston on April 24, 1862. Charles Prescott purchased her in Oct. 1862 as part of the Texas Adventure. After one voyage to Havana, she departed New York for New Orleans and collided with the SS *North Star* and sunk Feb. 9, 1863.

SS *Emma Dean* (aka *John Jewett*): 243-ton British brig, built 1860 at Brooklyn, New York, Capt. Robert Mount. Owned by Charles Stillman, whose agent reflagged and named her the *Emma Dean* in Sept. 1862 to honor a partner's wife. Made seven round trips from New York to Matamoros during the Civil War and carried 1,392 bales of cotton.

General C.C. Pinckney: 38-ton schooner, built 1854 at Charleston, South Carolina, Capt. F. Gerety (Jan.–March 1863), and Capt. Fogarty (April 1863). Captured by the U.S. Navy attempting to run into Wilmington, North Carolina, on May 6, 1862. The Confederates recaptured the schooner March 22, 1863, off Boca Chica, but then wrecked it attempting to cross the bar at the mouth of the Rio Grande.

SS *General Rusk* (*Blanche*): 417-ton side-wheel steamer, built 1857 in Wilmington, Delware, Capt. Leon Smith (1860–May 1862), Capt. Davidson (May–July 1862), and Capt. Robert N. Smith (August–Oct. 1862). A Confederate armed steamer that Major T.S. Moïse illicitly leased to civilian owners; made one successful run from Galveston to Havana with 583 bales of cotton. On its second run out of Matagorda Bay, Capt. Hunter of the USS *Montgomery* captured and burned her in Cuban waters. The cotton was partially burned and sold for $30,000.

George: 108-ton schooner, built 1853 at Kennebunkport, Maine, Capt. J.S. Rogers. It made two round trips between New York and Matamoros during the war carrying a total of 173 bales of cotton, numerous bales of hides, and 22 bales of wool that Harris Hoyt consigned to W.H. Reynolds & Co.

SS *George Washington*: 978-ton U.S. screw steamer, built 1862 at New York, Capt. Edwin V. Gager. It was a regular passenger and cargo packet between New Orleans and New York during the war.

Geziena Hilligonda: 180-ton Dutch brig, built 1859 at Groningen, Holland (Netherlands), Capt. B.P. Janson. The USS *Pembina* captured the brig off the Rio Grande on Dec. 4, 1864, as it arrived from Liverpool. The U.S. Supreme Court ordered its release on March 5, 1865, with the vessel and cargo restored to the owners.

SS *Grampus No. 2*: 252-ton side-wheel steamer, built 1861 at McKeesport, Pennsylvania, Capt. G.L. Smith. M. Kenedy & Co. used the steamer as a lighter operating outside the Rio Grande. They sold it to Chapple Dutton & Co. on behalf of Droege, Oetling & Co. who registered the steamer in Mexico. She did not return to M. Kenedy & Co. after the war.

172   Appendix 2. Sails, Steamers, and the Texas Cotton Trade

USS *Hatteras*: 1,126-ton side-wheel steamer, with 4 × 32-pounders and one 20-pounder, built 1861, Wilmington, Delaware. Commander George F. Emmons. The U.S. Navy purchased her in 1861 as the *St. Mary's*. She captured 7 blockade runners including the sloop *Elizabeth* on July 6, 1862 off Sabine Pass; detained and released the SS *Indian No. 2* on July 19, 1862 off Berwick Bay. The CSS *Alabama* sank her on Jan. 11, 1863, off Galveston Island.

Henry Dodge: (See: *Mary Sorley*).

Herbert: 1,387-ton British bark, built 1860 at East Boston, Massachusetts, Capt. C. Slater. The bark arrived at the Rio Grande from Liverpool via Havana in April 1863 with Henry Brastow as a passenger. She returned to Liverpool with 2351 bales of cotton and made two additional round trips with another 4,836 bales. (2386 + 2450).

HBMS *Immortalité*: 3,058-ton Royal Navy screw steam frigate, 51 guns, built 1859 at Pembroke Dock, UK. Capt. George Hancock. This British warship was in port at Havana during Christmas holidays 1862.

USS *Iosco*: 1,173-ton side-wheel steamer, with 2 × 100-pounders, 4 × 9" smoothbores, 2 × 24-pounder rifled, 2 × 12-pounder howitzers, Commander John Guest. She was built for the U.S. Navy in 1862 at Bath, Maine; on Nov. 20, 1864, and captured the British schooner *Sybil* off North Carolina as it sailed from the Rio Grande to New York.

SS *Isabel*: British side-wheel steamer, built at Brooklyn, New York, Capt. Edward P. Blake. Formerly Spanish-flagged, she escaped from Galveston with 700 bales of cotton on April 30, 1863, in company with the steamers *Harriet Lane* (*Lavinia*) and *Alice* (aka *Matagorda*). The USS *Admiral* captured her on the return voyage from Havana on May 28, 1864.

J.J. McNeil: Confederate schooner, built ca. 1852 in Texas, Capt. Alexander McCoffin (the U.S. Navy erroneously identified him as Alfred Coffin). The USS *Arthur* captured her on Jan. 25, 1862, off Pass Cavallo after running 100 bales of cotton to Vera Cruz and with the owner, Mr. Hopper and his wife on board.

SS *James Hale*: 173-ton side-wheel steamer, built 1860 at Freedom, Pennsylvania. Capt. Florencio Sallas. Built for M. Kenedy & Co. as an up-river transport on the Rio Grande, she arrived in April 1861. Union forces used her and the *Mustang* as river transports during their occupation of Brownsville, Nov. 1863–July 1864.

SS *John Jewett* (See: *Emma Dean*).

USS *Kensington*: 1052-ton screw steamer, with 2 × 32-pounders, one 30-pounder rifled, built 1858 at Philadelphia, Acting Volunteer Lieutenant Frederick Crocker. The U.S. Navy purchased her in 1862. On

Appendix 2. Sails, Steamers, and the Texas Cotton Trade 173

Sept. 30, 1862, she captured the *Velocity* off Sabine Pass and used the schooner as a tender to help blockade shallow Texas-Louisiana coastal waters.

Lecompt (*Le Compte*): 25-ton Confederate schooner, built 1854 at Algiers, Louisiana, Capt. & part owner James Mainland (1861–Oct. 1862 & June 1863), Capt. Samuel Doebner (June 1863–Jan. 1864). A Matagorda Bay pilot boat leased to Confederate Army for $20 per day until the U.S. Navy captured and towed her to Galveston Bay to join the blockading fleet (Oct. 1862). The Confederates recaptured her during Battle of Galveston Jan. 1, 1863, and restored her to Capt. Mainland, who leased her to the Marine Department as a Galveston Bay guard boat.

Lehman (*Lehman Jr.*, aka *Lamon, Lamar*): ca. 180-ton British schooner, built ca. 1854 at Biloxi, Mississippi, Capt. W. Maynard. A Louisiana-based schooner that ran into Galveston from Tampico via Matamoros (June 1863). The schooner arrived at Matamoros on Nov. 11, 1863, with 187 bales of cotton (weighing 88,721 lbs.) for Weil and Loeb and owner Daniel Goos of Louisiana.

Mack Canfield: 51-ton Swiss schooner, built 1853, at Essex, Massachusetts; Capt. Heinrich (Henry) Schmidt. Owned by the Swiss Consul in Galveston, Jacob C. Kuhn, it was captured off the Rio Grande from Galveston by the USS *W.G. Anderson* (August 25, 1863) with 133 bales of cotton and condemned for a total of $33,445.11.

Mary Sorley: (formerly *Henry Dodge*): 93-ton schooner, built 1856 at Portsmouth, Virginia, Capt. William F. Rogers. A former U.S. Revenue Cutter surrendered in March 1861 to Texans by her captain, she served as an armed gunboat at Galveston Bay and was named for the Galveston custom agent's wife. The government sold it to Thomas W. House. It was captured on its first blockade running attempt on April 3, 1864, under Capt. Charles Diericks with 257 bales of cotton.

SS *Matagorda* (*Alice*): 1250-ton British side-wheel steamer; built 1858 at Wilmington, Delaware, Capt. Cole. Renamed *Alice* (July–August 1862). She made ten successful Mobile runs (5 in and 5 out) and eight Texas runs (seven successful, 4 in and 3 out), including Sabine Pass and Brazos River, one round trip each, and Galveston Bay, twice (captured on its final run to Havana in Sept. 1864).

SS *Matamoros*: 240-ton Confederate/Mexican side-wheel steamer, built 1860 at Shousetown, Pennsylvania, Capt. Robert Dalzell. One of M. Kenedy & Co.'s outside lighters, it was chartered during the Union occupation under the Mexican flag. It provided Union logistic support at Matagorda Bay, but returned to Rio Grande and M. Kenedy &

Co.'s beneficial ownership when Union forces evacuated Brownsville in July 1864.

SS *Mexico*: 280-ton side-wheel U.S. steamer, built 1859 at Stockton, New Jersey, Master John S. Crowell. It was an ocean steamer that sailed from the Rio Grande in August 1864 and arrived in Havana with 303 bales of cotton and Harris Hoyt as a passenger. She made four additional round trips carrying about 300 bales of cotton on each voyage to Havana.

SS *Mexico*: 120-ton Confederate/Mexican side-wheel steamer, built 1859 at Wheeling, Virginia, Capt. Joseph Aschenberg. She was an outside and up river Rio Grande lighter owned by M. Kenedy & Co. until sold to Benito Vinas in June 1862. She remained in service until sunk June 22, 1865, between Matamoros and Bagdad with Robert Dalzell as captain.

Monarch: 300-ton British brig, built 1859, Guernsey, UK, Capt. G.G. Strickland. She arrived at the Rio Grande July 16, 1864, from Liverpool via Bermuda with the cargo from the *Caracas*. After clearing from Matamoros on Nov. 15, 1864, she arrived at Liverpool Jan. 12, 1865, with 747 bales of cotton.

USS *Montgomery*: 787-ton screw steamer, with one 10" smoothbore, one 32-pounder rifled, 4 × 32-pounder smoothbores, built 1858 at New York, Capt. Charles Hunter. The U.S. Navy purchased her in 1861. Her captain illegally boarded and burned the SS *Blanche* (former CSS *General Rusk*) on Oct. 7, 1862, in Cuban waters causing an international incident.

SS *Mustang*: 172-ton Confederate/Mexican side-wheel steamer, built 1860 at Pittsburgh, Pennsylvania, Capt. Martin. M. Kenedy & Co. Rio Grande up river steamer; controlled by Union quartermaster corps (Nov. 1863–August 1864), but leased from nominal Mexican owners with payments and ownership eventually reverting to M. Kenedy & Co.

SS *North Star*: 1,867-ton side-wheel steamer, built 1853 at New York, Capt. P.E. Lefevre. She collided with the *Ella Warley* on the evening of Feb. 9, 1863, on return voyage to New York from New Orleans via Key West. The *North Star* was heavily damaged but the smaller *Ella Warley* sank.

SS *Peterhoff*: 669-ton British side-wheel steamer, built 1862 at Hull, England, Capt. Stephen Jarman. Captured by the USS *Vanderbilt* coming out of St. Thomas, Danish Virgin Islands bound for Matamoros, she was taken into the U.S. Navy and mistakenly rammed and sunk off Wilmington, North Carolina, in 1864. After the war, the U.S. Supreme Court ruled the seizure as illegal and ordered compensation for the British owners.

Appendix 2. Sails, Steamers, and the Texas Cotton Trade

Plantagenet: 718-ton British screw steamer, built 1859 at Greenock, Scotland. Capt. Beard. A bulk cargo and passenger transport that carried Harris Hoyt as a passenger on its regular transit from Kingston, Jamaica to Port-au-Prince, Haiti, and New York (April–Sept. 1862 & June–Sept. 1863).

USS *Quaker City*: 1,428-ton side-wheel steamer, with one 100-, one 30-, and one 20-pounder rifled, 6 × 8" smoothbores, built 1854 in Philadelphia, Commander William F. Spicer. U.S. Navy purchased her in 1861. She captured a total of 19 blockade runners, including the SS *Cora* as it sailed from Matagorda Bay to join M. Kenedy & Co.'s fleet of river transports in March 1865.

Rimac: 593-ton British ship, built 1864 at Liverpool, Capt. R. Sewell. She made two round trips between Liverpool and Matamoros in late 1864 and 1865 with 1,360 bales of cotton (400 + 966).

SS *Roanoke*: 1071-ton side-wheel steamer, built 1851 at New York, Capt. Francis A. Drew. She was a regular packet that carried Harris Hoyt to New York from Havana on Sept. 13, 1864.

Rob Roy (formerly *Francis Marguez, Jr.*): 48-ton British schooner, built 1855 at Madisonville, Louisiana, Capt. Henry Laverty (Jan.–July 1863), Capt. J. (August–Nov. 1863), and William Watson (Nov. 1863–Feb. 1865). Probably the best known blockade running schooner of the Civil War, she was rebuilt on the keel of the *James Cartey* which had been built in 1849 at Bon Secours, Alabama (retained the same 48 4/95 tonnage and dimensions of 58' × 22'4" × 4'7"). Watson purchased and renamed her in April–May 1863, but retained Henry Laverty as captain. The registered dimensions are at slight variance with William Watson's claim that it was 78' × 22'6" × 4'9". The difference in length probably reflects the registered measurement of 58 feet as the distance between the perpendiculars rather than Watson's 78 feet which would have been the overall length from the end of the bowsprit to the stern. Watson ran the blockade from the Brazos River with 146 bales of cotton (Jan. 1864) and from Galveston twice (Sept. 1864 & Jan. 1865) with 198 & 150 bales. He sold the *Rob Roy* at Havana (Feb. 1865). Under a different captain, the *Rob Roy* was chased ashore and burned at Steinhatchee River, Florida (March 1865).

Roger A. Heirn: 1088-ton ship, build 1857 at New York, Capt. J. Stewart. Charles Stillman was a part-owner with his New York partners Smith & Dunning. To avoid attention from Northern officials, Stillman joined the crew as the supercargo in April 1865 for its voyage from Matamoros to Liverpool with 2274 bales of cotton.

USS *Sachem* (SS *Clarinda*): 197-ton screw steamer, with one 20-pounder rifled, 4 × 32 pounder smoothbores, built 1844 at New York City, Acting Master Amos Johnson. A former coast survey vessel; the U.S. Navy purchased her in 1861. She captured the schooner *Lecompt* at Matagorda Bay Oct. 23, 1862, but the Confederates disabled and captured her at the Battle of Sabine Pass Sept. 8, 1863. The Confederates sold her to Thomas W. House under Capt. Henry Scherffius who renamed her the *Clarinda* and ran the blockade to Vera Cruz with 500 bales of cotton in Oct. 1864.

Snow Drift (*Cora*): 70-ton U.S./British schooner, built 1858 at Essex, Mississippi, Capt. Joseph C. Witham. A Texas Adventure schooner that carried Harris Hoyt to Havana where it was reflagged and renamed the *Cora* and then sailed to Matamoros. Henry Brastow sold her to Henry Scherffius. She made five successful runs from Texas to Belize and Vera Cruz with about 720 bales of cotton, until captured on Dec. 19, 1864, out of Galveston with a new captain and 175 bales of cotton.

Sol Wildes (aka *Sol Wilder*): 485-ton bark, built 1863 at Cutler, Maine, Capt. Bunker. Based out of Boston, it made regular voyages to New Orleans in its first year of construction. The bark carried and sold the cotton that USS *W.G. Anderson* had illicitly taken directly from the captured schooner *America*.

USS *South Carolina*: 1,165-ton screw steamship, with 4 × 8" smoothbores, one 32-pounder, built 1860 at Boston, Commander James Alden. The U.S. Navy acquired her 1861. She was the first U.S. Navy warship to blockade the Texas coast, arriving off Galveston on July 2, 1861.

HBMS *Steady*: 570-ton screw steamer, with 1 × 68-pdr, 2 × 24-pdr howitzers, 2 × 20-pdr breech-loading smoothbores, built 1860 at Devonport, UK, Commander Henry D. Grant. A *Philomel*-class warship, she was commissioned on June 12, 1861 and was at Havana over the Christmas holidays in 1862. Commander James D. Bulloch used its design as a basis for the CSS *Florida*, a Confederate commerce raider built by William C. Miller & Sons at Liverpool.

Sybil (brig): 178-ton British brig, built 1848 at Kennebunkport, Maine, Capt. H.B. Townsley. She made three voyages out of Matamoros during the Civil War, delivering a total of 703 bales of cotton to New York in Oct. 1863, April 1864, and March 1865.

Sybil (former U.S.-flagged *Eagle*): 166-ton British schooner, built 1862 at Camden, Maine. Capt. William E. Askins. She changed her name and registry at Nassau (April 1863) and made four voyages to Matamoros (April 1863–Dec. 1864) carrying 1,230 bales of cotton to New York. Captured by the USS *Iosco* on her fourth voyage, she was later released at New York.

Thomas H. Terry: 519-ton British bark, built 1862 at St. Andrews, New Brunswick, Capt. Richardson. The bark arrived at New York May 24, 1863, from Matamoros with 105 bales of cotton and passengers Horace and son Thomas Hoyt. It made one other Civil War voyage from Matamoros with 695 bales of cotton to New York in Dec. 1864.

USS *Tyler*: 420-ton side-wheel steamer, with 6 × 8" smoothbores, 3 × 30-pounder rifled, 4 × 32- and one 12-pounder smoothbores, built 1857 at Cincinnati, Lieutenant Frederic S. Hill. From Sept. 1864, the *Tyler* operated on the White River in Arkansas under the command of the former captain of the USS *William G. Anderson*.

USS *Velocity*: 87-ton schooner, with 2 × 12-pound brass howitzers, built 1857 at Key West, Acting Master George Taylor. The USS *Kensington* captured the *Velocity* running into Sabine Pass from Belize via Sisal in Sept. 1862 and converted it into armed gunboat (aka USS *Fairy*) for the U.S. Navy. The Confederates recaptured her in Jan. 21, 1863 along with the USS *Morning Light* off Sabine Pass and sold her to Thomas W. House. She ran the blockade under several different captains as the *Vigilant* and *Nellie Blair* and was named the *Chaos* when captured in April 1865 under Capt. Peter Anderson.

HBMS *Vesuvius*: 970-ton side-wheel steamer, built 1839 at Sheerness, Captain Richard V. Hamilton. She was a British warship that was in port at Havana with the Royal Navy's *Steady* and *Immortalité* for the Christmas holidays in Dec. 1862.

West Florida (aka *Cephize* & *Hanover*): 93-ton schooner, built 1853 at Santa Rosa, Florida, Capt. Joseph H. Ashby (aka Ashbey). She was captured by the USS *Velocity* on Oct. 10, 1862 near the Sabine River with a Butler pass, but released. She arrived at Matamoros from New Orleans on Feb. 7, 1863, but wrecked May 10, 1863, attempting to run into Galveston Bay at San Luis Pass. Fifty bales of cotton bagging were saved, but all the whiskey was lost. The U.S. Navy identified her as the *Hanover* and the Confederates as the *Cephize*.

USS *William G. Anderson*: 593-ton bark, with one 20-pounder and one 12-pounder rifled, 6 × 32-pounders, built 1959 at East Boston, Acting Volunteer Lieutenant Frederic Stanhope Hill. U.S. Navy purchased the warship in 1861. It captured five prizes plus the cotton salvaged from the wreck of Harris Hoyt's chartered schooner, the *America*.

SS *William G. Hewes*: 747-ton side-wheel steamer, built 1860 at New York, Capt. Smith (August 1862–March 1863) and James Carlin (April–August 1863). Seized by the Louisiana officials in May 1861 and auctioned to a Louisiana company represented by Addison Cammack. After Harris Hoyt unsuccessfully attempted to purchase the steamer in Havana, the Exporting Company of South Carolina acquired and renamed her the *Ella and Annie*. Under this name, she made eight successful blockade runs with James Carlin as captain (three at Charleston, and one each at Wilmington, North Carolina, and Nassau). She was captured under a new captain in Nov. 1863 and renamed the USS *Malvern*.

Chapter Notes

Abbreviations:
BCAH—Dolph Briscoe Center for American History, The University of Texas, Austin, TX
Conf—Confederate
BG—Brigadier General
Cong—Congress
Doc.—Document
Ex.—Executive
GPO—Government Printing Office
Houghton—Houghton Library, Harvard University, Cambridge, MA
JSR—José San Román
LOC—Library of Congress
LtG—Lieutenant General
Maj—Major
MG—Major General
NARA—National Archives and Records Administration
NYT—New York Times
ORA—*Official Records of the Army During the War of the Rebellion*
ORN—*Official Records of the Navy During the War of the Rebellion*
Pt.—Part
RG—Record Group
Seq.—Sequence
Ser.—Series
SHQ—*Southwestern Historical Quarterly*
Sess—Session
University—University
Unk—Unknown

Preface

1. Stillman to Capt. King, Mar 11, 1862, King Ranch Archives, Kingsville, TX (quoted material).
2. Smith to Morell, Apr 1, 1864, Charles Stillman papers, MS Am 800.27, Houghton; New Orleans *Daily Delta*, May 27, 1859.

Chapter 1

1. J. David Hacker, "A Census-Based Count of the Civil War Dead," *Civil War History* 57, No.4 (Dec 2011), 307–348.
2. James A. Irby, *Backdoor at Bagdad: the Civil War on the Rio Grande* (El Paso: Texas Western Press, 1977), 17.
3. Philip Leigh, *Trading with the Enemy: The Covert Economy During the American Civil War* (Yardley, PA: Westholme Publishing, 2014), 15.
4. Leigh, *Trading with the Enemy*, 15; Ludwell H. Johnson, "Commerce Between Northeastern Ports and the Confederacy, 1861–1865," *The Journal of American History*, Vol. 54, No.1 (Jun 1976), 30–42.
5. David G. Surdam, "Traders or Traitors: Northern Cotton Trading During the Civil War," *Journal of Economic History*, Vol. 41 (1981), 867–888); Welles to Seward, Jun 8, 1863, ORN I: 20, 119 (quoted material).
6. Leigh, *Trading with the Enemy*, 24; Robert L. Kerby, *Kirby Smith's Confederacy: The Trans-Mississippi South, 1863–1865* (New York: Columbia University Press, 1972), 157–161.
7. David G. Surdam, *Northern Naval Superiority and the Economics of the American Civil War* (Columbus: University of South Carolina Press, 2001), 177; Kerby, *Kirby Smith's Confederacy*, 84–85; Smith to Stillman, Sep 27, 1864, Charles Stillman business papers, MS Am 800.27 Houghton.
8. B.P. Gallaway (ed.), *The Dark Corner of the Confederacy: Accounts of Civil War Texas as Told by Contemporaries* (Dubuque, IA: W. M. Brown Book Co., 1968), iii; Alden to Mervine, Jul 8, 1861, ORN 1: 16, 576–577 (quoted material);

179

L. Tuffly Ellis, "Maritime Commerce on the Far Western Gulf, 1861-1865," *SHQ*, Vol. 77, No. 2 (Oct 1973), 167–169; Richard V. Francaviglia, *From Sail to Steam: Four Centuries of Texas Maritime History, 1500–1900* (Austin: University of Texas Press, 1998), 193–194; Paul H. Silverstone, *Civil War Navies, 1855–1883* (Annapolis, MD: Naval Institute Press, 2001), 59–60.

9. Alden to Mervine, Jul 8, 1861, *ORN* 1: 16, 576–577.

10. Walter E. Wilson, "The Civil War Blockade Running Adventures of the Louisiana Schooner William R. King," *Louisiana History*, 56 (Summer 2015), 298; James W. Daddysman, *The Matamoros Trade: Confederate Commerce: Diplomacy, and Intrigue* (Newark: University of Delaware Press, 1984), 112–116; Turner to Bradfute, Nov 26, 1863, and Magruder to Boggs, Dec 22, 1863, *ORA* I: 26 pt. 2, 446–447, 523–525.

11. Chicago *Daily Tribune*, Jun 28, 1861; Walter E. Wilson, "Rebels at the Rio Grande: Naval Actions on the International Border in 1863," in *New Studies in Rio Grande Valley History*, 16, ed. Milo Kearney et al., 125–166 (Edinburg, TX: The University of Texas Rio Grande Valley, 2018), 130.

12. Stephen R. Wise, *Lifeline of the Confederacy: Blockade Running During the Civil War* (University of South Carolina Press, 1988), 107–108.

13. Note: The sailing distance is 1380 nautical miles from Galveston to Belize, compared to 1090 from New Orleans, and 1473 from Wilmington.

14. Wilson, "The Louisiana Schooner William R. King," 303.

15. *Ibid.*, 310–311; Frank Lawrence Owsley, *King Cotton Diplomacy* (Chicago: University of Chicago Press, 1931), 252–253; Wise, *Lifeline of the Confederacy*, 19–24; William Watson, *Adventures of a Blockade Runner* (T. Fisher Unwin, London, 1892), 113.

16. Raphael Semmes, *Memoirs of Service Afloat, During the War Between the States* (Baltimore: Kelly Piet & Co., 1869), 103; James Russell Soley, *The Blockade and the Cruisers* (New York: Charles Scribner's Sons, 1883), 16–20. Ernest McNeill Eller (ed.), *Civil War Naval Chronology 1861–1865* (Washington: GPO for the U.S. Navy Department, Naval History Division, 1971), II-54–57; IV-95–97.

17. George Minot (ed.), *The Statues at Large and Treaties of the United States of America*, Vol. IX (Boston: Little Brown & Co., 1862), 928–943 (Articles V and VII); Blacker to Crawford, Feb 9, 1862, *ORN* I: 17, 109–111; Wilson, "The Louisiana Schooner William R. King," 307; Farragut to French, Aug 25, 1862, *ORN* I: 19, 168. Note: many historians have been confused by the term "Marine League" and have erroneously calculated the distance the boundary extended into the Gulf.

18. Wilson, "Captain King's Cotton, the Civil War Blockade-Running Adventures of Richard King and Mifflin Kenedy," in *Supplementary Studies in Rio Grande Valley History*, 15, ed. Milo Kearney et al., 91–130 (Edinburg, TX: The University of Texas Rio Grande Valley, 2017), 93; Ellis, "Maritime Commerce on the Far Western Gulf, 1861–1865," 204–205.

19. *Ibid.*

20. Marilyn McAdams Sibley, "Charles Stillman: a Case Study of Entrepreneurship on the Rio Grande, 1861–1865," *SHQ*, 77, No. 2 (Oct 1973): 232; United States, 38th Cong., 2nd Sess. House Rep. No. 25, *New York Custom-House* (Washington: GPO, 1865), 1–37.

21. Consular Note for *Belasario*, Jan 26, 1863, JSR Papers, Box 2G 65, BCAH; Smith to Morell [for Stillman], Oct 19, 1863, and Nov 6, 1863 (1st quote), Charles Stillman business papers, MS Am 800.27 Houghton; U.S. Government, *New York Custom-House*, 1 (2nd quote). David Montejano, "Mexican Merchants and Teamsters on the Texas Cotton Road, 1862–1865," in *Mexico and Mexicans in the Making of the United States*, ed. John Tutino, 141–170 (Austin: University of Texas Press, 2012), 157; Milo Kearney and Anthony Knopp, *Boom and Bust: The Historical Cycles of Matamoros and Brownsville* (Austin: Eakin Press, 1991), 74.

22. Robert B. Vezzetti, ed. *Tidbits: A Collection from the Brownsville Historical Association and the Stillman House Museum* (Brownsville, TX: Brownsville Historical Association, ca. 2016), 26–27.

23. *Ibid.*; John Salmon Ford, *Rip Ford's Texas*, Stephen B. Oates (ed.) (Austin: University of Texas Press, 1963), 460 (quoted material).

24. Vezzetti, *Tidbits*, 26–27; Ford, *Rip Ford's Texas*), 460: Tom Lea, *The King*

Ranch (Boston: Little, Brown, and Co., 1957), 247–248, 251–252; Frank Daniel Yturria, *The Patriarch: The Remarkable Life and Extraordinary Times of Francisco Yturria* (Brownsville: University of Texas Brownsville, 2006), 24, 51, 83, 148; Jane Clements Monday and Frances Brannen Vick. *Petra's Legacy: the South Texas Ranching Empire of Petra Vela and Mifflin Kenedy* (College Station: Texas A&M University Press, 2007), 350–351.

25. George Walton Dalzell, *Flight from the Flag* (Chapel Hill: University of North Carolina Press, 1940), 239–248; Ford, *Rip Ford's Texas*, 329.

26. Meredith Willson, *But He Doesn't Know the Territory* (New York: G.P. Putnam & Sons, 1959 reprint (Minneapolis: University of Minnesota Press, 2009), 15, 26. Note: In addition to Harris Hoyt and Harold Hill, Marian and Marie, there's also Willson and Wilson.

27. U.S. Customs Records, Passenger Lists of Vessels arriving at New York, 1820–1897, NARA RG36, M237, *Plantagenet*.

Chapter 2

1. Edward H. Hall, *The Northern Counties Gazetteer and Directory, for 1855–6* (Chicago: R. Fergus, 1855), 30, 31; S.J. Clarke, *Biographical Record of Kane County, Illinois* (Chicago: S.J. Clarke Publishing Co., 1898), 326–329; Pliny A. Durant, H.C. Bradsby, and Samuel W Durant, *Biographical and Historical Record of Kane County, Illinois* (Chicago: Beers, Leggett & Co., 1888), 977; Batavia Historical Society (bataviahistoricalsociety.org); Statement of Hoyt, Dec 12, 1864, 41st Cong 3rd Sess, Senate Ex. Doc. No. 10, Pt. 3 (Washington: GPO, 1871); Hoyt to Stanton, Sep 15, 1862, NARA RG 94, M619 Letters Received by the Adjutant General's Office, R0107, Hoyt; W. & D. Richardson, Galveston City Directory, 1859–1860, 15, Rosenberg Library, Galveston, TX.

2. Illinois State Census, 1855, Illinois State Archives, Ancestry.com; FindaGrave.com; Hoyt family Bible records, 1811–1930, familysearch.org. Hoyt had seven children by his first wife Ann Elizabeth Sayre who died in Clinton County, NY, in 1842; He had three children by his second wife Charlotte Elizabeth Winchell, who died at Batavia, IL, in 1852. He had one child (Cora Louise) with his third wife, the widow Marie Emma Bryant Carpenter (1831–1919), who had one son, William, from a previous marriage.

3. Galveston *Weekly Civilian and Gazette*, Aug 2, 1859; Houston *Weekly Telegraph*, Sep 28, 1859 and Feb 1, 1860; *The Beaumont Banner*, May 30, 1861.

4. Wilson, "Captain King's Cotton," 92.

5. Statement of Hoyt, Dec 12, 1864, 41st Cong 3rd Sess, Senate Ex. Doc. No. 10, Pt. 3; Hoyt to Stanton, Sep 15, 1862, NARA RG 94, M619 Letters Received by the Adjutant General's Office, R0107, Harris Hoyt.

6. Note: Confidence man or con man is a term for a swindler developed before the Civil War.

7. Daddysman, *The Matamoros Trade*, 31; Kerby, *Kirby Smith's Confederacy*, 156; Owsley, *King Cotton Diplomacy*, 25–26; Ronnie C. Tyler, "Cotton on the Border, 1861–1865," *SHQ*, 73. No. 2 (Jul 1970), 457; United States, 63rd Congress, 1st Session, Apr 7–Dec 1, 1913, Senate Doc., No. 181 *Quotations from Statutes at Large of the Confederate States of America* (Washington: GPO, 1913) (quoted material).

8. Statement of Hoyt, Dec 12, 1864, 41st Cong 3rd Sess, Senate Ex. Doc. No. 10, Pt. 3; Laws of the Ninth Legislature, Passed at the Regular Session of November and December, 1861 and January, 1862, Condensed, Special Laws, Chapter 1, 24, *The Texas Almanac for 1863* (Austin, TX: D. Richardson, 1862), 20; H.P.N. Gammel (comp.). *Laws of Texas, 1822–1897*, Vol. V (Austin: The Gammel Book Co., 1898), 12–13; Houston *Weekly Telegraph*, Vol. 27, No. 47, Feb 5, 1862. Note: John M. Brown, J.D. McAdoo, Gabriel Felder, L.W. Groce Wm. L. Crump, Harris Hoit [Sic], N. Cavanaugh, Samuel Holliday, J. L. Farquhar, James P. Flewellen, Terrell J. Jackson, T.B. Traynham, R. H. Felder, and R.T. Flewellen were all commissioners of the Texas Manufacturing Company.

9. Statement of Hoyt, Dec 12, 1864, 41st Cong 3rd Sess, Senate Ex. Doc. No. 10, Pt. 3.

10. Ibid.

11. Ibid.

12. Ibid.; W.T. Block, *Schooner Sail to*

Starboard: Confederate Blockade Running on the Louisiana-Texas Coastlines (Woodville, TX: Dogwood Press, 1997), 119–120.

13. Work Projects Administration (WPA), *Ship Registers and Enrollments of New Orleans, Louisiana*, Vol. V, 1851–1860 (Baton Rouge: Louisiana State University, 1941), No. 149; Statement of Hoyt, Dec 12, 1864, 41st Cong 3rd Sess, Senate Ex. Doc. No. 10, Pt. 3; Louisville *Daily Courier*, Oct 4, 1856; A.T. Lynn Log entry, Aug 7, 1861, J.O.L.O. Observatory record book, 1861: 27–0701, Rosenberg Library, Galveston; Charles S. Davis, and J. Barto Arnold, III, *Colin J. McRae: Confederate Financial Agent: Blockade Running in the Trans-Mississippi as Affected by the Confederate Governments Direct European Procurement of Goods* (College Station, TX: Institute of Nautical Archeology, Texas A&M University, 2008), 168 (NARA, Galveston Weekly Customs Reports); Edmondson & Calwell to Hébert, May 2, 1862, NARA RG:109, Conf Vessel Papers, R-2, Seq.: A-54 1/2, *Andromeda*. Note: The 109 bales weighed 56,908 lbs., for an average of 522 lbs. each.

14. Davis and Arnold, *Colin J. McRae* (NARA, Galveston Weekly Customs Reports), 168; Statement of Hoyt, Dec 12, 1864, 41st Cong 3rd Sess, Senate Ex. Doc. No. 10, Pt. 3.

15. Eller (ed.), *Civil War Naval Chronology 1861–1865*, II-54, II-57.

16. U.S. Customs Records, Passenger Lists of Vessels arriving at New York, 1820–1890, NARA RG36, M237, 7, *Plantagenet*; Wise, *Lifeline of the Confederacy*, 274, 312; Statement of Hoyt, Dec 12, 1864, 41st Cong 3rd Sess, Senate Ex. Doc. No. 10, Pt. 3; *Galveston Weekly News*, May 21, 1862; Cate to McKean, May 26, 1862, *ORN* I: 17, 253; *NYT*, May 11, 1862.

17. Eller (ed.), *Civil War Naval Chronology 1861–1865*, I-40, II-75–76; Emmons to Welles, Jul 6, 1862, *ORN* I: 18, 666–667, and Jul 28, 1862, *ORN* I: 19, 94–95; Silverstone, *Civil War Navies*, 48, 51; Handbook of Texas Online, Robert Wooster and W.T. Block, "GILMER, ALEXANDER," accessed June 25, 2019, http://www.tshaonline.org/handbook/online/articles/fgi30. Note: The Author's wife grew up near Sabine Lake on a road named for Gilmer.

18. Emmons to Welles, Jul 6, 1862, *ORN* I: 18, 666–667, and Jul 28, 1862, *ORN* I: 19, 94–95.

19. William E. Gloag, Alexander Nicolson, Hubert Hamilton, and James Paterson, *The Scottish Jurist: Being Reports of Cases Decided in the Supreme Courts of Scotland, and in the House of Lords on Appeal from Scotland*, Vol. 38 (Edinburgh: Thomas Constable, 1866), 309–315; Sir John Rankine *The Scots Revised Reports: Court of Session*, Ser. 3 Vol. 4, Clements v. Macaulay, 1866 (Edinburg: William Green and Sons, 1903), 603–615; Eller, *Civil War Naval Chronology 1861–1865*, VI-235.

20. Wise, *Lifeline of the Confederacy*, 26, 114–115, 232, 270, 327; Colin Carlin, *Captain James Carlin: Anglo-American Blockade Runner* (Columbia: University of South Carolina Press, 2017), 123.

21. Davis and Arnold, *Colin J. McRae* (NARA, Galveston Weekly Customs Reports), 168, 170; New Orleans *Times-Picayune*, May 26, 1889; Gloag, et al., *The Scottish Jurist*, 309–315 (quoted material).

22. Houston *Tri-Weekly Telegraph*, Jun 9, 1862; *Philadelphia Inquirer*, Jun 19, 1862; Zacharie to Charles Stillman, Jun 28, 1862, Charles Stillman business papers, MS Am 800.27, Houghton; Wise, *Lifeline of the Confederacy*, 272, 274; Macaulay to Hébert, Aug 25, 1862, NARA RG:109, M3465, Conf Citizens File, J. L. Macanlay.

23. *NYT*, Oct 26, 1862; Macaulay to Hébert, Sep 19, 1862, NARA, RG:109, M346, Conf Citizens File, J. L. Macanlay; T.S. Moïse to P.O. Hébert, Sep 20, 1862, NARA, RG:109, M331, Conf Officer Records, T.S. Moïse; Leon Smith to Charles Mason, Sep 17, 1862, NARA RG:109, Conf Vessel Papers, R: 12, *General Rusk*; Burke to Mason, Sep 22, 1862, NARA RG109, M347 Miscellaneous Conf Records, Jno Burke; Rankine *The Scots Revised Reports*, 603–615; James M. Day, "Leon Smith: Confederate Mariner," *East Texas Historical Journal* 3, No. 1 (Mar 1965), 34.

24. Hunter to Farragut, Oct 11, 1862, *ORN* I: 19, 269; Silverstone, *Civil War Navies*, 48–49.

25. Lyons to Seward, Jan 8, 1863, *ORN* I: 273–274; Farragut to Welles, Dec 10, 1862, *ORN* I: 19, 272–273; Stuart L. Bernath, *Squall Across the Atlantic. American Civil War Prize Cases and Diplomacy*

(Berkeley: University of California, 1970), 101; London *Evening Star*, Nov 11, 1862.
26. Lyons to Seward, Jan 8, 1863, *ORN* I: 273–274; Robert M., Browning, Jr., *Lincoln's Trident: The West Gulf Blockading Squadron During the Civil War* (Tuscaloosa: University of Alabama Press, 2015), 206–208; Hunter to Farragut, Oct 11, 1862, *ORN* I: 19, 269; Welles to Farragut, Dec 9, 1862, *ORN* I: 19, 272; Farragut to Welles, Dec 10, 1862, and Court Martial of CDR Charles Hunter, Jan 20, 1863, *ORN* I: 19, 272–273, 275–277; *NYT* Oct 26, 1862 and Nov 8, 1862; *GWN* Oct 29, 1862; *NYT*; *ILN* Oct 8, 1862; *London Times*, Nov 11, 1862; *Baltimore Sun* Dec 2, 1873.

Chapter 3

1. Statements of Hoyt, Dec 7, 12, 1864, 41st Cong 3rd Sess, Senate Ex. Doc. No. 10, Pt. 3; Durant, et al., *Biographical and Historical Record of Kane County, Illinois*, 847; William Coffin, *Life and Times of Hon. Samuel D. Lockwood* (Chicago: Knight & Leonard Co., 1889), 128.
2. Statement of Hoyt, Dec 7, 1864, 41st Cong 3rd Sess, Senate Ex. Doc. No. 10, Pt. 3.
3. *Ibid.*; Statements of Hoyt, Dec 12, 1864, and W.H. Reynolds, Dec 10, 19, 1864, 41st Cong 3rd Sess, Senate Ex. Doc. No. 10, Pt. 3.
4. Norman C. Delaney, *The Maltby Brothers' Civil War* (College Station: Texas A&M University Press, 2013), 63, 77; Kittredge to McKean, Jan 25, 1862, *ORN* I: 17, 80–81; D.D. Shea to Garland, Mar 4, 1862, *ORA* I: 9, 703–705.
5. Kittredge to McKean, Jan 25, 1862, *ORN* I: 17, 80–81; Shea to Garland, Mar 4, 1862, *ORA* I: 9, 703–705; McKean to Kittredge, Feb 10, 1862, *ORN* I: 17, 81; Gray to Bee, Sep 16, 1862, *ORN* I: 19, 204.
6. Statements of Byron Sprague, Dec 9, 1864, and Reynolds, Dec 10, 1864, and Prescott, Dec 19, 1864, 41st Cong 3rd Sess, Senate Ex. Doc. No. 10, Pt. 3.
7. Hoyt to Stanton, Sep 15, 1862, NARA RG 94, M619 Letters Received by the Adjutant General's Office, R0107, Harris Hoyt; Carl Sandburg, *Abraham Lincoln: The Prairie Years and the War Years* (Pleasantville, NY: The Reader's Digest Association, 1954), 240–242, 627; James McPherson, *Battle Cry of Freedom: The Civil War Era* (New York: Oxford University Press, 1988), 324.
8. Statement of Hoyt, Dec 7, 1864, 41st Cong 3rd Sess, Senate Ex. Doc. No. 10, Pt. 3; Sandburg, *Abraham Lincoln*, 169. Barrett published a biography of Lincoln in Jun 1864 to boost his reelection campaign. See: Joseph H. Barrett, *Life of Abraham Lincoln* (New York: Moore, Wilstach & Baldwin, 1865).
9. John Hay recommendation for Harris Hoyt, Sep 17, 1862, 41st Cong, 3d Session, Senate Ex. Doc. No. 10, Pt. 4; Peg A. Lamphier, *Kate Chase and William Sprague: Politics and Gender in a Civil War Marriage* (Lincoln: University of Nebraska Press, 2003), 46. Note: In an otherwise excellent discussion of Harris Hoyt and the Texas Adventure, Lamphier questions the authenticity of the John Hay letter. The JAG report entered the letter into evidence, and it is cited in two different Congressional Reports without any indication of it not being genuine.
10. John Hay letter of recommendation for Harris Hoyt, Sep 17, 1862, 41st Cong., 3d Session, Senate Rep. No. 377.
11. John Russell Bartlett. *Memoirs of Rhode Island Officers Who Were Engaged in the Service of Their Country During the Great Rebellion of the South* (Providence: Sidney S. Rider & Brother, 1867), 105–120; John Oller, *American Queen: the Rise and Fall of Kate Chase—Civil War "Belle of the North" and Gilded Age Woman of Scandal*. (Da Capo Press, 2014), 214–220; *Washington Evening Star*, Aug 15, 1862, Sep 4, 26, 1862. Note: William Sprague, IV (Sep 12, 1830–Sep 11, 1915) was the RI governor (1860–1863) and senator (1863–1875).
12. Statement of Hoyt, Dec 7, 1864, 41st Cong 3rd Sess, Senate Ex. Doc. No. 10, Pt. 3; John Russell Bartlett. *Memoirs of Rhode Island Officers Who Were Engaged in the Service of Their Country During the Great Rebellion of the South* (Providence: Sidney S. Rider & Brother, 1867), 105–120; Lamphier, *Kate Chase and William Sprague*, 33; Leigh, *Trading with the Enemy*, 22.
13. Statement of L.B. Frieze. January 26, 1865, 41st Cong 3rd Sess, Senate Ex. Doc. No. 10, Pt. 3 (quoted material); Lamphier, *Kate Chase and William Sprague*, 33.
14. Wm. Sprague to Dix, Feb 10, 1865,

41st Cong 3rd Sess, Senate Ex. Doc. No. 10, Pt. 3.

15. Statements of Prescott, Dec 6, 1864, and Hoyt, Dec 7, 1864, 41st Cong 3rd Sess, Senate Ex. Doc. No. 10, Pt. 3; *Washington Evening Star*, Sep 20, 1862; ancestry.com. Charles L. Prescott.

16. Statements of Hoyt, Dec 7, 1864, and Prescott, Dec 6, 19, 1864, 41st Cong 3rd Sess, Senate Ex. Doc. No. 10, Pt. 3.

17. *Ibid.*; Statement of Frieze. January 26, 1865, 41st Cong 3rd Sess, Senate Ex. Doc. No. 10, Pt. 3.

18. W.H. Sprague to Dix, Feb 10, 1865 (quoted material), Statements of Prescott, Dec 6 and 19, 1864 1864, and Byron Sprague, Dec 8–9, 1864, and Hoyt, Dec 7, 1864, and Frieze. Jan 26, 1865, 41st Cong 3rd Sess, Senate Ex. Doc. No. 10, Pt. 3; J. Holt JAG Report, Jun 15, 1865, 41st Cong 3rd Sess, Senate Ex. Doc. No. 10, Pt. 1; Lamphier, *Kate Chase and William Sprague*, 160; Ancestry.com. Byron Sprague: 1824–1866; Providence *Evening Press*, Jul 31, 1866.

19. Statements of Prescott, Dec 6, 19, 1864, 41st Cong 3rd Sess, Senate Ex. Doc. No. 10, Pt. 3; Edwin Winchester Stone, *Rhode Island in the Rebellion*. (Providence: George H. Whitney, 1864), xxv–xxvii, 48, 305, 373, 374; Lamphier, *Kate Chase and William Sprague*, 46; Thomas Graham Belden and Marva Robins Belden, *So Fell the Angels* (Boston: Little, Brown, & Co., 1956), 58.

20. Leigh, *Trading with the Enemy*, 32–34. NARA, U.S. Passport Applications, Mar 10, 1863, William H. Reynolds (ancestry.com); Belden and Belden, *So Fell the Angels*, 58; Frederick J. Blue, *Salmon P. Chase: a Life in Politics* (Kent, OH: Kent State University Press, 1987), 184–186.

21. J. Holt, JAG Report, Jun 15, 1865, 41st Cong 3rd Sess, Senate Ex. Doc. No. 10, Pt. 1; Statements of Prescott, Dec 6, 1864, Dec 10, 19, 1864, and Frieze. January 26, 1865, and Byron Sprague, Dec 8, 9, 1864, and Hoyt, Dec 7, 1864, 41st Cong 3rd Sess, Senate Ex. Doc. No. 10, Pt. 3. Note: Taft & Co. included Orray Taft. Cyrus Taft, Edward P. Taft, and Jabez C. Knight; B.B. & R. Knight included Benjamin Brayton and Robert Knight; Reynolds & Co. included Reynolds, William H. Taylor, and Francis W. Reynolds: William's brother, Amasa, was the third partner in the company. Byron left the company on Nov 7, 1862.

22. Statements of Prescott, Dec 6, 1864, Dec 19, 1864, and Reynolds, Dec 10, 1864, 41st Cong 3rd Sess, Senate Ex. Doc. No. 10, Pt. 3.

23. Statement of Prescott, Dec 19, 1864, 41st Cong 3rd Sess, Senate Ex. Doc. No. 10, Pt. 3; Ivan Musicant, *Divided Waters: The Naval History of the Civil War* (Edison, NJ: Castle Books, 2000), 54; Owsley, *King Cotton Diplomacy*, 252–253; Wise, *Lifeline of the Confederacy*, 12–13, 19–24; Watson, *Adventures of a Blockade Runner*, 113.

24. Statements of Byron Sprague, Dec 9, 1864, and Reynolds, Dec 10, 1864, and Prescott, Dec 19, 1864, 41st Cong 3rd Sess, Senate Ex. Doc. No. 10, Pt. 3.

25. Statement of Byron Sprague, Dec 9, 1864, and Reynolds, Dec 10, 1864 (quoted material), and Hoyt, Dec 12, 1864, 41st Cong 3rd Sess, Senate Ex. Doc. No. 10, Pt. 3; ancestry.com.

26. *Ibid.*

27. Statement of Reynolds, Dec 10, 1864, 41st Cong 3rd Sess, Senate Ex. Doc. No. 10, Pt. 3.

28. Gideon Welles, *Diary of Gideon Welles: Secretary of the Navy Under Lincoln and Johnson*, Vol. I. Edgar T. Welles (ed.) (Boston: Houghton Mifflin Co., 1911), 166; Statement of Reynolds, Dec 10, 1864, 41st Cong 3rd Sess, Senate Ex. Doc. No. 10, Pt. 3.

29. Statements of Hoyt, Dec 7, 1864 (1st quote) and Dec 12, 1864 (2nd quote), and Prescott, Dec 6, 1864, 41st Cong 3rd Sess, Senate Ex. Doc. No. 10, Pt. 3; Lamphier, *Kate Chase and William Sprague*, 45.

30. Welles, *Diary of Gideon Welles*, 166; Belden and Belden, *So Fell the Angels*, 59; Sandburg, *Abraham Lincoln*, 191, 630; James M. McPherson, *War on the Waters: The Union & Confederate Navies, 1861–1865* (Chapel Hill: University of North Carolina Press, 2012), 14.

31. Statement of Hoyt, Dec 7, 1864, 41st Cong 3rd Sess, Senate Ex. Doc. No. 10, Pt. 3; W.H. Sprague to Gideon Welles, Oct 14, 1862, 41st Cong, 3d Session, Senate Ex. Doc. No. 10, Pt. 4.

32. Statement of Hoyt, Dec 7, 1864, 41st Cong 3rd Sess, Senate Ex. Doc. No. 10, Pt. 3.

33. Statement of Prescott, Dec 6, 1864, 41st Cong 3rd Sess, Senate Ex. Doc. No.

10, Pt. 3; Lamphier, *Kate Chase and William Sprague* 45, 48; Welles, *Diary of Gideon Welles*, 306 (quoted material dated May 19, 1863); Oller, *American Queen: The Rise and Fall of Kate Chase*, 146.

34. Statements of Reynolds, Dec 10, 1864, and Byron Sprague, Dec 9, 1864, and Hoyt, Dec 7, 1864, 41st Cong 3rd Sess, Senate Ex. Doc. No. 10, Pt. 3.

35. Statement of Prescott, Dec 19, 1864, 41st Cong 3rd Sess, Senate Ex. Doc. No. 10, Pt. 3; Abstract log of the C.S.S. *Bayou City*, *ORN* I: 18, 829.

36. Ibid.

37. Statement of Hoyt, Dec 12, 1864, 41st Cong 3rd Sess, Senate Ex. Doc. No. 10, Pt. 3. Note: Most Anglo-Americans spelled the Mexican city of Matamoros as "Matamoras" during the Civil War era.

38. Statements of Byron Sprague, Dec 9, 1864, and Reynolds, Dec 10, 1864, and Prescott, Dec 19, 1864, 41st Cong 3rd Sess, Senate Ex. Doc. No. 10, Pt. 3.

Chapter 4

1. Statements of Prescott, Dec 6, 19, 1864, and Reynolds, Dec 10, 1864, 41st Cong 3rd Sess, Senate Ex. Doc. No. 10, Pt. 3; Wise. *Lifeline of the Confederacy*, 251, 255, 276, 297.

2. Draper to Prescott, Oct 15, 1862, Statements of Prescott, Dec 6, 19, 1864, and Reynolds, Dec 10, 1864, 41st Cong 3rd Sess, Senate Ex. Doc. No. 10, Pt. 3.

3. Statements of Prescott, Dec 6, 1864, and Hoyt, Dec 7, 1864, 41st Cong 3rd Sess, Senate Ex. Doc. No. 10, Pt. 3. Note: Traditional bagging for cotton bales made from Kentucky hemp was being replaced by locally grown hemp as the Civil War progressed.

4. Frank P. Bennett, *History of American Textiles: with Kindred and Auxiliary Industries* (Boston: American Wool and Cotton Reporter, 1922), 38.

5. Statement of Reynolds, Dec 10, 1864, 41st Cong 3rd Sess, Senate Ex. Doc. No. 10, Pt. 3.

6. Ibid.; Hoyt to Stanton, Sep 15, 1862, NARA RG 94, M619 Letters Received by the Adjutant General's Office, R0107, Harris Hoyt; Statement of Byron Sprague, Dec 9, 1864, 41st Cong 3rd Sess, Senate Ex. Doc. No. 10, Pt. 3.

7. Hoyt to Stanton, Sep 15, 1862, NARA RG 94, M619 Letters Received by the Adjutant General's Office, R0107, Harris Hoyt; Statements of John W. Boynton, Dec 18, 1864, and Prescott, Dec 6, 19, 1864, 41st Cong 3rd Sess, Senate Ex. Doc. No. 10, Pt. 3.

8. Statements of Hoyt, Dec 7, 1864 Reynolds, Dec 10, 1864, 41st Cong 3rd Sess, Senate Ex. Doc. No. 10, Pt. 3.

9. Statement of Prescott, Dec 19, 1864, 41st Cong 3rd Sess, Senate Ex. Doc. No. 10, Pt. 3; Francis Richard Lubbock, *Six Decades in Texas or Memoirs of Francis Richard Lubbock, Governor of Texas in War-Time, 1861–1863*. C.W. Raines (ed.) (Austin: Ben C. Jones & Co., 1900), 38, 371.

10. Statement of Prescott, Dec 19, 1864, 41st Cong 3rd Sess, Senate Ex. Doc. No. 10, Pt. 3.

11. *Providence Evening Press*, Oct 28, 1862; *Boston Daily Advertiser*, Nov 6, 1862; ShipIndex.com. Note: The *Citizen* was registered at 95 tons.

12. W.H. Sprague to MG Butler Commanding Dept. New Orleans, Oct 30, 1862 (1st quote) and W.H. Sprague to Officer Commanding Gulf Squadron [RADM Farragut], Oct 30, 1862 (2nd quote), 41st Cong, 3d Sess, Senate Ex. Doc. No. 10, Pt. 4; Lamphier, *Kate Chase and William Sprague*, 47.

13. W.H. Sprague to MG Butler Commanding Dept. New Orleans, Oct 30, 1862 (1st quote), Oct 30, 1862 (2nd quote), 41st Cong, 3d Sess, Senate Ex. Doc. No. 10, Pt. 4; Leigh, *Trading with the Enemy*, 70; New York *World*, May 27, 1864; New York *Tribune*, June 1, 1864.

14. MG Butler to Officers of the Blockading Squadron, Sep 24, 1862, *ORA* I: 15, 584.

15. Parole of Honor, J.H. Ashby, et al., Oct 12, 1862, NARA RG:109, Conf Vessel Papers, R-32, Seq.: W-59, *West Florida*: Silverstone, *Civil War Navies*, 82, 109; Philadelphia *Inquirer*, Nov 19, 1862; Houston *Tri-Weekly News*, Jan 26, 1863; WPA, *Ship Registers*, Vol. V, No. 1309, Vol. VI, No. 1444.

16. Crocker to Farragut, Oct 12, 1862, *ORN* I: 19, 226; Cate to McKean, May 26, 1862, *ORN* I: 17, 253; U.S. vs Schooner *Andromeda*, Jun 13, 1862, and Jul 21, 1862, NARA RG:21, M1360 Admiralty final

record books, 1829–1911, Roll 7, Vol. 6; *NYT,* Jun 4, 1862.

17. Farragut to Butler, *ORN* I: 19, 231, Oct 28, 1862; MG Butler permit, May 21, 1862, *ORN* I: 19, 78; Davis statement to Emmons, July 17, 1862, *ORN* I: 19, 79 (quoted material); Emmons to Welles, Sep 1862, *ORN* I: 19, 76–77; Johnson to Broadwell, Mar 24, 1863, *ORA* I: 24 pt. 1, 291, May to Anderson, Mar 17, 1864, *ORA* I: 34 pt. 2, 1051; Linda Sue Newland, "The Persistence of Antebellum Planter Families in Postbellum East Texas" (Thesis, University of North Texas, Denton, 1998), 46.

18. Butler to Chase, Oct 22, 1862, *ORA* I: 15, 582–583.

19. *Ibid.*

20. Chester G. Hearn, *When the Devil Came Down to Dixie: Ben Butler in New Orleans* (Baton Rouge: LSU Press, 2000), 182–185.

21. Butler to Chase, Oct 22, 1862, *ORA* I: 15, 582–583; Order of Secretary of War Stanton to Butler, *ORN* I: 19, 231, Nov 11, 1862.

22. Prescott and Hoyt Agreement, Nov 4, 1862, and Statements of Prescott, Dec 6, 1864, and Hoyt, Dec 7, 1864, 41st Cong 3rd Sess, Senate Ex. Doc. No. 10, Pt. 3. Note: $100,000 in 1862 is equivalent to over $2.6 million in 2019 (www.wolframalpha.com).

23. *NYT,* Nov 8, 1862; J. Holt JAG Report, Jun 15, 1865. 41st Cong 3rd Sess, Senate Ex. Doc. No. 10, Pt. 1; Statements of Prescott, Dec 6, 19, 1864, and Byron Sprague, Dec 8, 9, 1864, and Hoyt, Dec 7, 1864, and Frieze. January 26, 1865, 41st Cong 3rd Sess, Senate Ex. Doc. No. 10, Pt. 3.

24. Ulrici y Barroso to JSR, Jan 17, 1863, BCAH, JSR Papers Box 2G63; *NYT,* Nov 8, 1862; Statements of Hoyt, Dec 7, 1864, and Prescott, Dec 19, 1864, 41st Cong 3rd Sess, Senate Ex. Doc. No. 10, Pt. 3; New York *Tribune,* May 2, 1897.

25. Statement of Hoyt, Dec 7, 1864, 41st Cong 3rd Sess, Senate Ex. Doc. No. 10, Pt. 3.

26. *NY Commercial Advertiser,* Feb 2, 1861, and Aug 28, 1861, and Sep 10, 1861, and Dec 12, 1861; *NY Herald,* Feb 3, 1861; *NY Tribune,* Feb 28, 1861; *NY Evening Post & NY Herald,* Mar 1, 1861; *Boston Post,* Aug 19, 1861; *NY World,* Sep 26, 1861; Donahue to Stillman, Aug 26, 1861, and Nov 9, 1861; Stillman business papers, MS Am 800.27 Houghton; Romero to Seward, Sep 2, 1861, British Parliamentary Paper, Foreign Office. "North America, No. 8. Papers Relating to the Blockade of the Ports of the Confederate States." (London: Harrison & Sons, 1862), 93–94; Daddysman, *The Matamoros Trade,* 156; Rodman L. Underwood, *Waters of Discord the Union Blockade of Texas During the Civil War* (Jefferson, NC: McFarland, 2003), 73. Notes: Accounts claiming that only about one vessel per year cleared from New York to Matamoros are misleading. Brazos Santiago was the principal port for both Brownsville and Matamoros prior to the declaration of the blockade in 1861.

27. Statement of Prescott, Dec 19, 1864 (quoted material), 41st Cong 3rd Sess, Senate Ex. Doc. No. 10, Pt. 3; Dix to Kennedy, NY Police, Jun 12, 1865, 41st Cong 3rd Sess, Senate Ex. Doc. No. 10, Pt. 2.

28. Invoice of *Snow Drift's* goods, Dec 2, 1862, Statements of Hoyt, Dec 7, 1864, and Prescott, Dec 6, 19, 1864, 41st Cong 3rd Sess, Senate Ex. Doc. No. 10, Pt. 3.

29. Statement of Hoyt, Dec 12, 1864, 41st Cong 3rd Sess, Senate Ex. Doc. No. 10, Pt. 3; Richard Henry Dana, *To Cuba and Back: A Vacation Voyage* (London: Smith, Elder & Co., 1859), 19–20.

30. Dana, *To Cuba and Back,* 21.

31. Statement of Hoyt, Dec 12, 1864, 41st Cong 3rd Sess, Senate Ex. Doc. No. 10, Pt. 3; Houston *Tri-Weekly Telegraph,* Mar 27, 1863.

32. Shufeldt to W.H. Seward, Dec 19, 1862, BCAH, Charles Ramsdell Collection Havana Consular Despatches; Statements of Hoyt, Dec 7, 1864, and Prescott, Dec 19, 1864, 41st Cong 3rd Sess, Senate Ex. Doc. No. 10, Pt. 3.

33. Galveston Special Orders No. 39, Feb 3, 1864, Ashbel Smith Papers, Box 4L262, BCAH; 136 Chase to FW Seward, Feb 17, 23, 1864; Tampico Consular Despatches, Ramsdell, BCAH; J. L. Burkhardt to Anna Burkhardt, May 12, 1864, NARA Fort Worth RG 21, Admiralty Case No. 7899, U.S. vs. SS *Isabel* (quoted material); Eaton to Welles, May 28, 1864, *ORN* I: 21, 306; Cayce to Robinson, May 29, 1864, NARA RG:109, M323 Conf Soldiers TX 13th Vol, R:0369, John H. Robinson.

34. Ulrici y Barroso to JSR, Jan 17, 1863, BCAH, JSR Papers Box 2G63; Shufeldt to W.H. Seward, Dec 19, 1862, BCAH,

Charles Ramsdell Collection Havana Consular Despatches.
35. Shufeldt to Farragut, Dec 1, 1862, *ORN* I: 19, 836–837; Charles Stuart Kennedy, *The American Consul: a History of the United States Consular Service 1776–1924*, 2nd ed. (Washington, D.C.: New Academia Publishing, 2015), 155–157.
36. Shufeldt to W.H. Seward, Dec 19, 1862, BCAH, Charles Ramsdell Collection Havana Consular Despatches; Statement of Prescott, Dec 6, 1864, 41st Cong 3rd Sess, Senate Ex. Doc. No. 10, Pt. 3
37. Shufeldt to W.H. Seward, Dec 19, 1862 (quoted material), BCAH, Charles Ramsdell Collection Havana Consular Despatches; Statements of Prescott, Dec 6, 1864, and Hoyt, Dec 7, 12, 1864, 41st Cong 3rd Sess, Senate Ex. Doc. No. 10, Pt. 3; Peter Andreas, *Smuggler Nation: How Illicit Trade Made America* (New York: Oxford University Press, 2013), 173.
38. Shufeldt to W.H. Seward, Dec 19, 1862, BCAH, Charles Ramsdell Collection Havana Consular Despatches.
39. Statement of Prescott, Dec 19, 1864, 41st Cong 3rd Sess, Senate Ex. Doc. No. 10, Pt. 3.
40. *Ibid.* (quoted material); Statements of Reynolds, Dec 9–10, 1864, and Invoice of goods per steamer *Ella Warley*, for Havana, Dec 12, 1862, and Invoice of *Snow Drift's* goods not on manifest, Jan 10, 1863, 41st Cong 3rd Sess, Senate Ex. Doc. No. 10, Pt. 3.
41. Economic History Association, EH.net; Andreas, *Smuggler Nation*, 173; John J. Rickley Testimony, Apr 19, 1864, "New York Custom-House," 38th Cong., 2nd Sess., House Report no 25 (quoted material).
42. Biographical Note, Hiram Barney Papers, The Huntington Library, San Marino, CA.
43. Sprague to Barney, Aug 15, 1861 (1st and 2nd quotes) and Sprague to Barney, Apr 24, 1862 (3rd quote), Hiram Barney Papers, Box 27, folder 13, Huntington Library, San Marino, CA.
44. *NY Herald*, Dec 9, 1862; *NYT,* Dec 14, 1862; *NY Daily Tribune*, Dec 15, 1862; ancestry.com; Statements of Reynolds, Dec 9–10, 1864, and Prescott, Dec 19, 1864 (quoted material), 41st Cong 3rd Sess, Senate Ex. Doc. No. 10, Pt. 3.
45. Statements of Hoyt, Dec 7, 12, 1864, and Reynolds, Dec 10, 1864, and Prescott, Dec 6, 1864 (quoted material), and Dec 19, 1864, 41st Cong 3rd Sess, Senate Ex. Doc. No. 10, Pt. 3.
46. *NY Daily Graphic*, Feb 13, 1875; Statement of Reynolds, Dec 10, 1864, 41st Cong 3rd Sess, Senate Ex. Doc. No. 10, Pt. 3.
47. Statement of Hoyt, Dec 7, 1864, 41st Cong 3rd Sess, Senate Ex. Doc. No. 10, Pt. 3.
48. *Ibid.*; Statement of Hoyt, Dec 12, 1864, 41st Cong 3rd Sess, Senate Ex. Doc. No. 10, Pt. 3.
49. Shufeldt to W.H. Seward, Dec 19, 1862, BCAH, Charles Ramsdell Collection Havana Consular Despatches; Statements of Hoyt, Dec 7, 1864, and Reynolds, Dec 10, 1864 (quoted material), 41st Cong 3rd Sess, Senate Ex. Doc. No. 10, Pt. 3.
50. Statements of Prescott, Dec 6, 1864, and Reynolds, Dec 10, 1864, 41st Cong 3rd Sess, Senate Ex. Doc. No. 10, Pt. 3.
51. Cammack to [Harris Hoyt?] Jan 1, 1863, 41st Cong 3rd Sess, Senate Ex. Doc. No. 10, Pt. 3; *NYT,* Feb 6, 1901; Helm to Benjamin Mar 6, 1863, *ORN* II: 3, 705.
52. *N.O. Times-Picayune*, Apr 25, 1861; *NY World*, May 26, 1862; Incorporation Articles, Jan 20, 1862, RG:109, M346 Conf Citizens Business File, Conf Bank of Louisiana; Carlin, *Captain James Carlin*, 123.
53. *NYT,* Dec 23, 1862; Paul A. Tenkottr and James C. Claypool (eds.), *The Encyclopedia of Northern Kentucky* (Lexington: University Press of Kentucky, 2009), 441; Kennedy, *The American Consul*, 153–155.
54. *NYT,* Dec 23, 1862; Houston *Tri-Weekly Telegraph*, Mar 27, 1863 (quoted material); Samuel Bernard Thompson, *Confederate Purchasing Operations Abroad* (Chapel Hill: University of North Carolina Press, 1935), 8–9; Bell to Farragut, Feb 27, 1863, *ORN* I: 19, 636.
55. Shufeldt to Farragut, Dec 1, 1862, *ORN* I: 19, 836–837.
56. *Ibid.*
57. *NYT,* Sep 6, 1862; Gloag, et al., *The Scottish Jurist*, 309–315; Rankine *The Scots Revised Reports*, 603–615; London *Evening Star*, Nov 11, 1862; Benjamin to Slidell, Mar 26, 1863, *ORN* I: 19, 282–284.
58. Benjamin to Slidell, Mar 26, 1863, *ORN* I: 19, 282–284; Macaulay to Hébert, Sep 15, 1862, NARA RG:109, M346 Conf

Citizens File, J. L. Macanlay [Sic]; Wise, *Lifeline of the Confederacy*, 84.

59. T.S. Moïse Service Record, NARA, RG:109 M331 Conf Officer and Enlisted Records, T.S. Moïse; Harold Moïse, *The Moïse Family of South Carolina* (Columbia: R.L. Bryan Co., 1961), 26–30; Donald G. Shomette, *Shipwrecks, Sea Raiders, and Maritime Disasters Along the Delmarva Coast 1632–2004* (Baltimore: John Hopkins University Press, 2007), 158. Note: Shomette erroneously states that Maj Moïse was court martialed before the *General Rusk/Blanche* sailed to Cuba and acquired its British registry. Moïse signed the charter party in May, but was not court martialed until December 1862.

60. Gloag, et al., *The Scottish Jurist*, 309–315; Rankine *Scots Revised Reports*, 603–615; W.P. Ballinger to Tom Ballinger, Jul 20, 1862, Ballinger Papers Box 2A 186, BCAH; Handbook of Texas Online, Thomas W. Cutrer, "Hebert, Paul Octave," accessed June 25, 2019, http://www.tshaonline.org/handbook/online/articles/fhe09.

61. *Civil War Naval Chronology 1861–1865*, II-100–101; Kenneth W. Howell (ed.), *The Seventh Star of the Confederacy* (Denton: University of North Texas Press, 2009), 119, 133, 235; Handbook of Texas Online, Thomas W. Cutrer, "Magruder, John Bankhead," accessed June 29, 2019, http://www.tshaonline.org/handbook/online/articles/fma15.

62. Kerby, *Kirby Smith's Confederacy*, 169–170; Carl H. Moneyhon, *Edmund J. Davis of Texas* (Fort Worth: TCU Press, 2010), 43; Handbook of Texas Online, Cutrer, "Hebert, Paul Octave."

63. Benjamin to Slidell, Mar 26, 1863, *ORN* I: 19, 282–284; Helm to Benjamin, Jun 3, 1863, *Confederate States of America. Confederate States of America Records: Reel 34* to 1889, 1854, Manuscript/Mixed Material, www.loc.gov/item/mss16550034/.

64. Cammack to [Harris Hoyt?] Jan 1, 1863, 41st Cong 3rd Sess, Senate Ex. Doc. No. 10, Pt. 3. Wise, *Lifeline of the Confederacy*, 114–115, 232, 270, 327; Carlin, *Captain James Carlin*, 123–125.

65. Smith to Ball, Hutchings & Co., May 15, 1864, NARA Fort Worth, RG 21, Admiralty Case No. 7899, U.S. vs. SS *Isabel*; Wise, *Lifeline of the Confederacy*, 272, 274, 312; Herndon to Bates, Mar 21, 1864, NARA M323, RG:109, R: 0365, Conf Soldiers TX 13th Vol., W.S. Herndon; Magruder to Hewes, Jul 23, 1864, NARA RG:109, Conf Vessel Papers, Seq.: A-24 1/8, *Alice/Matagorda*; Hawes to Lindsey, Jul 24, 1864, Ashbel Smith Papers, Box 4L261, BCAH. Note: Stephen Wise's normally reliable *Lifeline of the Confederacy* credits the *Alice/Matagorda* with 14 runs at Mobile (7 in and 7 out) and 14 Texas runs (6 in and 8 out); the more accurate total is ten Mobile runs (5 in and 5 out) and eight Texas runs (seven successful, 4 in and 3 out).

66. Hoyt to Prescott, Jan 12, 1863, and statement of Hoyt, Dec 7, 1864, 41st Cong 3rd Sess, Senate Ex. Doc. No. 10, Pt. 3.

67. *NYT*, Jan 1, 1863; Statements of Prescott, Dec 6, 19, 1864, 41st Cong 3rd Sess, Senate Ex. Doc. No. 10, Pt. 3.

68. Brastow to Prescott, Dec 17, 1862, 41st Cong 3rd Sess, Senate Ex. Doc. No. 10, Pt. 3.

69. Statements of Prescott, Dec 6, 19, 1864, 41st Cong 3rd Sess, Senate Ex. Doc. No. 10, Pt. 3 (quoted material); Ezra Lincoln to Banks, Nov. 18, 1862, and Banks to Chase, Nov. 27, 1862, N.P. Banks papers, LOC, box 25.

70. Brastow to Prescott, Dec 17, 1862, Hoyt to Prescott, Jan 2, Jan 12, 1863, 41st Cong 3rd Sess, Senate Ex. Doc. No. 10, Pt. 3.

71. Statement of Prescott, Dec 19, 1864 (quoted material), 41st Cong 3rd Sess, Senate Ex. Doc. No. 10, Pt. 3.

72. Brastow to Prescott, Dec 17, 1862, Hoyt to Prescott, Jan 2, 12, 1863, and statements of Hoyt, Dec 7, 1864 (quoted material), and Dec 12, 1864, and Reynolds, Dec 10, 19, 1864, 41st Cong 3rd Sess, Senate Ex. Doc. No. 10, Pt. 3; Belden and Belden, *So Fell the Angels*, 62. Note: In a generally accurate and insightful account Belden and Belden omit Hoyt's refusal to sail for New Orleans and erroneously have the *Snow Drift* departing Havana in Dec 1862.

73. Statements of Prescott, Dec 6, 19, 1864, and Reynolds, Dec 10, 1864, and Hoyt, Dec 12, 1864, and Frieze. January 26, 1865, 41st Cong 3rd Sess, Senate Ex. Doc. No. 10, Pt. 3; Leigh, *Trading with the Enemy*, 55; *NYT*, Jan 1, 1863.

74. Statements of Prescott, Dec 6, 19,

1864, 41st Cong 3rd Sess, Senate Ex. Doc. No. 10, Pt. 3.

75. Statements of Reynolds, Dec 10, 1864 (quoted material), and Prescott, Dec 19, 1864, 41st Cong 3rd Sess, Senate Ex. Doc. No. 10, Pt. 3; *Boston Post*, Dec 25, 1862; *NYT*, Dec 30, 1862.

76. Statements of Prescott, Dec 6, 1864, and Reynolds, Dec 10, 1864 (quoted material), 41st Cong 3rd Sess, Senate Ex. Doc. No. 10, Pt. 3; ShipIndex.com, schooner *Citizen*.

77. Statements of Prescott, Dec 6, 19, 1864, and Reynolds, Dec 10, 1864, 41st Cong 3rd Sess, Senate Ex. Doc. No. 10, Pt. 3; Leigh, *Trading with the Enemy*, 55.

78. Reynolds to Brastow, Feb 7, 1863 (quoted material), 41st Cong 3rd Sess, Senate Ex. Doc. No. 10, Pt. 3.

79. Statement of Prescott, Dec 6, 1864, 41st Cong 3rd Sess, Senate Ex. Doc. No. 10, Pt. 3; Stephen A. Dupree, *Planting the Union Flag in Texas: The Campaigns of Major General Nathaniel P. Banks in the West* (College Station: Texas A&M University Press, 2008), 20–21; *NY Herald*, Feb 11, 1863; Leigh, *Trading with the Enemy*, 53. Note: Leigh erroneously identifies the vessel that collided with the *Ella Warley* as the *Star of the West* and lists Charles Prescott as a ship captain rather than nominal owner/supercargo.

Chapter 5

1. *NY Herald*, Feb 2, 1863, Statement of Hoyt, Dec 12, 1864, 41st Cong 3rd Sess, Senate Ex. Doc. No. 10, Pt. 3; Pierre Fourier Parisot. *The Reminiscences of a Texas Missionary* (San Antonio: St. Mary's Church, 1899), 56. Note: The number of vessels at anchor (41 on Jan 25, 1863) is the author's compilation based on numerous contemporary newspaper, customs, and archival sources.

2. Invoice of *Snow Drift*'s goods, Dec 2, 1862, and statement of Hoyt, Jan 4, 1865, 41st Cong 3rd Sess, Senate Ex. Doc. No. 10, Pt. 3.

3. Corpus Christi *Ranchero*, Mar 26, 1863 (quoted material); Bee to Lopez, Mar 22, 1863, *ORA* I: 15, 1034.

4. Luckett to Gray, Mar 24, 1863, *ORA* II: 5, 856; Hale to Stillman, Jul 30, 1861, Charles Stillman business papers, MS Am 800.27, Houghton; Houston *Tri-Weekly Telegraph*, Nov 02, 1864. Note: Jockusch opened his own trading office at Rio Grande City in November 1864.

5. Smith to Morell [for Stillman], Mar 10, 1864, Charles Stillman business papers, MS Am 800.27, Houghton; Houston *Tri-Weekly Telegraph*, Nov 02, 1864; Statement of facts, Jockusch v. Zacharia, May 27, 1864, Ballinger Papers, 2A 188b; *Houston Daily Post*, Feb 27, 1898.

6. Statements Hoyt, Dec 12, 1864, and Jan 4, 1865, 41st Cong 3rd Sess, Senate Ex. Doc. No. 10, Pt. 3; Mifflin Kenedy & Co., Ledger and Journals (Oct 15, 1857 to December 31, 1866) (1859–1864), and (January 1st, 1861– March 31st, 1864), King Ranch Archives, Kingsville, TX; Brownsville *Daily Ranchero*, Jun 23, 1865. Note: The *Alamo* arrived at the Rio Grande in late Oct 1863.

7. Pierre Fourier Parisot. *The Reminiscences of a Texas Missionary* (San Antonio: St. Mary's Church, 1899), 55 (1st quote); Watson, *Adventures of a Blockade Runner*, 26 (2nd quote); *NY Herald*, Jan 9, 1865; Semmes, *Memoirs of Service Afloat*, 791–792; Sir Arthur James Lyon Fremantle, Walter Lord (ed.), *The Fremantle Diary, Being the Journal of Lt. Col. Fremantle Coldstream Guard on His Three Months in the Southern States* (Boston: Little, Brown, & Co., 1954), 6; JSR to Martenand, Jan 5, 1863, JSR Letters Box 2G120, BCAH (3rd quote).

8. *NY Herald*, Jan 9, 1865; Fremantle, *The Fremantle Diary*, 6; Semmes, *Memoirs of Service Afloat*, 792 (quoted material).

9. Pierre Fourier Parisot. *The Reminiscences of a Texas Missionary* (San Antonio: St. Mary's Church, 1899), 55–56 (1st quote); Semmes, *Memoirs of Service Afloat*, 792 (2nd quote); Wood to Seward, Feb 21, 1865, Ramsdell, Matamoros Consular Despatches, BCH; Watson, *Adventures of a Blockade Runner*, 22 (3rd quote), 26 (4th quote).

10. Statement of Hoyt, Dec 12, 1864 (1st quote), 41st Cong 3rd Sess, Senate Ex. Doc. No. 10, Pt. 3; *NYT* and *NY World*, Jun 16, 1863, U.S. Census, 1860, Morris, Grundy, IL, and 1850 Ava, Oneida, NY, ancestry.com; Family History Library Film: 803181; Morris IL, Jun 1863, NARA, RG:110, Civil War Union Draft Records, Harris Hoyt; M.M. McAllen, "Life Lived

along the Lower Rio Grande Valley during the Civil War," in the *Civil War on the Rio Grande, 1846–1876*, No. 46, ed. Roseann Bacha-Garza, Christopher L. Miller, and Russell K. Skowronek, 59–81 (College Station: Texas A&M University Press, 2019), 67; Fort and Fort, "*Los Algodones*," 165–166. Note: Horace Hoyt's eldest son, who was also named Harris, remained in Illinois, despite the risk of being drafted into the Union Army.

11. Clapp to Allen, Apr 26, 1865 (quoted material), NARA, RG:365, Records of the Cotton Bureau (archive.org), 539–543; Daddysman, *The Matamoros Trade*, 160; "Statistics of Iron and Cotton 1830–1860." *The Quarterly Journal of Economics* 2, No. 3 (1888): 383.

12. Irby, *Backdoor at Bagdad*, 9; Ulrici y Barroso to JSR, Jan 17, 1863, BCAH, JSR Papers Box 2G63; Ryder to JSR, Apr 19, 1864, Monterey, BCAH, JSR Papers Box 2G72; Statements of Hoyt Dec 7, 12, 1864, 41st Cong 3rd Sess, Senate Ex. Doc. No. 10, Pt. 3.

13. Watson, *Adventures of a Blockade Runner*, 27; Laverty to JSR, Jul 13, 1863, JSR Papers, 2G 65d, BCAH. John Maloney was introduced in the Preface.

14. Wood to Seward, Feb 21, 1865, Ramsdell, Matamoros Consular Despatches, BCAH (quoted material); Fremantle, *The Fremantle Diary*, 14.

15. Stillman to King, Mar 11, 1862, King Ranch Archives, Kingsville, TX; Wilson, "*Captain King's Cotton*," 94; Edward Hertslet (comp.), *The Foreign Officer List and Diplomatic and Consular Hand Book* (London: Harrison, 1877), 60; Ford, *Rip Ford's Texas*, 329; Fremantle, *The Fremantle Diary*, 11 (quoted material); Brownsville *Ranchero*, Mar 26, 1868; Yturria, *The Patriarch*, 15; Lea, *The King Ranch*, 185–186. Note: Tom Lea's transcription of the March letter erroneously lists "Judge Trevino" rather than "Judge Devine" as a participant in this meeting. Thomas Devine (1820–1890) was the Confederate judge for the Western District of Texas (1861–1864). Other authors have interpreted "Judge Trevino" to be one of the Trevino Brothers and have also included Francisco Yturria and Richard King in this meeting without citing primary source documentation. Charles Stillman described the meeting in a letter to Richard King who was at Santa Gertrudis, making it unlikely that King was a participant.

16. Stillman to King, Mar 11, 1862, King Ranch Archives, Kingsville, TX; Wilson, "*Captain King's Cotton*," 94.

17. Statement of Hoyt, Dec 12, 1864, 41st Cong 3rd Sess, Senate Ex. Doc. No. 10, Pt. 3.

18. Statement of Hoyt, Dec 7, 1864 (quoted material), 41st Cong 3rd Sess, Senate Ex. Doc. No. 10, Pt. 3; Hoyt to Hart, Jul 24, 1863, NARA M346, RG:109, R:0473, Conf Citizens File, Harris Hoyt: Luckett to Gray, Mar 24, 1863, *ORA* II: 5, 856; Handbook of Texas Online, Thomas W. Cutrer, "Luckett, Philip Noland," accessed June 29, 2019, http://www.tshaonline.org/handbook/online/articles/flu05.

19. Statement of Hoyt, Dec 7, 1864, 41st Cong 3rd Sess, Senate Ex. Doc. No. 10, Pt. 3; Hoyt to Hart, Jul 24, 1863, NARA M346, RG:109, R:0473, Conf Citizens File, Harris Hoyt: Luckett to Gray, Mar 24, 1863, *ORA* II: 5, 856; www.rockislandauctions.com; Corpus Christi, *Ranchero*, Feb 23, 1861.

20. Handbook of Texas Online, Cutrer, "Luckett, Philip Noland"; Ian V. Hogg, *Weapons of the Civil War* (New York: Military Press, 1987), 18–22.

21. Statements of Prescott, Dec 6, 19, 1864, and Hoyt Dec 12, 1864 and Jan 4, 1865, 41st Cong 3rd Sess, Senate Ex. Doc. No. 10, Pt. 3.

22. Ulrici and Barroso to Reynolds & Co., Jan 24, 1863, 41st Cong 3rd Sess, Senate Ex. Doc. No. 10, Pt. 3.

23. Statement of Reynolds, Dec 9, 1864 (quoted material), and Reynolds & Co. books entry, Apr 11, 1863, 41st Cong 3rd Sess, Senate Ex. Doc. No. 10, Pt. 3. Note: Wm. H. Reynolds witnessed Henry B. Brastow's passport application that showed him as 35 years-of-age, 5'11" brown hair, hazel eyes, aquiline nose (ancestry.com).

24. Statements of Reynolds, Dec 10, 1864, and Frieze, Jan 26, 1865, 41st Cong 3rd Sess, Senate Ex. Doc. No. 10, Pt. 3; *Gore's Liverpool General Advertiser*, Sep 24, 1863, Sep 15, 1864, and Apr 6, 1865.

25. *Galveston Weekly News*, Sep 30, 1863; Houston *Tri-Weekly Telegraph*, Jan 12, 1864; Manifest, May 28, 1864, and Health Clearance, Aug 27, 1864, New Orleans Admiralty Case #7961 NARA Fort Worth, U.S. vs Schooner *Cora*.

26. Davis and Arnold, *Colin J. McRae*

(Galveston Quarterly Customs Report), 173 *Galveston Daily News*, Nov 26, 1894; John Greenough Deposition, Jan 2, 1865, NARA, RG109 Record Books of the Confederate Govt. Chief Signal Reports for Houston Observatory, 1863–1864, 277; Galveston *Daily News*, Nov 23, 26, 1864; New Orleans Admiralty Case #7961 NARA Fort Worth, U.S. vs Schooner *Cora*; Woolsey to Welles, Dec 20, 1864, *ORN* I: 21, 763–764; ancestry.com, Henry Scherffius.

27. Statement of Hoyt, Dec 12, 1864 (quoted material), 41st Cong 3rd Sess, Senate Ex. Doc. No. 10, Pt. 3.

28. *NYT* and *NY World*, Jun 16, 1863; Statement of Hoyt, Dec 12, 1864 (quoted material), and Prescott, Dec 19, 1864, 41st Cong 3rd Sess, Senate Ex. Doc. No. 10, Pt. 3.

29. Statements of Hoyt, Dec 12, 1864, and Prescott, Dec 19, 1864, 41st Cong 3rd Sess, Senate Ex. Doc. No. 10, Pt. 3. Note: Prescott confused the dates of the shipment and the arrival of Hoyt's brother who accompanied the 20 bales to New York in May of 1863. Hoyt's father-in-law arrived at Matamoros on the *Lehman* in Nov 1864.

30. Statements of Reynolds, Dec 9, 10, 1864, and Prescott, Dec 19, 1864, and Frieze. January 26, 1865, 41st Cong 3rd Sess, Senate Ex. Doc. No. 10, Pt. 3.

31. *Passenger Lists of Vessels Arriving at New York, New York, 1820–1897*. Microfilm Publication M237, 675 rolls. NAI: 6256867. Records of the U.S. Customs Service, Record Group 36. National Archives at Washington, D.C.; Allen Nevins, *The War for the Union Vol. III, The Organized War 1863–1864* (New York: Charles Scribner's Sons, 1971), 121.

32. Wilson, *Bulloch Belles* 114–115.

33. Nevins, *The War for the Union*, Vol. III, 121–123; McPherson, *Battle Cry of Freedom*, 610–611.

34. Brastow to Reynolds, Jun 18, 1863 (1st quote) and Jul 5, 1863 (2nd quote), 41st Cong 3rd Sess, Senate Ex. Doc. No. 10, Pt. 3.

35. Brastow to Reynolds, Jul 5, 1863 (quoted material), 41st Cong 3rd Sess, Senate Ex. Doc. No. 10, Pt. 3.

36. Statement of Reynolds, Dec 10, 1864, 41st Cong 3rd Sess, Senate Ex. Doc. No. 10, Pt. 3; *NY Shipping & Commercial List*, Oct 21, 1863; *NY World* and *NYT*, Oct 20, 1863; Smith to Morell, Oct 19, 1863, and Account Current José Morell with J. & N. Smith & Co., Statements and Accounts, Dec 16, 1863, Charles Stillman business papers, Houghton. Note: Prescott said that Brastow loaded the cotton on the *Emma* and then departed in September. The *Emma Dean* best fits this description since the brig *Emma* did not arrive until after Brastow had already departed from Matamoros.

37. Ellis, "Maritime Commerce on the Far Western Gulf, 1861-1865," and Sibley, "Charles Stillman," 227–240; Smith to Morrell, Sep 23, 1863 and to Stillman, Oct 4, 1864 (quoted material), Charles Stillman papers, 1847–1884. MS Am 800.27, Houghton.

38. Statements of Prescott, Dec 6, 19, 1864, and Reynolds, Dec 10, 1864 (quoted material), 41st Cong 3rd Sess, Senate Ex. Doc. No. 10, Pt. 3.

Chapter 6

1. Statements of Prescott, Dec 6 & Dec 19, 1864, & Reynolds, Dec 10, 1864 (quoted material), 41st Cong 3rd Sess, Senate Ex. Doc. No. 10, Pt. 3.

2. *Handbook of Texas Online*, Barbara Stock, "Prairie Lea, TX," accessed Feb 9, 2019, http://www.tshaonline.org/handbook/online/articles/hlp50.

3. Statement of Hoyt, Dec 7, 1864, 41st Cong 3rd Sess, Senate Ex. Doc. No. 10, Pt. 3; Houston *Tri-Weekly Telegraph*, Apr 21, 1863 (quoted material).

4. Houston *Tri-Weekly Telegraph*, Apr 21, 1863.

5. *Ibid*.

6. *Ibid*. (1st quote); Statement of Reynolds, Dec 13, 1864 (2nd quote), 41st Cong 3rd Sess, Senate Ex. Doc. No. 10, Pt. 3.

7. Houston *Tri-Weekly Telegraph*, Apr 21, 1863 (quoted material); Statement of Hoyt, Dec 7, 1864, 41st Cong 3rd Sess, Senate Ex. Doc. No. 10, Pt. 3.

8. Statement of Hoyt, Dec 7, 1864, and Jan 4, 1865, 41st Cong 3rd Sess, Senate Ex. Doc. No. 10, Pt. 3.

9. Houston *Tri-Weekly Telegraph*, May 30, 1862; Daddysman, *The Matamoros Trade*, 112.

10. Magruder to Cooper, Jun 8, 1863, *ORA* I: 26/2, 61–62 (quoted material); Wilson, "Captain King's Cotton," 95–96.

11. Townsend, *The Yankee Invasion of Texas*, 50; Kerby, *Kirby Smith's Confederacy*, 179.
12. Daddysman. *The Matamoros Trade*, 107–110; Tyler, "Cotton on the Border," 461–463; Jerry Thompson and Lawrence T. Jones III, *Civil War and Revolution on the Rio Grande Frontier; a Narrative and Photographic History* (Austin: State Historical Association, 2004), p. 43; Wilson, "Captain King's Cotton," 95–96; Lea, *The King Ranch*, 215; Dana to Kimmey, Dec 18, 1863, *ORA* I: 26 pt. 2, 865 (quoted material).
13. Statement of Hoyt, Jan 4, 1865, 41st Cong 3rd Sess, Senate Ex. Doc. No. 10, Pt. 3; Wilson, "Captain King's Cotton," 95–96.
14. Farragut to Welles, Jun 1, 1863, *ORN* I: 20, 282.
15. Lance E. Davis and Stanley L. Engerman, *Naval Blockades in Peace and War; an Economic History Since 1750* (New York: Cambridge University Press, 2006), 116–121; *Hansard's Parliamentary Debates*, Sep. 3, 162, 166, 2077–2082 (api.parliament.uk).
16. *Ibid.*; Bernath, *Squall Across the Atlantic*, 11–12, 19–20. Note: The accomplished historians Lance Davis, Engerman, and Surdam are among those who erroneously equate blockade running with smuggling.
17. Carlin, *Captain James Carlin*, 28–33.
18. Hoyt to Hart, Jul 24, 1863, NARA, RG:109, M346, Conf Citizens File, R:0473, Harris Hoyt.
19. New Orleans Admiralty Case #7961 NARA Fort Worth, U.S. vs Schooner *Cora*; Woolsey to Welles, Dec 20, 1864.
20. New Orleans *Times-Picayune*, May 20, 1863; Watson, *Adventures of a Blockade Runner*, 3; Watson to Reid, Oct 13, 1863, NARA RG:109, Conf Vessel Papers, R-25, Seq.: R-24.
21. NARA Proofs of Citizenship Seamen's Protection Certificates Port of New Orleans, Louisiana, 1850–1851, Henry Laverty; Watson, *Adventures of a Blockade Runner*, 17; Enrique Laverty Invoice for the C.P. Knapp; Jan 27, 1862, JSR Papers 2G61, BCAH. Note: Henry Laverty's name sometimes appears with a Spanish first name (Enrique) or his surname is misspelled as "Lafferty."

22. New Orleans *Times-Picayune*, Apr 7, 1863, and May 20, 1863.
23. Laverty to JSR, Jul 13, 1863, JSR Papers 2G65, BCAH.
24. Bates to Turner, Oct 11, 1863, NARA Conf Vessel Papers, Reel: 25, Seq.: R-24, *Rob Roy*; Watson, *Adventures of a Blockade Runner*, 35–38, 44–46.
25. Watson, *Adventures of a Blockade Runner*, 39, 41–42, 46; Luckett to Turner Sep 27, 1863, *ORA* I: 26/2, 263.
26. Watson, *Adventures of a Blockade Runner*, 54, 56–57; Keaton to Bates, Oct 21, 1863, NARA RG:109, Conf Vessel Papers, Reel: 25, Seq.: R-24, *Rob Roy*; Yancey to Lynn, Oct 21, 1863, *ORN* I: 20, 844.
27. Watson, *Adventures of a Blockade Runner*, 65, 68–70, 76–78.
28. NARA, 1860 U.S. Census, M653, Galveston Ward 3; A.W. & D. Richardson. Galveston City Directory, 1859–1860, Galveston, Texas. Rosenberg Library (texashistory.unt.edu); Muster Report, Mar 28, 1863, NARA RG:109, M323, Conf Soldiers Texas, R:0437 William R. Evans.
29. Handbook of Texas Online, Steve Hooper, "Sorley, James," accessed July 06, 2019, http://www.tshaonline.org/handbook/online/articles/fsorl; Special Orders, No. 266, Houston *Tri-Weekly Telegraph*, Oct 7, 1863.
30. Hoyt to Hart, Jul 24, 1863, NARA, RG:109, M346, Conf Citizens File, R:0473, Harris Hoyt.
31. *Ibid.*; Luckett to Gray, Mar 24, 1863, *ORA* II: 5, 856.
32. *NY Cronica*, May 21, 1864; *NY World* and *NYT*, Dec 1, 1863; *Gore's Liverpool General Advertiser*, May 5, 1864; Cotton Account, Oct 30, 1863, and Smith to Morell [for Stillman], Dec 26, 1863, and Account Sale, Jan 1, 1864, Charles Stillman business papers, MS Am 800.2, Houghton.
33. Statements and Accounts, Oct 30, 1863, and Smith to Morell [for Stillman], Dec 30, 1863 & Jan 8, 1864, Charles Stillman business papers, MS Am 800.2, Houghton; *NY World* & *NYT*, Dec 1, 15, 1864; *NY Shipping & Commercial List*, Jan 16, 1864.
34. Smith to Morell [for Stillman], Dec 26, 1863, and Mar 2, 1864, Charles Stillman business papers, MS Am 800.2, Houghton.
35. Hoyt to Hart, Jul 24, 1863, NARA,

RG:109, M346, Conf Citizens File, R:0473, Harris Hoyt; Handbook of Texas Online, Carolyn Hyman, "Greer, Elkanah Bracken," accessed June 25, 2019, http://www.tshaonline.org/handbook/online/articles/fgr42.

36. Statements of Prescott, Dec 6, 19, 1864, and Court-martial of Harris Hoyt, Jan 24, 1865, 41st Cong 3rd Sess, Senate Ex. Doc. No. 10, Pt. 3. *NYT,* Jan 2, 1865.

37. Weil to Loeb, Nov 17, 1863, and May 2, 1864, 48th Cong, 1st Sess, Ex. Doc. No. 103, GPO, 1884; Sisnero to Legrand & Co., Jul 21, 1863, BCAH:, JSR Papers, Box 2G 63. Deposition of Roeld Hendrik, Dinkela, Jan 18, 1865, and Prize Appraisers' Report, Jun 8, 1865, NARA Fort Worth, NO Admiralty case 7945 U.S. vs Brig *Geziena Hilligonda*. Note: It is possible that the *America* was the schooner *Central America* which arrived at the Rio Grande from New Orleans in Mid-July of 1863. The *Central America* could have run into Texas and had its name shortened or perhaps the *America* was a different undocumented schooner that formerly had a name similar to *Zara Gosher*.

38. Log of the U.S. bark *W. G. Anderson,* Aug 27, 1863, *ORN* I: 20, 487; Manuscript Map of Caney Creek and San Bernard River, NARA RG:109, M258 Conf Engineers R0104 Oswald Dietz.

39. Log of the U.S. bark *W. G. Anderson,* Aug 27, 1863, *ORN* I: 20, 487; Farragut to Welles, Feb 23, 1863, *ORN* I: 19, 622; *Cambridge Tribune,* Sep 27, 1913; Frederic Stanhope Hill, *Twenty Years at Sea or Leaves from My Old Log-Books* (Boston: Houghton, Mifflin & Co., 1893), 137, 142, 175–181, 191.

40. Log of the U.S. bark *W. G. Anderson,* Aug 27, 1863, *ORN* I: 20, 487; Silverstone, *Civil War Navies,* 106.

41. Log of the U.S. bark *W. G. Anderson,* Aug 27, 1863 & Statement of *William G. Anderson* crew, Aug 27, 1863, and Farragut to Welles, Mar 16, 1864, *ORN* I: 20, 486–487; Statement of Prescott, Dec 19, 1864, 41st Cong 3rd Sess, Senate Ex. Doc. No. 10, Pt. 3. Note: Prescott got the story confused about the *America.* He thought the *America* went aground but claimed that Hoyt was able to sell the cotton.

42. Farragut to Welles, Mar 16, 1864, *ORN* I: 20, 486.

43. Hill to Mullany, *ORN* I: 20, 482; Hill, *Twenty Years at Sea,* 220–221, 224–229 (quoted material), 240.

44. *Ibid.*; United States, *Compilation of Laws and Decisions of the Courts Relating to War Claims* (Washington: GPO, 1908), 215, 247, 272.

45. Master Hartney Statement, Jun 27, 1864, and Judgement, Aug 5, 1864, NARA RG:21, Admiralty Case No. 7891, U.S. vs *Caroline.*

46. Muster Report, Mar 28, 1863, NARA RG:109, M323, Conf Soldiers Texas, R:0437 William R. Evans; Depositions of William Evans and John Curley, Apr 28, 1865, NARA RG:21, Admiralty Case No. 8032, U.S. vs. SS *Cora*; Gripon Power of Attorney to Kenedy, Aug 8, 1863, Mifflin Kenedy Papers, Box 2A,The South Texas Archives and Special Collections, Texas A&M University Kingsville, Kingsville, TX; Lea, *The King Ranch,* 197–200; Wilson, "Captain King's Cotton," 102–103.

47. Moses to JSR, Nov 15, 1863, JSR Papers 2G 66e; M. Kenedy Ledger, Oct 31, 1863, pg. 59, King Ranch Archives; Depositions of William Evans and John Curley, Apr 28, 1865, NARA RG:21, Admiralty Case No. 8032, U.S. vs. SS *Cora*; Spicer to Thatcher, Mar 25, 1865. *ORN* I: 22, 110; Silverstone, *Civil War Navies,* 53; Wilson, "Captain King's Cotton," 102–103.

48. Hill to Welles, Aug 30, 1863, *ORN* I: 20, 488.

49. *Ibid.*; Farragut to Welles, Mar 16, 1864, *ORN* I: 20, 486.

50. *Boston Daily Advertiser,* Oct 23, 1863; *NY Shipping & Commercial List,* Nov 14, 1863; Andrew W. Hall, *Civil War Blockade Running on the Texas Coast.* (Charleston: History Press, 2014), 81–82; Underwood, *Waters of Discord,* 36–37. Note: Some accounts erroneously identify the bark as the *Sol Wilder.*

51. Statement of William G. Anderson crew, Aug 27, 1863, and Farragut to Welles, Mar 16, 1864, *ORN* I: 20, 486–487; Court-martial record of Frederic S. Hill, Jun 7, 1864, *ORN* I: 20, 488–489; Underwood, *Waters of Discord,* 35.

52. Farragut to Welles, Mar 16, 1864, *ORN* I: 20, 486.

53. Court-martial record of Frederic S. Hill, Jun 7, 1864, *ORN* I: 20, 488–489; Hall, *Civil War Blockade Running on the Texas Coast,* 82; Underwood, *Waters of Discord,* 37.

54. Statement of Reynolds, Dec 10, 1864, 41st Cong 3rd Sess, Senate Ex. Doc. No. 10, Pt. 3.

55. Loeb to Carrington, Oct 19, 1863, NARA, RG:109, M346, Conf Citizen Files, R:0596, D.E. Loeb.

56. Statement of Prescott, Dec 6, 19, 1864, 41st Cong 3rd Sess, Senate Ex. Doc. No. 10, Pt. 3; Belden and Belden, *So Fell the Angels*, 100–101; *Texas Handbook Online*, Hooper, "Sorley, James," Special Orders, No. 266, Houston *Tri-Weekly Telegraph*, Oct 7, 1863.

Chapter 7

1. Loeb to Carrington, Oct 19, 1863, NARA, RG:109, M346, Conklin to Gray Nov 1, 1862, *ORN* I: 19, 800–801.

2. Statement of Hoyt, Dec 7, 1864, 41st Cong 3rd Sess, Senate Ex. Doc. No. 10, Pt. 3.

3. *Ibid.*

4. Davis and Arnold, *Colin J. McRae: Confederate Financial Agent* (NARA, Galveston Monthly Customs Report), 172; Loeb to Carrington, Oct 19, 1863, NARA, RG:109, M346, Conf Citizen Files, R:0596, D.E. Loeb.

5. Special Orders, No. 266, Houston *Tri-Weekly Telegraph*, Oct 7, 1863; *Waco News-Tribune*, May 31, 1924; *Handbook of Texas Online*, Julia Beazley, "House, Thomas William," accessed Jun 07, 2019, http://www.tshaonline.org/handbook/online/articles/fho68.

6. Loeb to Carrington, Oct 19, 1863, NARA, RG:109, M346 Conf. Citizen Files, R0596, D.E. Loeb; Marks to Best, Sep 04, 1863, and Shea to McCulloch, Jan 7, 1862, NARA RG:109, Conf. Vessel Papers, Seq. L-33 3/8, R-19, *LeCompte*; Conklin to Gray Nov 1, 1862, *ORN* I: 19, 800–801; WPA, *Ship Registers*, Vol. V, No. 739.

7. Admiralty Case, Jun 29, 1863, NARA RG:109, NARA RG:109, Conf. Vessel Papers, Seq. L-33 3/8, R-19, *LeCompte*; Bradford to Lecour, Dec 11, 1863, NARA RG:109, M346 Confederate Civilian Files, R0089 Samuel Bradford; Smith to Aldrich, Mar 30, 1864, *ORN* I: 888; Log of the *Royal Yacht*, Oct 3, 1862, Rosenberg Library, Galveston; Handbook of Texas Online, Diana J. Kleiner, "Chubb, Thomas B.," accessed July 12, 2019, http://www.tshaonline.org/handbook/online/articles/fch40; *Dallas Morning News*, Aug 27, 1890. Note: As of the access date, the Handbook of Texas article on Chubb has numerous errors and omissions.

8. Statement of Hoyt, Dec 7, 1864, 41st Cong 3rd Sess, Senate Ex. Doc. No. 10, Pt. 3; Leon Smith to Turner, Sep 8, 1863, *ORN* I: 20, 555–557; Silverstone, *Civil War Navies*, 77.

9. Debray to Mills, Aug 11, 1863 and to Turner, Aug 12, 1863, *ORA* I: 261, 242–244; Houston *Tri-Weekly Telegraph*, Sep 7, 1863.

10. Belden and Belden, *So Fell the Angels*, 101.

11. *Ibid.*; Statement of Prescott, Dec 6, 1864 (quoted material), 41st Cong 3rd Sess, Senate Ex. Doc. No. 10, Pt. 3.

12. Loeb to Carrington, Oct 19, 1863, NARA, RG:109, M346, Conf Citizen Files, R:0596, D.E. Loeb.

13. *Ibid.*; Loeb to Weil, Oct. 23, 1863 (quoted material), Mexican Claims, U.S. Congress, House, 48th Congress, 1st Session, Ex. Doc. No. 103, Washington: GPO, 1884.

14. Galveston Special Orders No. 111, Sep 25, 1864, Ashbel Smith Papers, Box 4L262, BCAH; Chubb to Hewes, Jun 1, 1864, NARA RG:109, Conf Vessel Papers, R:25, Seq. R-24, *Rob Roy*; Watson, *Adventures of a Blockade Runner*, 149, 171–173, 198 (quoted material), 199, 203–205, 285.

15. Statement of Hoyt, Dec 7, 1864, 41st Cong 3rd Sess, Senate Ex. Doc. No. 10, Pt. 3.

16. *Ibid.* (quoted material); Statement of Hoyt, Dec 12, 1864, 41st Cong 3rd Sess, Senate Ex. Doc. No. 10, Pt. 3. Note: It is unclear whether Hoyt's son traveled with him to Texas or if he had remained behind when Hoyt ran the blockade in 1862.

17. Turner to Bee Nov 26, 1863, *ORA* I: 26/2, 445–446.

18. Jerry Thompson, *Tejano Tiger: Jose De Los Santos Benavides and the Texas-Mexico Borderlands, 1823–1891* (Fort Worth: TCU Press, 2017), 253–254; Thompson and Jones, *Civil War and Revolution on the Rio Grande Frontier*, 59–60; Galveston *Tri-Weekly News*, Jun 25, 1863 (quoted material).

19. Hugo L. Black III, "Richard Fitzpatrick's South Florida, 1822–1840, Part II" *Tequesta: the Journal of the Historical*

Association of Southern Florida. Vol. 1, No. 41 (1981), 63 (digitalcollections.fiu.edu/tequesta/); Fitzpatrick to Benjamin, Mar 8, 1864, *ORA* I: 34/2, 1030–1032 (quoted material).

20. Lyman Brightman Russell, *Genealogy of the Russell Family* (San Antonio: The Naylor Company, 1959), 7–10; Handbook of Texas Online, Cutrer, "Luckett, Philip Noland."

21. Handbook of Texas Online, Thomas W. Cutrer, "Bee, Hamilton Prioleau," accessed July 09, 2019, http://www.tshaonline.org/handbook/online/articles/fbe24; *Handbook of Texas Online*, Harold J. Weiss, Jr., "Hays, John Coffee," accessed August 25, 2019, http://www.tshaonline.org/handbook/online/articles/fhabq.

22. Statements of Hoyt, Dec 7, 1864, and Reynolds, Dec 10, 1864, and Prescott, Dec 19, 1864, 41st Cong 3rd Sess, Senate Ex. Doc. No. 10, Pt. 3; Tarver to Dickinson, Nov 8, 1863, *ORA* I: 26/1, 436.

23. Karen G. Fort and Tom A. Fort, "*Los Algodones*: The Cotton Times on the Rio Grande," in *The Civil War on the Rio Grande, 1846–1876*, No. 46, ed. Roseann Bacha-Garza, Christopher L. Miller, and Russell K. Skowronek, 159–196 (College Station: Texas A&M University Press, 2019), 167; Kerby, *Kirby Smith's Confederacy*, 179; David Montejano, "Mexican Merchants and Teamsters on the Texas Cotton Road, 1862–1865," 164; Statement of Prescott, Dec 19, 1864, 41st Cong 3rd Sess, Senate Ex. Doc. No. 10, Pt. 3 (quoted material).

24. Ledger entry, June 1864, Ballinger Papers, Box 2A 189, BCAH; Rio Grande Ferry service application, May 22–21, 1862, Cameron County Commissioner's Court Minutes, Book A, Aug 29, 1848 to May 24, 1862. 33–37, 41–42.

25. Ronnie C. Tyler, *Santiago Vidaurri, and the Southern Confederacy* (Austin: Texas State Historical Society, 1973), 117–118; Daddysman, *The Matamoros Trade*, 117–119.

26. Watson, *Adventures of a Blockade Runner*, 29–30.

27. Statement of Prescott, Dec 19, 1864, 41st Cong 3rd Sess, Senate Ex. Doc. No. 10, Pt. 3.

28. Kerby, *Kirby Smith's Confederacy*, 168–169; Daddysman, *The Matamoros Trade*, 123–125.

29. Kerby, *Kirby Smith's Confederacy*, 171; Seddon to E. Kirby Smith, Oct 29, 1863, *ORA* I: 53, 904–905 (quoted material).

30. E. Kirby Smith to Jefferson Davis, Sep 11, 1863, *ORA* I: 22 pt. 2, 1003–1005; Townsend, *The Yankee Invasion of Texas*, 45.

31. Trans-Mississippi Dept. General Order No. 35, Aug 3, 1863, *ORA* I: 22/2, 953 (1st quote); Kerby, *Kirby Smith's Confederacy*, 138; E. Kirby Smith to Davis, Sep 11, 1863, *ORA* I: 22 pt. 2, 1003–1010; E. Kirby Smith to Davis, Sep 11, 1863, *ORA* I: 22/2, 1008 (2nd quote).

32. Judy Gentry, "Confederates and Cotton in East Texas," *East Texas Historical Journal* 48, No. 1 (2010), 25, Townsend, *The Yankee Invasion of Texas*, 46; Special Orders No. 198 and 327, Nov 22, 1863, and Dec 1, 1863, *ORA*: I 26/2, 437–438; Daddysman, *The Matamoros Trade*, 127; Handbook of Texas Online, Julia Beazley, "Hutchins, William J.," accessed July 26, 2019, http://www.tshaonline.org/handbook/online/articles/fhu51; Bryan to Broadwell, Nov 19, 1863, and Broadwell to Hutchins, Sorley, et al., Nov 20, 1863, United States, 62nd Cong 3rd Sess, Senate Doc. No. 987, *Cotton Sold to the Confederate States* (Washington: GPO, 1912), 308–310; Handbook of Texas Online, Hooper, "Sorley, James"; New Orleans *Times*, Feb 11, 1869.

33. Kerby, *Kirby Smith's Confederacy*, 141–142; Lea, *The King Ranch*, 191.

34. Kerby, *Kirby Smith's Confederacy*, 171; Daddysman, *The Matamoros Trade*, 131–135; Handbook of Texas Online, Julia Beazley, "Nichols, Ebenezar B.," accessed July 29, 2019, http://www.tshaonline.org/handbook/online/articles/fni01; Charles W. Ramsdell, "The Texas State Military Board, 1862–1865," *SHQ*, 27, No. 4 (Apr 1924), 255.

35. Kerby, *Kirby Smith's Confederacy*, 198–199; Handbook of Texas Online, Ralph A. Wooster, "Murrah, Pendleton," accessed July 26, 2019, http://www.tshaonline.org/handbook/online/articles/fmu15.

36. Gentry, "Confederates and Cotton in East Texas," 29, Kerby, *Kirby Smith's Confederacy*, 202–205; Handbook of Texas Online, Ralph A. Wooster, "Murrah, Pendleton"; Lea, *The King Ranch*, 191–192.

37. August Santleben, *A Frontier Pioneer: Early Staging and Overland Freighting Days on the Frontiers of Texas and Mexico*, 1910 Reprint (Castroville, TX: Castro Colonies Heritage Association, 1994), 28, 229.
38. Houston *Tri-Weekly Telegraph*, Jun 15, 1863.
39. Cherry to Turner, May 11, 1863, NARA RG:109, M346, Conf Citizen Files, Cherry, Saml; Houston *Tri-Weekly Telegraph*, Dec 14, 1863.
40. Ledger Feb 1, 1864–Sep 23, 1864, William Pitt Ballinger Papers, 2A 189, BCAH.
41. Statement of Prescott, Dec 19, 1864, 41st Cong 3rd Sess, Senate Ex. Doc. No. 10, Pt. 3.
42. Ibid. (1st quote); Lea, *The King Ranch*, 192; Judith F Gentry, "Edmund Kirby Smith's Early Leadership," in *The Battlefield and Beyond: Essays on the American Civil War*, ed. Clayton E. Jewett, 126–172 (Baton Rouge: LSU Press, 2012), 152–153; Kerby, *Kirby Smith's Confederacy*, 161–162; Ledger entry, Feb 1, 1864–Sep 23, 1864, William Pitt Ballinger Papers 2A 189, BCAH (2nd quote).
43. Daddysman, *The Matamoros Trade*, 135–136; Statement of Prescott, Dec 19, 1864, 41st Cong 3rd Sess, Senate Ex. Doc. No. 10, Pt. 3 (quoted material); Gentry, "Edmund Kirby Smith's Early Leadership," 152–153.
44. R.H. Williams. *With the Border Ruffians: Memories of the Far West, 1852–1868*, E.W. Williams (ed.) (Lincoln: University of Nebraska Press, 1982), 284, 285, 289.
45. Lea, *The King Ranch*, 189 (quoted material); Mary Margaret McAllen Amberson, James A. McAllen, and Margaret H. McAllen, *I Would Rather Sleep in Texas* (Austin: Texas Historical Association, 2003), 211–212; Webster III, *Entrepôt: Government Imports into the Confederate States* (Roseville, MN: Edinborough Press, 2020), 207; Handbook of Texas Online, W. H. Timmons, "Hart, Simeon," accessed May 09, 2019, http://www.tshaonline.org/handbook/online/articles/fhaak.
46. Seddon to Hart, Oct 29, 1863, *ORA* I: 53, 95 (quoted material); Daddysman, *The Matamoros Trade*, 132–133, 140.
47. Ralph A. Wooster (ed.), *Lone Star Blue and Gray, Essays on Texas in the Civil War* (Austin, Texas State Historical Society, 1995), 215–216, 221, 226–227; Tyler, "Cotton on the Border, 456–477; Tyler, *Santiago Vidaurri*, 29; Daddysman, *The Matamoros Trade*, 137–141; San Antonio *Daily Express*, Feb 16, 1899.
48. Webster, *Entrepôt*, 207; Daddysman, The Matamoros Trade, 136–137, Russell to Hale & Co. Nov 21, 1863 (quoted material), and Russell to Hutchins, Mar 1, 1864, NARA M331 Conf Officers & Enlisted, R0217 Charles Russell.
49. Handbook of Texas Online, James W. Daddysman, "Quintero, Jose Agustin," accessed July 03, 2019, http://www.tshaonline.org/handbook/online/articles/fqu05; Daddysman, *The Matamoros Trade*, 44, 140 (1st quote); Russell to Hale & Co. Nov 21, 1863 (1st quote), & David McKnight medical certificate, Feb 11, 1864 (2nd quote), and Russell to Hutchins, Mar 1, 1864, NARA M331 Conf Officers and Enlisted, R0217 Charles Russell.
50. Weil to Loeb, Nov 17, 1863 (quotes 1–3), Loeb to Weil and Levy, May 2, 1864 (4th quote), Mexican Claims, 48th Cong, 1st Sess, House Ex. Doc. No. 103 (Washington: GPO, 1884).
51. Weil to Loeb, Dec 4, 1863 (1st quote), Dec 26, 1863 (2nd and 3rd quote), Loeb to Weil and Levy, Houston, May 2, 1864, 48th Cong, 1st Sess, Ex. Doc. No. 103, GPO, 1884; Statement of Reynolds, Dec 10, 1864, U.S. Congress 41st Cong 3rd Sess, Senate Ex. Doc. No. 10, Pt. 3.
52. Statement Hoyt, Dec 12, 1864, 41st Cong 3rd Sess, Senate Ex. Doc. No. 10, Pt. 3; Davis and Arnold, *Colin J. McRae* (Galveston Monthly Customs Report), 172; NARA, RG:109, Conf. Vessel Papers, R-8, C-157; Woolsey to Welles, Dec 20, 1864, *ORN* I: 21, 763; Hoyt to Hart, Jul 24, 1863, NARA, RG:109, M346, Conf Citizens File, R:0473, Harris Hoyt.
53. Statement of Hoyt, Dec 12, 1864, 41st Cong 3rd Sess, Senate Ex. Doc. No. 10, Pt. 3; New Orleans *Daily True Delta*, Jan 16, 1864; *NYT,* Jan 23, 1864.

Chapter 8

1. Statements of Prescott, Dec 6, 1864, and Reynolds, Dec 10, 1864, and Hoyt, Dec 12, 1864, 41st Cong 3rd Sess, Senate Ex. Doc. No. 10, Pt.

2. Statement of Hoyt, Dec 7, 1864, 41st Cong 3rd Sess, Senate Ex. Doc. No. 10, Pt. 3

3. Statements of Hoyt, Dec 12, 1864 (1st quote), and Reynolds, Dec 10, 1864 (2nd quote), 41st Cong 3rd Sess, Senate Ex. Doc. No. 10, Pt. 3.

4. Statements of Reynolds, Dec 10, 13, 1864, 41st Cong 3rd Sess, Senate Ex. Doc. No. 10, Pt. 3.

5. Statement of Reynolds, Dec 10, 1864, 41st Cong 3rd Sess, Senate Ex. Doc. No. 10, Pt. 3.

6. Strong to MG Dix, Dec 9, 1864, and Statements of Reynolds, Dec 10, 1864, and Hoyt, Dec 12, 1864, & Prescott, Dec 19, 1864, 41st Cong 3rd Sess, Senate Ex. Doc. No. 10, Pt. 3.

7. Obituary, General Lyman C. Frieze, "Textile World," Vol. 53: 1 (Sep 8, 1917), 35 (963); Richard F. Miller (ed.). *States at War, Vol. 1: a Reference Guide for Connecticut, Maine, Massachusetts, New Hampshire, Rhode Island and Vermont in the Civil War* (Hanover: University Press of New England, 2013), 482, 536; John Russell Bartlett, "Index to the Acts & Resolves of Rhode Island 1850–1862" (1863). Library Archive. Paper 9.

8. Statements of Reynolds, Dec 10, 1864, and Frieze. January 26, 1865 (quoted material), and Robert Knight. Jan 28, 1865, 41st Cong 3rd Sess, Senate Ex. Doc. No. 10, Pt. 3.

9. Statement of Reynolds, Dec 10, 1864 (quoted material), and Prescott, Dec 19, 1864, 41st Cong 3rd Sess, Senate Ex. Doc. No. 10, Pt. 3.

10. Statement of Reynolds, Dec 10, 1864, 41st Cong 3rd Sess, Senate Ex. Doc. No. 10, Pt. 3.

11. Ibid.

12. Wise, *Lifeline of the Confederacy*, 184–185, 316; Turner to Bee, Jul 29, 1863, and Bee to Turner, Aug 10, 1863 & Aug 27, 1863, & Bee to Clements, Oct 3, 1863, ORA I: 26/2, 123–125, 157–158 (1st quote), & 286–286 (2nd quote); Galveston *Tri-Weekly News*, Jun 25, 1863; *Handbook of Texas Online*, Allen Kibler and Dawn Kibler, "Redgate, Samuel Joseph," accessed June 20, 2019, http://www.tshaonline.org/handbook/online/articles/frehu.

13. Statement of Reynolds, Dec 10, 1864, 41st Cong 3rd Sess, Senate Ex. Doc. No. 10, Pt. 3.

14. Statements of Prescott Dec 6, 1864, and Reynolds, Dec 10, 1864 (quoted material), and Hoyt, Jan 4, 1865; 41st Cong 3rd Sess, Senate Ex. Doc. No. 10, Pt. 3.

15. Statement of Reynolds, Dec 10, 1864, 41st Cong 3rd Sess, Senate Ex. Doc. No. 10, Pt. 3.

16. *NY Herald*, Mar 23, 1864, and Apr 20, 1864, & Statements of Prescott Dec 6, 1864, and Reynolds, Dec 10, 1864, 41st Cong 3rd Sess, Senate Ex. Doc. No. 10, Pt. 3.

17. Mrs. Hoyt to Prescott, Jan 9, 1863, & Statements of Prescott, Dec 6, 19, 1864, and Reynolds, Dec 10, 1864, 41st Cong 3rd Sess, Senate Ex. Doc. No. 10, Pt. 3; *NYT*, Apr 23–24, 1864 (quoted material).

18. Statements of Hoyt, Dec 12, 1864, and Compton. Dec 21, 1864, 41st Cong 3rd Sess, Senate Ex. Doc. No. 10, Pt. 3; Bances to JSR, Apr 28, 1864, BCAH, JSR Box 2G 72; Barcelona *El Lloyd Español*, May 21, 1864; Carbonell & Co. to JSR, May 17, 1864, BCAH, JSR Box 2G 69; JSR to del Regato, May 20, 1864, and JSR to Echeverria & Co., Sep 20, 1864, BCAH, JSR Box 2G 121; Ryder to JSR, BCAH:, JSR Box 2G 72; Smith to Morell [for Stillman], Apr 1, 1864, Charles Stillman business papers, MS Am 800.27, Houghton. Note: The Spanish brig was either the *Conde De Reus* or *Neptuno*.

19. *NYT*, Aug 21, 1864; Statements of Reynolds, Dec 10, 1864; and Wm. Compton. Dec 21, 1864, and Hoyt, Jan 4, 1865, 41st Cong 3rd Sess, Senate Ex. Doc. No. 10, Pt. 3; Ancentry.com.

20. *NYT*, Aug 21, 1864, *NY Shipping & Commercial List*, Aug 24, 1864; and statements of Reynolds, Dec 10, 1864, and Hoyt, Dec 12, 1864, 41st Cong 3rd Sess, Senate Ex. Doc. No. 10, Pt. 3; Thomas A. Jenckes interview, Feb 27, 1871, 41st Cong., 3d Sess, Senate Rep. No. 377.

21. Marilyn McAdams Sibley, *George W. Brackenridge; Maverick Philanthropist* (Austin: University of Texas Press, 1973), 41–46, 55–56.

22. Dana to Stone, Dec 11, 1863, *ORA* I: 26/1, 842–844 (quoted material); Sibley, *George W. Brackenridge*, 41–46, 79–80; Sibley, "Charles Stillman," 235–238.

23. Benjamin F. McIntyre, *Federals on the Frontier; the Diary of Benjamin F. McIntyre, 1862–1864*, Nannie M. Tilley (ed.) (Austin: University of Texas Press,

1963), 376; Mifflin Kenedy & Co. Journal, July 16, 1864, Pg. 123, King Ranch Archives, Kingsville, TX; Fort, T.A. "Steamboats on the Lower Rio Grande." (Unpublished manuscript, 2015), 54.

24. Mifflin Kenedy & Co., Ledger and Journals (Oct 15, 1857 to December 31, 1866) (1859–1864), and (January 1st, 1861–March 31st, 1864), King Ranch Archives, Kingsville, TX; Wilson, "Captain King's Cotton," 120. Note: In 1865, $159,140 is equivalent to about $2.7 million in 2019.

25. Statements of Prescott, Dec 19, 1864, and Compton. Dec 21, 1864, 41st Cong 3rd Sess, Senate Ex. Doc. No. 10, Pt. 3; Consular Notes, Aug 20, 1864, BCAH, JSR Papers, Box 2G70.

26. NARA, RG:36, M237 Passenger Lists of Vessels Arriving at New York, New York, 1820–1897, *Roanoke*; *NYT*, Sep 14, 1864; Statements of Prescott Dec 6, 1864, and Hoyt, Dec 7, 1864, and Reynolds, Dec 10, 1864, 41st Cong 3rd Sess, Senate Ex. Doc. No. 10, Pt. 3.

27. Selfridge to Porter Aug 23, 1864 and Pennock to Porter, Sep 8, 1864, *ORN* I: 26, 517, 553, 555; Hill to Lee, Nov 13, 1864, *ORN* I: 26, 721–722.

28. Statement of Reynolds, Dec 10, 1864, 41st Cong 3rd Sess, Senate Ex. Doc. No. 10, Pt. 3.

29. Statements of Prescott Dec 6, 1864, and Reynolds, Dec 10, 1864 (quoted material) and Dec 13, 1864, 41st Cong 3rd Sess, Senate Ex. Doc. No. 10, Pt. 3; *NY Shipping & Commercial List & New Yorker Handels Zeitung*, Mar 4, 1865.

30. Statement of Reynolds, Dec 10, 1864, 41st Cong 3rd Sess, Senate Ex. Doc. No. 10, Pt. 3.

31. Etchison to Hurlbut, Feb 27, 1865, *ORA* I: 48/1, 1048–1049; Amberson, McAllen, and McAllen, *I Would Rather Sleep in Texas*, 246.

32. C.S. Seward to F.W. Seward, Nov 8, 1864, Consular Despatches, Ramsdell Collection (quoted material).

33. Etchison to Hurlbut, Feb 27, 1865, aqnd Wallace to Grant, Mar 14, 1865 (quoted material), *ORA* I: 48/1, 1048–1049, and 1276–1279; Amberson, McAllen, and McAllen, *I Would Rather Sleep in Texas*, 250–253; Daddysman, *The Matamoros Trade*, 183.

34. Statement of Prescott, Dec 19, 1864, 41st Cong 3rd Sess, Senate Ex. Doc. No. 10, Pt. 3.

35. *Ibid.*

36. Statement of Reynolds, Dec 10, 1864 (quoted material), 41st Cong 3rd Sess, Senate Ex. Doc. No. 10, Pt. 3; Blatchford Cases in Prize, NY, Betts, 615; *NYT*, Dec 1, 1864; Silverstone, *Civil War Navies*, 40.

37. Statement of Reynolds, Dec 10, 1864 (quoted material), 41st Cong 3rd Sess, Senate Ex. Doc. No. 10, Pt. 3; Blatchford Cases in Prize, NY, Betts, 615.

38. Statement of Reynolds, Dec 10, 1864, 41st Cong 3rd Sess, Senate Ex. Doc. No. 10, Pt. 3.

39. Houston *Tri-Weekly News*, Dec 12, 1864; *NY World*, Dec 28, 1864; *Gore's Liverpool General Advertiser*, Jan 19, 1865; Statements of Prescott Dec 6, 10, 1864, and Reynolds, Dec 10, 1864, and Wm. Compton, Dec 21, 1864, 41st Cong 3rd Sess, Senate Ex. Doc. No. 10, Pt. 3.

40. Statement of Prescott Dec 6, 1864 (quoted material), 41st Cong 3rd Sess, Senate Ex. Doc. No. 10, Pt. 3; Belden and Belden, *So Fell the Angels*, 142. Note: The Beldens and other authors have assumed that information aboard the *Sybil* led to Prescott's arrest in November 1864. However, the *Sybil* did not arrive at New York harbor until December 1 and there was no cotton onboard for any of the Texas Adventure partners.

Chapter 9

1. Walter E. Wilson and Gary L. McKay, *James D. Bulloch: Secret Agent and Mastermind of the Confederate Navy* (Jefferson, NC: McFarland, 2012), 105–106, 301; Walter E. Wilson, *The Bulloch Belles* (Jefferson, NC: McFarland, 2015), 127–128.

2. MG Dix to MG Draper, Dec 13, 1864, and MG Dix to Perkins, Dec 15, 1864, 41st Cong 3rd Sess, Senate Ex. Doc. No. 10, Pt. 2; MG Dix to Ludlow, Dec 7, 1864, and Hazard telegram to Reynolds, Dec 8, 1864, 41st Cong 3rd Sess, Senate Ex. Doc. No. 10, Pt. 3.

3. Leigh, *Trading with the Enemy*, 94–94.

4. Hazard telegram to Reynolds, 41st Cong 3rd Sess, Senate Ex. Doc. No. 10, Pt. 3.

5. Bolles to MG Dix, May 5, 1865, and statements of Frieze and Reynolds, Dec 10, 1864, and January 26, 1865, and Prescott, Dec 6, 1864, and Robert Knight. Jan 28, 1865, 41st Cong 3rd Sess, Senate Ex. Doc. No. 10, Pt. 3; *NY World*, Feb 20, 1865; Peyton O. Abbott, "Business Travel Out of Texas," *SHQ*, 96. No. 2 (Oct 1992), 264, 271.

6. Oller, *American Queen: the Rise and Fall of Kate Chase*, 214–220; Holt JAG Report, Jun 15, 1865. 41st Cong 3rd Sess, Senate Ex. Doc. No. 10, Pt. 1.

7. W.H. Sprague to MG Dix, Dec 10, 1864, 41st Cong 3rd Sess, Senate Ex. Doc. No. 10, Pt. 3.

8. Ibid.

9. Ibid.

10. Ludlow to MG Dix, Dec 8, 1864, and Parole of Byron Sprague, Dec 9, 1864, 41st Cong 3rd Sess, Senate Ex. Doc. No. 10, Pt. 3.

11. Statement of Reynolds, Dec 10, 1864, 41st Cong 3rd Sess, Senate Ex. Doc. No. 10, Pt. 3.

12. Ibid.

13. Strong to MG Dix, Dec 9, 1864, and Parole of Prescott, Dec 17, 1864, 41st Cong 3rd Sess, Senate Ex. Doc. No. 10, Pt. 3.

14. Statement of Hoyt, Dec 7, 1864, 41st Cong 3rd Sess, Senate Ex. Doc. No. 10, Pt. 3.

15. Ibid.

16. Belden and Belden, *So Fell the Angels*, 146; Statement of Hoyt, Dec 12, 1864, 41st Cong 3rd Sess, Senate Ex. Doc. No. 10, Pt. 3.

17. Statement of Hoyt, Dec 12, 1864 (quoted material), 41st Cong 3rd Sess, Senate Ex. Doc. No. 10, Pt. 3; Abraham Lincoln, Feb 18, 1864, Presidential Proclamation 110; and Apr 11, 1864, Presidential Proclamation 126, presidency.ucsb.edu. Note: Lincoln signed Proclamation 126, closing the ports of Brownsville and Brazos Santiago just three days before his assassination.

18. Statement of Hoyt, Dec 12, 1864, 41st Cong 3rd Sess, Senate Ex. Doc. No. 10, Pt. 3.

19. Court-martial of Harris Hoyt, Jan 23, 1865, 41st Cong 3rd Sess, Senate Ex. Doc. No. 10, Pt. 3; Spencer C. Tucker (ed.). *American Civil War: the Definitive Encyclopedia and Document Collection*, Vol. II (Santa Barbara, CA: ABC-CLIO, 2013), 677.

20. Court-martial of Harris Hoyt, Jan 21, 24, 1865, 41st Cong 3rd Sess, Senate Ex. Doc. No. 10, Pt. 3; *NYT*, Dec 26, 1896 (quoted material); William Richards Castle and Arthur Stanwood Pier (eds.), "Non-Academic," *The Harvard Graduates' Magazine*, Vol. V (1896–1897): 452.

21. Hardie to MG Dix, Feb 13, 1865, 41st Cong 3rd Sess, Senate Ex. Doc. No. 10, Pt. 3.

22. Bolles to MG Dix, Mar 22, 1865 (quoted material), and Dix to Stanton, Mar 23, 1865, 41st Cong 3rd Sess, Senate Ex. Doc. No. 10, Pt. 2.

23. Holt JAG Report, Jun 15, 1865. 41st Cong 3rd Sess, Senate Ex. Doc. No. 10, Pt. 1.

24. Holt JAG Report, Jun 15, 1865 (quoted material), 41st Cong 3rd Sess, Senate Ex. Doc. No. 10, Pt. 1; Lamphier, *Kate Chase and William Sprague*, 47.

25. Holt JAG Report, Jun 15, 1865. 41st Cong 3rd Sess, Senate Ex. Doc. No. 10, Pt. 1.

26. Bolles to MG Dix, Mar 22, 1865 (quoted material), and Dix to Stanton, Mar 23, 1865, and Thurston to MG Dix, Jun 26, 1865, 41st Cong 3rd Sess, Senate Ex. Doc. No. 10, Pt. 2. Note: Byron Sprague's lawyer also questioned the legality of his arrest and parole by a military tribunal.

27. MG Dix to Stanton, Mar 23, 1865, and Townsend to MG Dix, Jun 9, 1865, NARA, RG109 M347 Conf Combined Service Records R:0195, Harris Hoyt.

28. Hoyt to Townsend, Aug 13, 1865, and Van Buren, to Townsend, Aug 18, 1865, 41st Cong 3rd Sess, Senate Ex. Doc. No. 10, Pt. 2.

29. Oller, *American Queen: the Rise and Fall of Kate Chase*, 113–115.

30. Leigh, *Trading with the Enemy*, 52–54; Thomas G. Belden, "Kate Was Too Ambitious," *American Heritage*, Vol. 7, No. 5 (Aug 1956); United States Senate (senate.gov).

Chapter 10

1. Eller, *Civil War Naval Chronology 1861–1865*, V-104; Houston *Tri-Weekly News*, Jun 23, 1865; Andrew Johnson, Presidential Proclamation 141, Jun 23, 1865, presidency.ucsb.edu. Note: "Juneteenth" continues to be celebrated as "Emancipation Day" state holiday in Texas.

2. JSR to de Lizardi & Co, May 19, 1865, JSR 2G 121, BCAH.

3. Note: The listed cotton bale totals are derived from multiple primary sources that show 52 total shipments with 21,016.5 confirmed bales, 1,460 estimated, and 150 lost at sea. Liverpool was the destination of 35 of the shipments and 20,819.5 of the cotton bales (19,544.5+1125+150), 6 shipments went to New York, 4 to Havana, 4 to New Orleans, 1 to Baltimore, 1 to Barcelona, and one unknown.

4. *Gore's Liverpool General Advertiser*, Sep 7, 1865.

5. Lea, *The King Ranch*, 210, 242–243; Monday and Vick. *Petra's Legacy*, 212; Mifflin Kenedy & Co., Ledger and Journals (Oct 15, 1857 to December 31, 1866) (1859–1864), and (January 1st, 1861– March 31st, 1864), King Ranch Archives, Kingsville, TX (quoted material).

6. Wilson, "Captain King's Cotton," 120–121.

7. Lea, *The King Ranch*, 242–244.

8. Statements and accounts, José Morell, Mar 3, 1864. Charles Stillman Business Papers, MS Am 800.27, Houghton; Charles Stillman Oath of Allegiance, Dec 2, 1863, NARA RG:109, M346 Conf Citizens File, R:0985 Charles Stillman; Stillman to Elizabeth Pamela Goodrich Stillman, Feb 11, 1865, King Ranch Archives, Kingsville, TX (quoted material).

9. Sibley, "Charles Stillman," 239: Sibley, *George W. Brackenridge*, 83; Amberson, McAllen, and McAllen, *I Would Rather Sleep in Texas*, 321; Memphis *Public Ledger*, Jun 23, 1879 (quoted material); *Galveston Daily News*, Jul 3, 1979. Note: Sibley's otherwise reliable accounts state that Stillman suffered a stroke in the summer of 1864; while this may be true, he continued to actively conduct business at the Rio Grande until his departure in March 1865.

10. Amberson, McAllen, and McAllen, *I Would Rather Sleep in Texas*, 279; Handbook of Texas Online, John Mason Hart, "Stillman, Charles," accessed June 02, 2019, http://www.tshaonline.org/handbook/online/articles/fst57; Lea, *The King Ranch*, 247; Pat Kelley, *River of Lost Dreams; Navigation on the Rio Grande* (Lincoln: University of Nebraska Press, 1986), 77; Sibley, "Charles Stillman," 239: Sibley, *George W. Brackenridge*, 83.

11. Sibley, *George W. Brackenridge*, 79–80; Handbook of Texas Online, John Mason Hart, "Brackenridge, George Washington," accessed June 02, 2019, http://www.tshaonline.org/handbook/online/articles/fbr02.

12. Sibley, "Charles Stillman," 236; Charles Stillman Oath of Allegiance, Dec 2, 1863, NARA RG:109, M346 Conf Citizens File, R:0985 Charles Stillman.

13. Handbook of Texas Online, Hart, "Stillman, Charles" and "Brackenridge, George Washington"; Sibley, "Charles Stillman," 239–240: Sibley, *George W. Brackenridge*, 79–80, 92–93.

14. Sibley, "Charles Stillman," 237–238; Sibley, *George W. Brackenridge*, 15; Handbook of Texas Online, Hart, "Brackenridge, George Washington."

15. Sibley, *George W. Brackenridge*, 15; Handbook of Texas Online, Hart, "Brackenridge, George Washington."

16. Vezzetti, Tidbits, 26–27, 71; *Handbook of Texas Online*, Roberto Mario Salmón, "San Roman, Jose," accessed June 05, 2019, http://www.tshaonline.org/handbook/online/articles/fsa16; Celaya to JSR, May 24, 1863, BCAH, JSR Papers, 2G 64, BCAH; Monday and Vick. *Petra's Legacy*, 185–186.

17. *Handbook of Texas Online*, René Harris, "Mills, David Graham" and Marie Beth Jones, "Mills, Robert," accessed June 02, 2019, http://www.tshaonline.org/handbook/online/articles/fmi64.

18. Handbook of Texas Online, Seymour V. Connor, "Russell, Charles Arden," accessed July 11, 2019, http://www.tshaonline.org/handbook/online/articles/fru18; Russell, *Genealogy of the Russell Family*, 10; Camille Yeamans Neighbors, "The Old Town Saint Mary's on Copano Bay and Some Interesting People Who Once Lived There" (Thesis. Southwest Texas State Teachers College, San Marcos, TX, 1942), 63–65 (quoted material).

19. U.S. and Mexican Claims Commission. *Case of Mexico Upon the Newly Discovered Evidence of Fraud and Perjury in the Claims of Benjamin Weil and La Abra Silver Mining Company* (Washington, D.C.: Judd & Detweiler, Printers, 1878), iii.

20. Mexican Claims, *The Weil Case*, 48th Cong, 1st Sess, Ex. Doc. No. 100, GPO, 1884; Thompson, *Tejano Tiger*, 71, 104.

21. Mexican *Claims Commission. Claims of Benjamin Weil and La Abra Silver Mining Company*, viii (quoted material); W. Michael Reisman and Christina Parajon Skinner, *Fraudulent Evidence Before Public International Tribunals: the Dirty Stories of International Law* (Cambridge: Cambridge University Press, 2014), 9–12; New Orleans *Times-Picayune*, Oct 20, 1888; Civil District Court Case Papers, No 255–294, 322, 1880, Benjamin Weil (ancestry.com); Julian Costillo Slaughter et al., Richard A. Ford (ed.), "Appellants, v. Cecil R. Loeb, Executor of Samuel E. Loeb, Deceased," *The Washington Law Reporter*, Vol. 34, 1906, 480–483.

22. Benjamin to Slidell, Mar 26, 1863, ORN I: 19, 282–284; Loyalty Oath, U.S. Legation London, Aug 1, 1865, NARA RG:109 M1003 Conf Pardon Applications, John Laing Macanlay [*Sic*].

23. Gloag, et al., *The Scottish Jurist*, 309–315; Rankine, *The Scots Revised Reports*, 603–615; Bernath, *Squall Across the Atlantic*, 106–107. Note: In the Scottish courts Clements claimed £2700, the equivalent of 12,000 U.S. dollars.

24. Eller, *Civil War Naval Chronology 1861–1865*, VI-235; Bernath, *Squall Across the Atlantic*, 106–107; Robert M., Browning, Jr., *Lincoln's Trident: The West Gulf Blockading Squadron During the Civil War* (Tuscaloosa: University of Alabama Press, 2015), 206–208; Wilson and McKay, *James D. Bulloch*, 210–212; Boston *Herald*, Dec 6, 1897.

25. *Cambridge Tribune*, Sep 27, 1913.

26. Wilson and McKay, *James D. Bulloch*, 212, 235–243.

27. Public Document No. 3, Report of the Joint Special Committee of the General Assembly. (Providence: State of Rhode Island, 1866); Pawtucket *Evening Times*, Sep 6, 1917.

28. Public Document No. 3, Rhode Island, 1866.

29. Terry Halbert and Elaine Ingull, *Law and Ethics in the Business Environment*. 7th ed. (Boston: Cengage Learning, 2012), 72.

30. Providence *Manufacturers' and Farmers' Journal*, Mar 19, 1866, Mar 26, 1866, and Apr 2, 1866.

31. *Ibid.*; Obituary, General Lyman C. Frieze, "Textile World," Vol. 53: 1 (Sep 8, 1917), 35 (963); Richard F. Miller (ed.), *States at War, Vol. 1: a Reference Guide for Connecticut, Maine, Massachusetts, New Hampshire, Rhode Island and Vermont in the Civil War*. (Hanover: University Press of New England, 2013), 482, 536; Bartlett, "Index to the Acts & Resolves of Rhode Island 1850–1862" Paper 9; NY *Daily Tribune*, Aug 15, 1902 (quoted material).

32. Providence *Manufacturers' and Farmers' Journal*, Nov 7, 1864; Providence *Evening Press*, Oct 23, 1867; Harrisburg *Telegraph*, Dec 4, 1874; *Boston Post* Feb 6, 1879.

33. Robert V. Bruce, *Bell: Alexander Graham Bell and the Conquest of Solitude*, 1973 reprint (Ithaca: Cornell University Press, 1990), 238, 244; Charlotte Gray, *Reluctant Genius: Alexander Graham Bell and the Passion for Invention* (Toronto: HarperCollins, 2006), 160, 169, 181–182 (quoted material).

34. *Daily Deadwood Pioneer-Times*, Dec 12, 1908; *Boston Globe*, Jul 19, 1873; NY *Sun*, Mar 5, 1890; Rhode Island Historical Cemetery Commission. (rihistoriccemeteries.org); Find A Grave (findagrave.com).

35. Thomas A. Jenckes interview, Feb 27, 1871, 41st Cong., 3d Session, Senate Rep. No. 377; Belden and Belden, *So Fell the Angels*, 251–253.

36. Ibid.

37. Lamphier, *Kate Chase and William Sprague*, 120–121; Biographical Directory of the U.S. Congress (bioguide.congress.gov).

38. Belknap to U.S. Senate, Feb 27, 1871 (quoted material), 41st Cong, 3d Session, Senate Ex. Doc. No. 10, Pt. 4; Select Committee Report, "Alleged Traffic with Rebels in Texas," Mar 3, 1871, 41st Cong., 3d Sess, Senate Rep. No. 377, 17–18.

39. Belden and Belden, *So Fell the Angels*, 284–285, 291–297, 326–327; Oller, *American Queen: the Rise and Fall of Kate Chase*, 214–220, 239; *Boston Herald*, *Chicago Daily News*, Saint Paul, MN, *Daily Globe*, Eureka, NV, *Daily*, Evansville, IN, *Courier*, Washington, D.C. *Evening Star*, New Haven, RI, *Register*, NY *Herald*, NY *Tribune*, *Philadelphia Inquirer*, Cleveland *Plain Dealer*, Portland, ME, *Daily Press*, Saginaw, MI, *Courier-Herald*, *Salt Lake Herald*, Wheeling, WV, *Register*, Worcester, MA, *Daily Spy*, *Arkansas Gazette*, Feb 21, 1882; Lea, *The King Ranch*, 190.

40. *NY Daily Graphic*, Feb 13, 1875;

Census Returns of England and Wales, 1901. Kew, Surrey, England: The National Archives, 1901, Ancestry.com; John Russell Bartlett, *Genealogy of That Branch of the Russell Family Which Comprises the Descendants of John Russell, of Woburn, Massachusetts, 1640–1878* (Bowie, MD, Heritage Books, 1989), 139.

41. Philadelphia *Times*, Apr 28, 1879 (1st and 2nd quotes); and *NYT,* Apr 28, 1879; *NY World*, Oct 18, 1893 (3rd quote).

42. *NY Tribune* (1st quote), and *NYT,* Sep 1, 1889 (2nd and 3rd quotes).

43. *NY World*, Oct 18, 1893; Staunton VA *Spectator*, Apr 8, 1879.

44. *NYT,* Apr 28, 1879; *NY World*, Oct 18, 1893.

45. *NY Daily Graphic*, Feb 13, 1875; Census Returns of England and Wales, 1901. Kew, Surrey, England: The National Archives, 1901, Ancestry.com; Hoyt family Bible records, 1811–1930, familysearch.org.

Chapter 11

1. Bartlett. *Memoirs of Rhode Island Officers*, 105–120; Lamphier, *Kate Chase and William Sprague*, 33.

Bibliography

Archives, Official Publications, Diaries, and Primary Sources

Blatchford, Samuel. Reports of cases in prize, argued and determined in the circuit and district courts of the United States, for the southern district of New York, 1861–65. Washington, D.C.: Government Printing Office. 1866.

Cameron County, TX Archives, Brownsville, TX.

Dolph Briscoe Center for American History, The University of Texas at Austin, TX: Ashbel Smith Papers, José San Román Papers, William Pitt Ballinger Papers, and Charles Ramsdell Collection.

Ford, John Salmon. *Rip Ford's Texas*. Stephen B. Oates (Ed.), Austin: University of Texas Press, 1963.

Fort, T.A. "Steamboats on the Lower Rio Grande" (unpublished manuscript, 2015), courtesy of the author.

Fremantle, Sir Arthur James Lyon, *The Fremantle Diary, Being the Journal of Lt. Col. Fremantle Coldstream Guards on His Three Months in the Southern States*. Walter Lord (ed.), Boston: Little, Brown, & Co., 1954.

Gammel, H.P.N. (comp.). *Laws of Texas, 1822–1897*, Vol. V. Austin: The Gammel Book Co., 1898.

Gloag, William E., Alexander Nicolson, Hubert Hamilton, and James Paterson. *The Scottish Jurist: Being Reports of Cases Decided in the Supreme Courts of Scotland, and in the House of Lords on Appeal from Scotland*, Vol. 38. Edinburgh: Thomas Constable, 1866.

Hertslet, Edward (comp.) *The Foreign Officer List and Diplomatic and Consular Hand Book*. London: Harrison, 1877.

Hill, Frederic Stanhope. *Twenty Years at Sea or Leaves from My Old Log-Books*. Boston: Houghton, Mifflin & Co., 1893.

Houghton Library, Harvard University, Cambridge, MA, Theodore Roosevelt Collection, Charles Stillman business papers.

Huntington Library, San Marino, CA, Hiram Barney Papers. Box 1, Folder 22 and 35.

King Ranch Archives, Kingsville, TX, Mifflin Kenedy & Co. Journal (Oct 15, 1857 to December 31, 1866).

Library of Congress, N.P. Banks papers; Photos, Prints, Drawings.

Lubbock, Francis Richard. *Six Decades in Texas or Memoirs of Francis Richard Lubbock, Governor of Texas in War-Time, 1861–1863*. C.W. Raines (ed.). Austin: Ben C. Jones & Co., 1900.

McIntyre, Benjamin F. *Federals on the Frontier; the Diary of Benjamin F. McIntyre, 1862–1864*. Nannie M. Tilley (ed.). Austin: University of Texas Press, 1963.

Minot, George (ed.). *The Statutes at Large and Treaties of the United States of America*, Vol. IX. Boston: Little Brown & Co., 1862, 928–943 (Articles V & VII).

National Archives and Records Administration, RG: 109, Confederate Citizens File, Confederate Vessel Papers.

National Archives and Records Administration, RG: 36, M237, US Customs Records, Passenger Lists of Vessels arriving at New York, 1820–1897.

National Archives and Records Administration, RG; 94, Letters Received by the Adjutant General's Office.

National Archives and Records Administration Fort Worth, RG: 21, Admiralty Cases.
Parisot, Pierre Fourier. *The Reminiscences of a Texas Missionary.* San Antonio: St. Mary's Church, 1899.
Rankine, Sir John. *The Scots Revised Reports: Court of Session*, Ser. 3 Vol. 4. Edinburgh: William Green & Sons, 1903.
Rhode Island. *Public Document No. 3*, "Report of the Joint Special Committee of the General Assembly." Providence: State of Rhode Island, 1866.
Rosenberg Library, Galveston, TX, Richardson, W. & D. *Galveston City Directory, 1859–1860*; J.O.L.O. Observatory record book, 1861: 27–0701; Log of the *Royal Yacht*, 1862–186: 53–0001.
Santleben, August. *A Frontier Pioneer: Early Staging and Overland Freighting Days on the Frontiers of Texas and Mexico.* 1910. Reprint. Castroville, TX: Castro Colonies Heritage Association, 1994.
Semmes, Raphael. *Memoirs of Service Afloat, During the War Between the States.* Baltimore: Kelly Piet & Co., 1869.
Texas A&M University-Kingsville, Kingsville, TX, James C. Jernigan Library, The South Texas Archives & Special Collections.
Texas State Library and Archives Commission, Austin, Texas. Memorials and Petitions.
United Kingdom. British Parliamentary Papers, Foreign Office.
United Kingdom. National Archives, Census Returns of England and Wales, 1891, Kew, Surrey, England.
United States. *Compilation of Laws and Decisions of the Courts Relating to War Claims.* Washington, D.C.: GPO, 1908.
United States. *Official Records of the Union and Confederate Navies in the War of the Rebellion*, 30 Vol.s. Washington, D.C.: GPO, 1894–1921.
United States. *The War of the Rebellion: a Compilation of the Official Records of the Union and Confederate Armies*, 70 Vol.s. Washington, D.C.: GPO, 1880–1901.
United States, 38th Congress, 2nd Session, 1864–1865, House Rep. No. 25, *New York Custom-House*. Washington, D.C.: GPO, 1865.
United States, 41st Congress, 3rd Session, 1870–71, Vol. 1, Senate Ex. Doc. No. 10, Parts 1–4, *Letters of the Secretary of the War: Unlawful Traffic with Rebels in the State of Texas*; No. 377, *Alleged Traffic with Rebels in Texas*. Washington, D.C.: GPO, 1871.
United States, 48th Congress, 1st Session, 1883–84, House Ex. Doc. No. 103, *Mexican Claims*, Washington, D.C.: GPO, 1884.
United States, 62nd Congress, 3rd Session, Senate Doc. No. 987, *Cotton Sold to the Confederate States*, Washington, D.C.: GPO, 1912.
United States, 63rd Congress, 1st Session, Apr 7—Dec 1, 1913, Senate Doc., No. 181 *Quotations from Statutes at Large of the Confederate States of America*. Washington, D.C.: GPO, 1913.
Watson, William. *Adventures of a Blockade Runner.* London: Fisher Unwin, 1892.
Welles, Gideon. *Diary of Gideon Welles: Secretary of the Navy Under Lincoln and Johnson*, Vol. I. Edgar T. Welles (ed.), Boston: Houghton Mifflin Co., 1911.
Williams R.H. *With the Border Ruffians: Memories of the Far West, 1852–1868.* E.W. Williams (ed), Lincoln: University of Nebraska Press, 1982.
Work Projects Administration. *Ship Registers and Enrollments of New Orleans, Louisiana*, Vol. V (1851–1860) & VI (1861–1870). Baton Rouge: Louisiana State University, 1941.
The Young-Sanders Center, Franklin, Louisiana.

Newspapers

Baltimore *Sun.*
Barcelona *El Lloyd Español.*
Beaumont *Banner.*
Boston *Daily Advertiser.*
Boston *Herald.*
Boston *Post.*
Boston *Globe.*
Brownsville *Daily Ranchero.*
Brownsville *Ranchero.*
Cambridge [MA] *Tribune*
Chicago *Daily News.*
Deadwood, AZ, *Daily Deadwood Pioneer-Times.*
Galveston *Daily News.*
Galveston *Weekly Civilian and Gazette.*
Galveston *Weekly News.*

Harrisburg *Telegraph.*
Houston *Daily Post.*
Houston *Tri-Weekly Telegraph.*
Houston *Weekly Telegraph.*
Liverpool *Gore's General Advertiser.*
London *Evening Star*
Louisville *Daily Courier*
Memphis *Public Ledger.*
New Orleans *Daily True Delta.*
New Orleans *Times-Picayune.*
New Orleans *Times.*
New York *Commercial Advertiser.*
New York *Daily Graphic.*
New York *Daily Tribune.*
New York *Evening Post.*
New York *Herald.*
New York *Sun.*
New York *Times.*
New York *Tribune.*
New York *World.*
New York *Shipping & Commercial List.*
New Yorker *Handels Zeitung.*
Pawtucket *Evening Times.*
Philadelphia *Inquirer.*
Philadelphia *Times.*
Providence *Evening Press.*
Providence *Manufacturers' and Farmers' Journal.*
San Antonio *Daily Express.*
Waco *News-Tribune.*
The Washington (DC) *Law Reporter.*
Washington (DC) *Evening Star.*

Periodicals, Journals, Theses, Compilations

Abbott, Peyton O. "Business Travel Out of Texas." *Southwestern Historical Quarterly*, 96. no. 2 (Oct 1992): 259–271.

Bartlett, John Russell. "Index to the Acts & Resolves of Rhode Island 1850–1862" (1863). Library Archive. Paper 9.

Belden, Thomas G. "Kate Was Too Ambitious." *American Heritage*, Vol. 7, No. 5 (Aug 1956): 40–43.

Black, Hugo L. III. "Richard Fitzpatrick's South Florida, 1822–1840, Part Ii." *Tequesta: the Journal of the Historical Association of Southern Florida.* I, No. 41 (1981): 33–68.

Castle, William Richards, and Arthur Stanwood Pier (eds.). "Non-Academic." *The Harvard Graduates' Magazine.* Vol. V (1896–1897).

Day, James M. "Leon Smith: Confederate Mariner." *East Texas Historical Journal.* Vol. III, No. 1 (Mar 1965): 34–49.

Ellis, L. Tuffly. "Maritime Commerce on the Far Western Gulf, 1861–1865." *Southwestern Historical Quarterly*, 72, No. 2 (Oct 1973): 167–226.

Fort, Karen G., and Tom A. Fort. "*Los Algodones*: The Cotton Times on the Rio Grande." In *The Civil War on the Rio Grande, 1846–1876,* No. 46, edited by Roseann Bacha-Garza, Christopher L. Miller, and Russell K. Skowronek, 159–196. College Station: Texas A&M University Press, 2019.

Gentry, Judith F. "Edmund Kirby Smith's Early Leadership." In *The Battlefield and Beyond: Essays on the American Civil War,* edited by Clayton E. Jewett. 126–172. Baton Rouge: LSU Press, 2012.

Gentry, Judy. "Confederates and Cotton in East Texas." *East Texas Historical Journal* 48, No. 1 (2010): 20–39.

Hacker, J. David. "A Census-Based Count of the Civil War Dead." *Civil War History* 57, No. 4 (Dec 2011): 307–348.

Hall, Edward H. *The Northern Counties Gazetteer and Directory, for 1855–6* (Chicago: R. Fergus, 1855).

Johnson, Ludwell H. "Commerce Between Northeastern Ports and the Confederacy, 1861–1865." *The Journal of American History* 54, no.1 (Jun 1976): 30–42.

Kearney, Milo, and Anthony Knopp. *Boom and Bust: The Historical Cycles of Matamoros and Brownsville.* Austin: Eakin Press.

Larios, Avila. "Brownsville-Matamoros: Confederate Lifeline." *Mid-America: an Historical Quarterly* 40, no.2 (Apr 1958): 67–91.

McAllen, M.M. "Life Lived Along the Lower Rio Grande Valley During the Civil War." In *The Civil War on the Rio Grande, 1846–1876,* No. 46, edited by Roseann Bacha-Garza, Christopher L. Miller, and Russell K. Skowronek, 59–81. College Station: Texas A&M University Press, 2019.

Montejano, David. "Mexican Merchants and Teamsters on the Texas Cotton Road, 1862–1865." In *Mexico and Mexicans in the Making of the United States,* edited by John Tutino, 141–170. Austin: University of Texas Press, 2012.

Neighbors, Camille Yeamans. "The Old

Town Saint Mary's on Copano Bay and Some Interesting People Who Once Lived There." Thesis. Southwest Texas State Teachers College, San Marcos, TX, 1942.

Newland, Linda Sue. "The Persistence of Antebellum Planter Families in Postbellum East Texas." Thesis, University of North Texas, Denton, TX, 1998.

Ramsdell, Charles W. "The Texas State Military Board, 1862–1865." *Southwestern Historical Quarterly*, 27, No. 4 (Apr 1924): 253–275.

Richardson, David. *The Texas Almanac for 1863*. Austin, TX: Richardson & Co., 1862.

Sibley, Marilyn McAdams. "Charles Stillman: a Case Study of Entrepreneurship on the Rio Grande, 1861–1865." *Southwestern Historical Quarterly*, 72, No. 2 (Oct 1973): 227–240.

"Statistics of Iron and Cotton 1830–1860." *The Quarterly Journal of Economics* 2, No. 3 (1888): 379–84.

Surdam, David G. "Traders or Traitors: Northern Cotton Trading During the Civil War." *Business and Economic History* 28, No. 2 (Winter 1999): 301–312.

Tyler, Ronnie C. "Cotton on the Border, 1861–1865." *Southwestern Historical Quarterly*, 73, No. 4 (Apr 1970): 456–477.

Unknown. "Obituary, General Lyman C. Frieze." *Textile World*, Vol. 53, No. 1 (Sep 8, 1917): 35 (963).

Wilson, Walter E. "Captain King's Cotton: The Civil War Blockade-Running Adventures of Richard King and Mifflin Kenedy." In *Supplementary Studies in Rio Grande Valley History*, 15, edited by Milo Kearney et al., 91–130. Edinburg, TX: The University of Texas Rio Grande Valley, 2017.

Wilson, Walter E. "The Civil War Blockade Running Adventures of the Louisiana Schooner William R. King." *Louisiana History*, 56 (Summer 2015), 294–314.

Wilson, Walter E. "Rebels at the Rio Grande: Naval Actions on the International Border in 1863." In *New Studies in Rio Grande Valley History*, 16, edited by Milo Kearney et al., 125–165. Edinburg, TX: The University of Texas Rio Grande Valley, 2018.

Secondary Sources

Amberson, Mary Margaret McAllen, James A. McAllen, and Margaret H. McAllen. *I Would Rather Sleep in Texas*. Austin: Texas Historical Association, 2003.

Andreas, Peter. *Smuggler Nation: How Illicit Trade Made America*. New York: Oxford University Press, 2013.

Barrett, Joseph H. *Life of Abraham Lincoln*. New York: Moore, Wilstach & Baldwin, 1865.

Bartlett, John Russell. *Genealogy of That Branch of the Russell Family Which Comprises the Descendants of John Russell, of Woburn, Massachusetts, 1640–1878*. Bowie, MD: Heritage Books, 1989.

Bartlett, John Russell. *Memoirs of Rhode Island Officers Who Were Engaged in the Service of Their Country During the Great Rebellion of the South*. Providence: Sidney S. Rider & Brother, 1867.

Belden, Thomas Graham, and Marva Robins Belden. *So Fell the Angels*. Boston: Little, Brown, & Co., 1956.

Bennett, Frank P. *History of American Textiles: with Kindred and Auxiliary Industries*. Boston: American Wool and Cotton Reporter, 1922.

Bernath, Stuart L. *Squall Across the Atlantic: American Civil War Prize Cases and Diplomacy*. Berkeley: University of California Press, 1970.

Block, W.T. *Schooner Sail to Starboard: Confederate Blockade Running on the Louisiana-Texas Coastlines*. Woodville, TX: Dogwood Press, 1997.

Blue, Frederick J. *Salmon P. Chase: a Life in Politics*. Kent, OH: Kent State University Press, 1987.

Browning, Robert M., Jr. *Lincoln's Trident: the West Gulf Blockading Squadron During the Civil War*. Tuscaloosa: University of Alabama Press, 2015.

Bruce, Robert V. *Bell: Alexander Graham Bell and the Conquest of Solitude* 1973. Reprint, Ithaca: Cornell University Press, 1990.

Carlin, Colin. *Captain James Carlin; Anglo-American Blockade Runner*. Columbia: University of South Carolina Press 2017.

Clarke, S.J. *Biographical Record of Kane County, Illinois*. Chicago: S.J. Clarke Publishing Co., 1898.

Daddysman, James W. *The Matamoros*

Trade: Confederate Commerce, Diplomacy, and Intrigue. Newark: University of Delaware Press, 1984.

Dalzell, George Walton. *Flight from the Flag.* Chapel Hill: University of North Carolina Press, 1940.

Davis, Charles S., and J. Barto Arnold, III. *Colin J. McRae: Confederate Financial Agent: Blockade Running in the Trans-Mississippi as Affected by the Confederate Government's Direct European Procurement of Goods.* College Station, TX: Institute of Nautical Archeology, Texas A&M University, 2008.

Davis, Lance E., and Stanley L. Engerman. *Naval Blockades in Peace and War, an Economic History Since 1750.* New York: Cambridge University Press, 2006.

Delaney, Norman C. *The Maltby Brothers' Civil War.* College Station: Texas A&M University Press, 2013.

Dupree, Stephen A. *Planting the Union Flag in Texas: The Campaigns of Major General Nathaniel P. Banks in the West.* College Station: Texas A&M University Press, 2008.

Durant, Pliny A., H.C. Bradsby, and Samuel W Durant. *Biographical and Historical Record of Kane County, Illinois.* Chicago: Beers, Leggett & Co, 1888.

Francaviglia, Richard V. *From Sail to Steam: Four Centuries of Texas Maritime History, 1500–1900.* Austin: University of Texas Press, 1998.

Gallaway, B.P. (ed). *The Dark Corner of the Confederacy: Accounts of Civil War Texas as Told by Contemporaries.* Dubuque, IA: W. M. Brown Book Co., 1968.

Gray, Charlotte. *Reluctant Genius: Alexander Graham Bell and the Passion for Invention.* Toronto: HarperCollins, 2006.

Halbert, Terry and Elaine Ingull. *Law and Ethics in the Business Environment.* 7th ed. Boston: Cengage Learning, 2012.

Hall, Andrew W. *Civil War Blockade Running on the Texas Coast.* Charleston: History Press, 2014.

Hashim, Nadra O. *Hemp and the Global Economy: the Rise of Labor, Innovation, and Trade.* Lanham, MD: Lexington Books, 2017.

Hearn, Chester G. *When the Devil Came Down to Dixie: Ben Butler in New Orleans.* Baton Rouge: LSU Press, 2000.

Hogg, Ian V. *Weapons of the Civil War.* New York: Military Press, 1987.

Howell, Kenneth W. (ed). *The Seventh Star of the Confederacy.* Denton, University of North Texas Press, 2009.

Irby, James A. *Backdoor at Bagdad: the Civil War on the Rio Grande.* El Paso: Texas Western Press, 1977.

Kelley, Pat. *River of Lost Dreams; Navigation on the Rio Grande.* Lincoln: University of Nebraska Press, 1986.

Kennedy, Charles Stuart. *The American Consul: a History of the United States Consular Service 1776 –1924,* 2nd ed. Washington, D.C.: New Academia Publishing, 2015.

Kerby, Robert L. *Kirby Smith's Confederacy: The Trans-Mississippi South, 1863–1865.* New York: Columbia University Press, 1972.

Lamphier, Peg A. *Kate Chase and William Sprague: Politics and Gender in a Civil War Marriage.* Lincoln: University of Nebraska Press, 2003.

Lea, Tom. *The King Ranch.* Boston: Little, Brown, and Co., 1957.

Leigh, Philip. *Trading with the Enemy: The Covert Economy During the American Civil War.* Yardley, PA: Westholme Publishing, 2014.

McPherson, James M. *Battle Cry of Freedom: The Civil War Era.* New York: Oxford University Press, 1988.

McPherson, James M. *War on the Waters: The Union & Confederate Navies, 1861–1865.* Chapel Hill: University of North Carolina Press, 2012.

Miller, Richard F. (ed.). *States at War, Vol. 1: A Reference Guide for Connecticut, Maine, Massachusetts, New Hampshire, Rhode Island and Vermont in the Civil War.* Hanover: University Press of New England, 2013.

Moise, Harold. *The Moise Family of South Carolina.* Columbia: R.L. Bryan Co., 1961.

Monday, Jane Clements, and Frances Brannen Vick. *Petra's Legacy: the South Texas Ranching Empire of Petra Vela and Mifflin Kenedy.* College Station: Texas A&M University Press, 2007.

Moneyhon, Carl H. *Edmund J. Davis of Texas.* Fort Worth: TCU Press, 2010.

Musicant, Ivan. *Divided Waters: The Naval History of the Civil War.* Edison, NJ: Castle Books, 2000.

Nevins, Allen. *The War for the Union Vol. III, the Organized War 1863–1864.* New York: Charles Scribner's Sons, 1971.

Oller, John. *American Queen: the Rise and Fall of Kate Chase—Civil War 'Belle of the North' and Gilded Age Woman of Scandal.* Boston: Da Capo Press, 2014.

Owsley, Frank Lawrence, Jr. *King Cotton Diplomacy: Foreign Relations of the Confederate States of America.* Chicago: University of Chicago, 1931.

Reisman, W. Michael, and Christina Parajon Skinner. *Fraudulent Evidence Before Public International Tribunals: the Dirty Stories of International Law.* Cambridge: Cambridge University Press, 2014.

Russell, Lyman Brightman. *Genealogy of the Russell Family.* San Antonio: The Naylor Company, 1959.

Sandburg, Carl. *Abraham Lincoln: The Prairie Years and the War Years.* Pleasantville, NY: The Reader's Digest Association, 1954.

Shomette, Donald G. *Shipwrecks, Sea Raiders, and Maritime Disasters Along the Delmarva Coast 1632–2004.* Baltimore: Johns Hopkins University Press, 2007.

Sibley, Marilyn McAdams. *George W. Brackenridge: Maverick Philanthropist.* Austin: University of Texas Press, 1973.

Silverstone, Paul H. *Civil War Navies, 1855–1883.* Annapolis, MD: Naval Institute Press, 2001.

Soley, James Russell. *The Blockade and the Cruisers.* New York: Charles Scribner's Sons, 1883.

Stone, Edwin Winchester. *Rhode Island in the Rebellion.* Providence: George H. Whitney, 1864.

Surdam, David G. *Northern Naval Superiority and the Economics of the American Civil War.* Columbus: University of South Carolina Press, 2001.

Tenkotte, Paul A., and James C. Claypool (eds). *The Encyclopedia of Northern Kentucky.* Lexington: University Press of Kentucky, 2009.

Thompson, Jerry. *Tejano Tiger: Jose De Los Santos Benavides and the Texas-Mexico Borderlands, 1823–1891.* Fort Worth: TCU Press, 2017.

Thompson, Jerry, and Lawrence T. Jones III, *Civil War and Revolution on the Rio Grande Frontier; a Narrative and Photographic History.* Austin: State Historical Association, 2004.

Thompson, Samuel Bernard. *Confederate Purchasing Operations Abroad.* Chapel Hill: University of North Carolina Press, 1935.

Townsend, Stephen A. *The Yankee Invasion of Texas.* College Station: Texas A&M Press, 2006.

Tucker, Spencer C. (ed). *American Civil War: The Definitive Encyclopedia and Document Collection,* Vol. II. Santa Barbara, CA: ABC-CLIO, 2013.

Tyler, Ronnie C. *Santiago Vidaurri, and the Southern Confederacy.* Austin: Texas State Historical Society, 1973.

Underwood, Rodman L. *Waters of Discord: The Union Blockade of Texas During the Civil War.* Jefferson, NC: McFarland, 2003.

Vezzetti, Robert B. *Tidbits: A Collection from the Brownsville Historical Association and the Stillman House Museum.* Brownsville, TX: Brownsville Historical Association, ca 2003.

Webster III, C.L. *Entrepôt: Government Imports into the Confederate States.* Roseville, MN: Edinborough Press, 2010.

Willson, Meredith. *But He Doesn't Know the Territory.* 1959. Reprint, Minneapolis: University of Minnesota Press, 2009.

Wilson, Walter E. *The Bulloch Belles: Three First Ladies, a Spy, a President's Mother and Other Women of a 19th Century Georgia Family.* Jefferson, NC: McFarland, 2015.

Wilson, Walter E., and Gary L. McKay, *James D. Bulloch: Secret Agent and Mastermind of the Confederate Navy.* Jefferson, NC: McFarland, 2012.

Wise, Stephen R. *Lifeline of the Confederacy: Blockade Running During the Civil War.* Columbia: University of South Carolina Press, 1988.

Yturria, Frank Daniel. *The Patriarch: The Remarkable Life and Extraordinary Times of Francisco Yturria.* Brownsville: University of Texas at Brownsville, 2006.

Index

Numbers in **_bold italics_** indicate pages with illustrations

A. & W. Sprague & Co. *see* Sprague, William, IV
USS *Admiral* 172
admiralty court 4, 27, 44, 84, 86, 92–95, 123
Alabama 160, 175; *see also* Mobile Bay
CSS *Alabama* 141, 172
SS *Alamo* 69, 93, 135, 168, 189*n*6
Alden, James 11, 149, 176
SS *Alice see* SS *Matagorda*
Alleyton, TX 12, 72, 73, **_81_**, 108
America (schooner) 90–93, 95, 96, 105, 113, 114, 128, 141, 153, 155, 168, 176, 177, 193*n*37, 193*n*41
Andromeda 25, 26, 48, 149, 168
Anaconda Plan *see* blockade
Anderson, Peter 177
Aransas (Pass, Bay) **_11_**, 13, 81, 90, 92
Arizona 143, 161
Arkansas 106, 113, 120, 151, 159, 177
Army, British 1, 153
Army, Confederate (forces, military) 27–29, 32, 40, 42, 47, 59, 60, 73, 78, 85, 87, 93, 99, 100, 102, 103, 105–108, 110, 116, 152, 158–160, 163, 169–171, 173, 176, 177
Army, Texas 155
Army, U.S. (forces, military) 1, 9, 10, 12, 16–18, 36, 37, 42, 47, 49, 56, 72, 76, 77, 102, 108, 111, 118–122, 124, 126, 130, 133, 135, 137, 142, 144, 150, 151, 153, 159–163, 165, 172, 174, 198*n*10
USS *Arthur* 32, 157, 168, 172
Ashby, James H. 48, 149, 168, 177
Austin, TX 5, 24, 46, 137, 138, 150

Baffin Bay, TX 13, 81
Bagdad, MX iv, 6, 66, **_67_**, 68–70, 74, 75, **_81_**, 89, 109, 112, 121, 174
Ballinger, William Pitt 108, 109
Baltimore, MD 3, 122, 153, 157, 169, 170
Banks, Nathaniel Prentice 10, 34, 42, 54, 62, **_63_**, 64, 65, 113, 149, 153, 164
Banshee 89, 177
Barney, Hiram 55, 64, 149

Barrett, Joseph H. 33, 149, 183*n*8
Barry, William F. 55
Bartlett, Clarence R. 145, 149, 156
Bartlett, Cora Louise *see* Hoyt, Cora Louise
Batavia 21, 155, 156, 158, 181*n*2
Battle of Sabine Pass 152, 176
Beaumont, TX 12, 22, 25
Bee, Hamilton P. 61, 102, 103, 107, 110, 111, 115, 138, 149, 150
Belize **_14_**, 15, 18, 74, 75, 85, 86, 112, 158, 176, 177, 180*n*13
Belknap, William E. 144, 150
Bell, Alexander Graham 143, 150
Bell, Wilson 8
Belle Italia 169
Belle of Lamar 90, 169
SS *Belle Sulphur* 25, 26, 169
Bellot, De Miniers & Co. 116, 150, 161
Benjamin, Judah P. 61, 102, 150
Bermuda 3, 13, 18, 53, 116, 117, 121, 124, 169, 174
Bertram, Henry 119, 150
Berwick Bay, LA 25, 26, **_81_**, 169, 172
Bisbie (Bisbee), D.T. 115, 116, 150
SS *Black Warrior* 163
Blacker, Louis 71, 150
Blake, Edward P. 172
Blake Brothers & Company 94
SS *Blanche see* SS *General Rusk*
blockade (Anaconda Plan, fleet) 10, 12, 15, 16, 22, 23, 32, 33, 38–41, 48, 71, 83, 84, 91, 126, 149, 155, 156, 170, 172, 173, 175, 176, proclamations 9, 24, 129, 133, 135
blockade runners (running) 4, **_11_**, 13, 15, 16, 18, 25, **_26_**, 27, **_28_**, 29, 30, 32, 33, 35, 42, 44, 46–49, 53, 57–59, 61, 62, 70, 74, 80, **_81_**, 82–86, 89–94, 97, **_98_**, 99, 101, 105, 109, 111, 114, 128, 130, 139, 140, 149, 151–156, 158–160, 162, 163, 165, 170, 173, 175–178, 192*n*16, 194*n*16
blockading fleet *see* blockade
Boca Chica, TX 16, 17, 68, 171
Boca del Rio (mouth of the Rio Grande) *see* Rio Grande

Bolivia 143
Bolles, John A. 124, 125, 130, 131
Booth, John Wilkes 131
Bordeaux, France 116
Boston (East Boston) 3, 91, 94, 141, 155, 172, 176, 177
Boynton, John W. 46, 125, 150
Brackenridge, George W. 118, 119, 135, 137, 150, 153, 164; Brackenridge Park 138
Brastow, Henry B. 50–54, 62, 64, 65, 74–77, 79, 96, 112–115, 127, 150, 151, 172, 176, 190n23, 191n36
Brazos County 90
Brazos River *11*, 12, 13, 25, 42, 73, 85, 87, 91, 112, 165, 168, 170, 173, 175
Brazos Santiago Pass, TX *11*, 13, 16, 51, 66, 68, 93, 111, 129, 186n26, 199n17
Breaker 169
Brenham 22, 101-103, 117, 129, 152
British *see* United Kingdom
Broadwell, William A. 106, 151
Brownsville 1, 4, *14*, 17, 18, 51, 61, 70, 72, 79, *81*, 82, 86, 102, 104, 108, 109, *118*, 119, 129, 134, 135, 136, 137, 138, 144, 149–151, 154, 157, 161, 172, 174, 186n26, 199n17
Bryant, Samuel S. 22, 73, 80, 90, 97, 101, 112, 114, 151, 191n29
Buchanan, James 33, 125, 153
Bull Run, First Battle of (Manassas) 34, 36, 115, 128, 153, 164
Bulloch, James D. 3, 163, 164, 176
Burkhardt, Anna 53
Burkhardt, James T. 53, 151
Butler, Andrew J. 47, 49, 151
Butler, Benjamin F. 10, 47–50, 55, 62, 149, 151–153, 163, 177

Calcasieu, LA *11*
Cambridge, MA (*Chronicle, Tribune*) 5, 130, 141
Cammack, Addison J. 57, 61, 62, 151, 159, 178
Camp Chase, OH 116
Caney Creek, TX *11*, 13, 91, 129
Caracas 116, 117, 120, 121, 124, 125, 169, 174
cards (carding machinery for cotton or wool) *45*, 46, 54, 68, 72, 77, 79, 80, 88, 95, 116, 125, 128, 129, 150, 158, 160
Caribbean Sea *14*
Carioca 116, 117, 120, 121, 124, 125, 169, 174
Caroline 93, 169
Cavallo Pass *see* Pass Cavallo
Celaya, Simón 70, 138, 151
Charleston, SC (harbor) 9, *14*, 44, 170, 171, 178
Chase, Kate (Mrs. Kate Sprague) 2, 34, *35*, 40, 41, 42, 127, 132, 145, 151, 152, 164
Chase, Salmon P. 2, 9, 34, 36, 37, *39*, 40, 41, 49, 55, 125, 132, 151, 152
Chicago 21, 114, 121, 123, 124, 128, 131, 152

Chubb, Thomas B. 99, 152, 194n7
Citibank 137, 164
Citizen 47, 50, 62, 64–66, 74–77, 79, 88, 96, 112, 115, 169
SS *City of New York* 146, 169
Clinton County, NY 21, 155, 181n2
Clements, Nelson 27, 28, 52, 140, 152, 159, 160, 201n23
Clermont 31, 38, 114, 148
USS *Clifton* 99, 152, 155, 170
Clinton County, NY 21, 155, 181n2
Cocks, James 21, 22
Colorado 127, 151
Colorado River, TX 12, 138
Colt revolvers 5, 51, 55, 72, *73*
Columbia (West Columbia) 12, *81*, 87
Columbus, TX 12, 116, 162
Compton, Abraham 117
Compton, Rebecca 117
Compton, William Y. 111, 117, 119, 120, 126 127, 152
Confederate States Congress 24; Customs 25, 83, 87, 88, 97, 99, 104, 105, 112, 133, *134*, 163, 173; Government 2, 9, 12, 19, 25, 27, 30, 47, 59, 61, 80, 83, 88, 95, 100, 106, 109–111, 114, 115, 139–141, 160, 170; *see also* Army, Confederate
Conkling, Roscoe 145, 151, 152
Connecticut 19, 40, 164, 165; *see also* Hartford
Cora see Snow Drift
SS *Cora* 93, 136, 153, 155, 170, 175
Corpus Christi (City, Bay, Pass) *11*, 13, *14*, 32, *81*, 82, 91–93, 102, 103, 118, 158, 168, 169
SS *Corsica* 117, 170
cotton *23*, *26*; baling and compressing 45, 51, 67, 68, 70, 72, *101*, 156, 185n3; diplomacy (King Cotton) 17, 23, 30, 58, 141; expenses 75, 84, 100, 108, 109, 111, 115; *see also* blockade (runners, running)
C.P. Knapp 85, 86, 158, 169
Crawford, John 17, 152
Crocker, Frederick 48, 152
Cuba (Cuban) 15, 26–30, 48, 52, 56–59, 62, 111, 140, 156, 161, 163, 171, 173, 196n59; *see also* Havana

Dalzell, Robert 137, 173, 174
Dana, Napoleon J.T. 82, 145, 152
Davis, Jefferson 111, 161
USS *DeSoto* 27, 170
Devine, Thomas 71, 152, 153, 190n15
Dix, John A. 125, *126*, 127, 128, 130, 131, 144, 153
Donahue, John H. 77, 153
Dubuque 126
Duke University 4

Eagle Pass 82, 109, 162
East Boston *see* Boston

Edison, Thomas 143
Elizabeth 25–27, 31, 48, 61, 74, 128, 154, 170, 172
SS *Ella and Annie* see SS *William G. Hewes*
SS *Ella Warley* 44, 45, 47, 53–57, 62–66, 71, 74, 128, 129, 150, 161, 164, 170, 174, 189n79
SS *Emma Dean* (*John Jewett*) 77, 171, 172, 183n36
Emmons, George F. 27, 172
Etchison, Emanuel D. 122, 153
Europe (European) 13, 17, 23, 30, 61, 69, 140, 143, 150, 152, 161
Evans, Ophelia (Fillie) 88, 93, 153
Evans, William R. 85, 87–92, 105, 153, 162, 168–170
Evans, William R., Jr. 93, 153
Exporting Company of South Carolina 53, 178

Farnsworth John F. 31
Farragut, David Glasgow 28, 30, 47–49, 53, 58, 94, 153
Fitzpatrick, Richard 102
Florida 145, 156, 163, 175, 177; *see also* Key West; Pensacola
CSS *Florida* 176
Flour Bluff *81*, 82
Ford, John S. "Rip" 1, 2, 18, 71–73, 103, 153, 154, 158
Fort Lafayette 129
Fort Sumter 9, 38
France (French) 30, 72, 116, 140, 152, 153, 156, 158, 165; *see also* Navy, French
Francis Marguez Jr. see *Rob Roy*
Fremantle, Arthur J.L. 1, 71, 153
Frieze, Lyman B. 114, 115, 126, 127, 142, 153, 163

Galvan, Jerry (Jeremiah) 17, 18, 89, 136, 137, 154, 164
Galveston (Bay, city, island) 4, 10, *11*, 12, 13, *14*, 15, 20–22, 25, 27–29, 32, 35, 42, 46, 53, 60, 68, 73–75, *81*, 83, 85, 87, 88, 90, 95, 97, *98*, 99, 100, 101, 103, 105, 107, 111, 112, 133, *134*, 135, 136, 140, 151–153, 157–160, 162, 163, 165, 168, 170–173, 175–177, 180n13
Galveston Navigation Company 96
General C.C. Pinckney 68, 171
SS *General Rusk* (*Blanche*) 27–31, 57–62, 100, 140, 141, 152, 156, 159, 160, 169, 171, 174, 188n59
George 118, 121, 171
SS *George Washington* 112, 113, 171
Geziena Hilligonda 90, 171
Gilmer, Alexander 25, 27, 154, 182n17
Goos, Daniel 90, 173
SS *Grampus No. 2* 69, 171
Greer, Elkanah B. 90, 154

Gulf of Mexico 5, *11*, 12, 13, *14*, 15, 16, 25, 26, 35, 38, 47, 52, 56, 66, 67, *81*, 90–93, 97, 133, 149, 152, 153, 170, 180n17

Hale & Co. *see* Maloney, John P.
Hart, Simeon 85, 86, 90, 104–106, 110–112, 154, 162
USS & CSS *Harriet Lane* (*Lavinia*) 155, 172
Hartford 46, 150, 165
Harvard University 5
USS *Hatteras* 26, 27, 49, 170, 172
Havana 12, 13, *14*, 17–19, 25–27, 29–31, 43, 50–59, 61–64, 70, 71, 73, 74, 79, 84, 86, 94, 116, 117, 119, 120, 125, 129, 150–152, 154, 159, 161, 162, 165, 168–178, 188n72, 200n3
Hay, John M. 33, 35, 39, 127, 129, 144, 149, 154, 161, 183n9
Hayden, R. 169
Hays, John C. *73*, 103, 154
Hébert, Paul O. 5, 29, 59, *60*, 61, 107, 154, 159
Helm, Charles J. 58, 61, 154, 163
Henry Dodge see *Mary Sorley*
Herbert 74, 172
Herron, Francis J. 118, 150, 155
Hill, Frederic S. 91–95, 114, 120–122, 141, 155, 177
Hill, Professor Harold 19, 20, 147, 155, 165, 181n26
House, Thomas W. 98, 101, 155, 173, 176, 177
Houston 12, *14*, 21, 22, 25, 27, 46, 52, 60, 72, 74, 79, 80, *81*, 87, 90, 95, 96, 106, 111, 155, 156, 160, 162, 165
Houston, Sam 24, 79, 155
Hoyt, Ann Elizabeth (Sayre) 21, 155, 181n2
Hoyt, Charlotte E. Winchell 21, 155, 181n2
Hoyt, Cora Louise 21, 22, 56, 145, 146, 148, 149, 156, 160, 181n2
Hoyt, Elmira Smith 156
Hoyt, Harriet 21, 22, 156
Hoyt, Harris George 21, 22, 31, 101, 155, 156, 194n16
Hoyt, Horace 38, 70, 71, 73, 75, 76, 156, 177, 190
Hoyt, Margaret Morse 156
Hoyt, Marie Emma Bryant (Carpenter) 20–22, 31, 38, 70, 114, 117, 145–148, 151, 156, 181n26, 181n2
Hoyt, Susan Langdon 156
Hoyt, Thomas C. 70, 75, 156, 177
Hunter, Charles 29, 30, 58, 59, 156, 171, 174
Huntsville 24
Hutchins, William J. 106, 156

Illinois 19–22, 33, 38, 39, 75, 122, 154, 156, 158, 160, 190n10; *see also* Batavia; Chicago; Kane County; Kings County; Morris

Index

Illustrated London News 45
HBMS *Immortalite* 58, 172, 177
Indiana 19, 20, 22, 119, 156; *see also* Indianapolis
Indianapolis 31
Indianola 12, *81*, 134
Inman Steamship Company 145, 146, 149, 169
USS *Iosco* 123, 172, 176
Iowa 19–21, 39, 147, 150, 151, 155, 156, 165; *see also* Clermont; Dubuque
Ireland (Irish) 18, 85–87, 93, 110, 136, 154, 158, 159
SS *Isabel* 53, 170, 172
Italian 89

Jamaica *see* Kingston
James Cartey see *Rob Roy*
SS *James Hale* 69, 119, 172
J.B. Bostock, Freeman, & Co. 117
Jenckes, Thomas A. 144, 157
J.J. McNeil 32, 169, 172
Jockusch, John W. 88, 157, 189n4
SS *John F. Carr* 168
SS *John Jewett* see SS *Emma Dean*
Johnson, Amos 176
Johnson, Andrew 132, 133, 135, 151, 157, 163

Kane County, IL 21, 31, 158, 160
Kenedy, Mifflin (M. Kenedy & Co.) 1, 4, 5, 18, 66, 69, 71, 72, 77, 93, 104, 119, 135, 136, 138, 150, 157, 162, 160, 164, 168, 171–175
Kennedy, John A. 51, 55, 56, 76, 157
USS *Kensington* 48, 152, 172, 177
Key West *14*, 15, 27, 86, 92, 168, 174, 177
King, Richard (King Ranch) 4, 18, 66, 69, 72, *81*, 82, 93, 108, 119, 135–137, 138, 157, 158, 159, 162, 164, 170, 190n15
Kings County, IL 31
Kingston, Jamaica *14*, 25, 26, 170, 175
Kittredge, John W. 32, 157, 168
Knight, Robert (B.B. & R. Knight & Co.) 37, 126, 127, 157

La Abra Silver Mine 140
Labatt & Joseph 76, 77, 115
Laguna del Madre (lagoon) *11*, 13, 68
Lamar *81*
Lamar, Mirabeau B. 93
Lancy, John 74, 169
Lansing, Z.D. 145, 146
Laredo, TX *81*, 82, 102–105, 113, 114, 120, 121, 142
Laverty, Henry 85, 86, 158, 169, 175, 192n21
Lavinia see CSS *Harriet Lane*; USS *Harriet Lane*
Lea, Tom C. 110, 158, 190n15
Lecompt (*Le Compte*) 99, 173, 176
Lehman (*Lamon, Lamar*) 90, 95–101, 110–114, 128, 139, 156, 173, 191n29

Levy, Marx 98, 158, 163, 164, 165
Lincoln, Abraham 9, 12, 20, 24, 25, 31, 33, 40, 48, 55, 83, 119, 125, 128–130, 133, 142, 149, 151, 154, 158, 161, 163, 183n8, 199n17
Lincoln Mary Todd 21
Liverpool 10, 108, 109, 117, 123, 133, 134, 136, 146, 163, 164, 169–172, 174–176, 200n3
Lockwood, Mary N. 31, 158
Lockwood, Samuel D. 31, 158
Loeb, Samuel E. 90, 95, 98, 100, 111, 139, 140, 158, 165, 173
London 3, 143, 146, 156, 160
Louisiana 5, 10, 11, 25, 28, 47–50, 57, 59–61, 64, 86, 90, 100, 106, 107, 149–151, 154, 155, 159, 162, 163, 164, 165, 169, 173, 177, 178; *see also* Berwick Bay; Lake Charles; New Orleans; Shreveport
Louisiana State Museum 5, *60*
Louisiana State University 5
Lubbock, Francis R. 46, 72, 103, 105, 106, 158
Lubbock, Henry S. 158
Lubbock, Thomas S. 158
Luckett, Philip N. 72, 73, 78, 88, 99, 103, 107, 129, 158, 159

M. Kenedy & Co. *see* Kenedy, Mifflin
Macaulay, James A. 27, 57, 59, 62, 159, 160
Macaulay, John L. 27–29, 57, 59, 61, 62, 140, 141, 159, 160
Mack Canfield 92, 173
Maggio, G.B. 89, 169
Magruder, John Bankhead 12, 29, 42, 60, 81, 88, 90, 95, 97–102, 107, 108, 112–115, 154, 159, 160, 163
Maloney, John P (Hale & Co.) 2, 69, 71, 72, 76, 117, 159, 190n13
Martin, Edward 68
SS *Mary Hill* 168
Mary Sorley (*Henry Dodge*) 88, 155, 172, 173
Massachusetts 19, 47, 62, 102, 149, 161, 168, 172, 173; *see also* Boston; Cambridge
SS *Matagorda* (SS *Alice*) 25, 26, 61, 168, 172, 173
Matagorda Bay 3, *8*, *11*, 12, 13, *14*, 29, 32, 59, 81, 82, 91, 93, 99, 134, 149, 168, 170, 171, 173, 175, 176
Matamoros 1, 2, *14*, 17–19, 42, 43, 46–48, 50–54, 56, 57, 61–71, 73, 74, 76, 77, 79, *81*, 85, 86, 88, 90, 91, 93, 97, 100–104, 108–117, *118*, 119–123, 127, 129, 133, 134, 136, 138, 144, 150–154, 156, 158–162, 164, 165, 169, 171, 172, 174–177, 193n37, 186n26, 191n29, 191n36
SS *Matamoros* 69, 119, 173
McClellan, George B. 55, 56
McKean, William 32
Metropolitan Hotel 122, 124, 126

Index 213

Mexican War 18, 58, 72, 102, 103, 110, 150, 152–154, 157, 158, 162
Mexico (Mexican) 1, 11, *14*, 15–17, 24, 66, 67, 70, 71, 72, 82, 83, 92, 101, 102, 104, 105, 108–112, 121, 122, 129, 133, 135, 138, 139, 140, 141, 150, 151, 153, 156, 158–160, 162–165, 171, 173; *see also* Bagdad; Matamoros; Monterey; Sisal; Tampico; Vera Cruz
SS *Mexico* (Mexican lighter) 69, 71, 174
SS *Mexico* (U.S.) 119, 120, 174
Mills, David G. (R. & D.G. Mills & Co.) 76, 101, 135, 138, 144, 157, 159
Mills, Robert *101*, 135, 159; *see also* Mills, David G.
Milmo, Patricio 110, 111, 159
Minié ball 7, *8*, 34
Mississippi 159, 169, 173, 176
Mississippi River *14*, 20, 22, 26, 27, 64, 94, 106, 107, 120, 137, 148, 154
Mix, Charles 119
Mobile Bay (city) *14*, 15, 61, 153, 163, 173, 188n65
Moïse, Theodore S. 5, 27, 28, 29, 30, 58, 59, *60*, 61, 159, 171, 188n59
Monarch 117, 120–123, 125, 174
Monterey, MX 17, 111
USS *Montgomery* 29, 30, 58, 59, 156, 171, 174
Mooney, Thomas P. 79, 80, 95, 101, 160
Moore, Thomas C. 31, 160
Morgan, Charles 27, 28, 57, 61, 141
USS *Morning Light* 177
Morrell, Jose (Joseph) 17, 160
Morris, Theodore A. 116, 117, 119–124, 127
Morris, IL 38, 70, 117
Moss, D.N. 169
Mott, Robert 27, 28, 57, 59, 62, 159, 160
Murrah, Pendelton 106, 107, 160
The Music Man 19, 147, 155, 165
SS *Mustang* 69, 119, 172, 174

Narraganset Bay 47
Nassau 13, *14*, 17, 18, 53, 61, 112, 117, 120, 176, 188
National City Bank of New York 137, 164
Navy, French 17
Navy, Royal 17, 58, 172, 177
Navy, U.S. (Department, fleet) 1–3, 12, 15–17, 26, 27, 31, 32, 38, 42, 44, 48, 57, 60, 86, 87, 91–95, 97, 99, 110, 114, 116, 120, 123, 140, 141, 154, 156, 157, 163, 168, 170–177
New Jersey 65, 88, 174
New Orleans 3, 5, 12, 13, *14*, 15, 18, 19, 21, 22, 26–28, 47–49, 54, 59, 61–66, 68, 71, 74, 85, 86, 91–94, 106, 112, 113, 137, 149, 151–154, 158–163, 169–171, 174, 176, 177, 180n13, 188n72, 193n37, 200n3
New York (City, Port, State) 1, 10, 17, 19, 22, 25, 26, 32, 36–39, 42–47, 52–54, 57, 60, 62, 63, 65, 73, 75, 76, 77, 89, 94, 102, 112, 113, 115–118, 120–126, 128, 129, 131, 133, 134, 136, 137, 143, 145, 146, 148, 149, 151–153, 155–157, 160–162, 164, 165, 168–172, 174–177, 186n26, 191n29, 198n40, 200n3; Customs 50, 51, 55, 56, 62, 63, 77, 91, 93, 125, 149; *see also* Clinton County
Newport *see* Rhode Island
Nichols, Ebenezar B. 107, 160
Norfolk 126, 150
SS *North Star* 65, 171, 174

Oetling, George (Droege, Oetling, & Co.) 71, 72, 160, 171
Orange, TX 27

Paris, France 116, 150
Parkes, Franklin H. 146, 156, 160
Pass Cavallo *11*, 21, 32, 81, 172
Payne, John 169
Peel-Dumble & Co. 169
USS *Pembina* 171
Penascal 13, *81*, 82
Pensacola 15, 48
Pennsylvania 153, 169, 170, 171, 172, 173, 174; *see also* Philadelphia
percussion caps 32, 51, 55
SS *Peterhoff* 116, 174
Philadelphia 34, *63*, 172, 175; Navy Yard 94
Phillips, Thomas 122
Pierce, Edward L. 36, 37, 161
Pierce, Leonard, Jr. 121, 122, 161
SS *Plantagenet* 26, 175
Point Isabel (Port Isabel) *81*, 138
Port Lavaca, TX (Lavaca) 3, 12, 29, 32, 59, *81*, 134
Prairie Lea 79, 80, 88, 116
Prescott, Charles L. 35–38, 41, 42, 44–47, 50, 51, 53–57, 62–65, 95, 113, 117, 122–125, 128–130, 161, 164, 170, 189n79, 191n29, 191n36, 193n41, 198n40
Providence 35–37, 42, 43, 46, 48, 50, 54, 57, 62–66, 74, 75, 77, 78, 82, 95, 96, 112–115, 120, 123, 126, 143, 144, 177

USS *Quaker City* 93, 170, 175
Quintero, José A. 111, 161

R. & D.G. Mills & Co. *see* Mills, David G.
railroad (rail, railhead) 12, 25, 72, 87, 118, 126, 135, 136, 138, 143, 152, 155, 156, 164
Redgate, Samuel J. 115, 116, 161
Reindeer 169
Reynolds, Charles 143, 169
Reynolds, Francis W. 65, 184n21
Reynolds, William H. (W.H. Reynolds & Co.) 36–44, 46, 47, 50, 51, 56, 62, 64, 65, 71, 74–77, 80, 113–116, 118, 120–131, 143, 150, 158, 161, 169, 171, 184n21, 190n23

Rhode Island 2, 19, 20, 34–37, 47, 55, 63, 90, 115, 127, 142, 143, 144, 154, 157, 161, 163, 164; *see also* Providence
SS *Rimac* 134, 175
Rio Grande (anchorage, district, Rio Bravo, Boca del Rio) 1–4, 6, *11*, 13, 15–18, 27, 42, 43, 53, 62, 66, *67*, 68–77, 79, 81–83, 85, 86, 90–94, 96, 103, 104, 108–111, 113, 116–123, 126, 133–137, 139, 145, 150, 153, 155, 157–159, 162, 168–174, 189n6, 193n37, 200n9; Railroad Company 138
Rio Grande City 189n4
SS *Roanoke* 120, 175
Rob Roy (*Francis Marguez Jr.*; *James Cartey*) 5, 85–87, 101, 158, 165, 169, 175
Roger A. Heirn 136, 175
Roosevelt, Theodore, Jr. 33, 76, 94, 154, 161
Roosevelt, Theodore, Sr. 33, 76, 94, 154, 161
Russell, Charles A. 2, 5, 102, *103*, 107, 110, 111, 138, 139, 154, 162

Sabine (Lake, Pass, River) 3, *11*, 12, 13, *14*, 25–27, 48, 49, 61, 74, *81*, 99, 154, 162, 168–170, 172, 173, 177, 182n17
USS *Sachem* (SS *Clarinda*) 99, 155, 162, 175, 176
St. Nicholas Hotel 113
St. Thomas, Danish Virgin Islands 174
San Antonio (City, Express Publishing Co., National Bank, school board, Water Works) 4, 82, 90, 137, 138, 150, 153, 162
San Antonio Bay 3
San Antonio Breakfast Club 5
San Antonio River 103
San Barnard River *11*, 21
San Luis Pass *11*, 13, 97, 177
San Marcos River 24, 79, 160
San Román, José 1, 2, 5, 18, 70–71, 76, 86, 119, 120, 133, 135, 138, 151, 162
Santleben, August 116, 162
Santleben, Christian 116, 162
Schenck, George R. 65, 170
Scherffius, George Henry 25, 27, 74–76, 85, 87, 112, 162, 170, 176
Scotland 13, 140, 163, 170, 175
Scovel, Louis L. 94
Scurry, William Reed 90, 162
Seguin 138
Seward, William H. 30, 54, 58, 122, 125, 151, 162, 163, 165
Ship Island 15
Shreveport 106, 151
Shufeldt, Robert W. 53, 54, 57, 58, 63, 163
Sisal 177
Skaggs, Eli Harrison 48, 49, 163
Smith, E. Kirby 90, 106, 107, 109, 110, 156, 160, 163
Smith, Edward S. 21
Smith, Emma Dean 77
Smith, G.L. 171

Smith, James Y. 142, 163
Smith, Leon 29, 42, 87, 99, 158, 163, 168, 171
Smith, Newton 77, 164
Smith, Robert N. 171
Smith & Dunning 175
Snow Drift (*Cora*) 44–47, 50–58, 61–66, 68–71, 73–76, 79, 80, 85, 88, 93, 112–114, 129, 150, 162, 165, 170, 176, 188n72
Sol Wildes (*Sol Wilder*) 94, 176, 193n50
Sorley, James 88, 95, 105, 107, 163, 164
South Carolina 36, 37, 103, 158, 159, 161, 171
USS *South Carolina* 10, 149, 176
Southern Steamship Company *see* Morgan, Charles
Spain (Spanish) 12, 30, 51, 52, 57, 58, 61, 63, 70, 117, 138, 140, 141, 151, 162, 172, 192n21, 197n18
Sprague, Byron 36–38, 50, 115, 125, 126, 127, 128, 129, 131, 164, 199n26
Sprague, Mrs. Kate *see* Chase, Kate
Sprague, William IV (A. & W. Sprague & Co.) 2, *34*, 35–42, 47, 50, 55, 56, 62, 64, 114, 115, 125–132, 142–145, 150–153, 157, 158, 161, 163, 164
HBMS *Steady* 58, 176, 177
Stillman, Charles 1, 2, 4, 5, 17, 18, 68, 71, 72, 77, 89, 93, 118, 119, 135–138, 152–154, 157, 160, 162, 164, 165, 169, 170, 175, 190n15, 200n9
Suydam, James A. 38, 116, 121
Sybil (brig) 121, 176
Sybil (schooner, *Eagle*) 121, 123, 172, 176, 198n40

Taft, Edward P. 126, 184n21
Taft, Orray (Orray Taft & Co.) 37, 127, 164, 184n21
Tampico *14*, 53, 90, 112, 114, 151, 160, 173
Tenerife, Azores 169
Texas A&M University 150
Texas A&M University–Kingsville 4
Texas Legislature (Congress, congressman, Senate) 20, 24, 28, 46, 79, 103, 105, 116, 153, 162
Texas Manufacturing Company 24, 25, 46, 78, 79, 181n8
Texas Marine Department 29, 87, 99, 158, 163
Thomas H. Terry 75, 177
Townsend, George N. 145
Townsend, John D. 130, 164
Trans-Mississippi Department 90, 105–108, 151, 154, 163
Treaty of Guadalupe Hidalgo 16, 139
Trinity River 168, 170
USS *Tyler* 120, 121, 155, 177

Ulrici & Barroso 52, 53, 56, 57, 70, 71, 74
United Kingdom (British, Great Britain) 1, 3, 8, 14, 15, 17, 22, 25–28, 30, 56–58, 60,

68–71, 74, 75, 77, 85, 86, 87, 109, 116, 117, 121, 123, 134, 140, 141, 143, 145, 150, 152, 153, 159, 165, 167–177, 188n59; *see also* Ireland; Liverpool; London; Scotland
U.S. Congress (congressman, congressional, Senate, senator) 2, 31, 41, 42, 62, 115, 125, 127, 128, 130–132, 139, 142–145, 148–153, 155, 157, 162; investigation (investigators) 17, 24, 77, 144, 145, 148, 150, 153; legislation (act) 9, 76, 142; report 1, 183*n*9
U.S. Customs 64, 155, 189*n*1; *see also* New York Customs
U.S. Navy *see* Navy, U.S.
U.S. Pension Office 33, 149, 152
U.S. State Department 61, 122
University of Texas at Austin 5, 137, 138, 153
University of Texas, Rio Grande Valley 4

USS *Vanderbilt* 174
Vanderbilt, Cornelius 54, 65, 164
Velasco 14, 81
USS *Velocity* (USS *Fairy, Vigilant, Nellie Blair, Chaos*) 48, 155, 173, 177
Vera Cruz 14, 32, 74, 75, 162, 172, 176
Vermont 18, 21, 151, 152, 156
HBMS *Vesuvius* 58, 177
Victoria, Queen (Victorian) 139, 143
Victoria, TX 12, 73, 79
Vidaurri, Santiago 110, 159, 165
SS *Ville du Havre* 164
Vinas, Benito 69, 70, 174
Virginia 3, 55, 60, 126, 146, 150, 153, 158, 168, 173, 174; *see also* Norfolk; Richmond

Warrior 125, 126
Warwick Railroad Company 143
Washington County 22

Washington, D.C. 3, 19, 25, 28, 30, 31, 33–36, 39, 41, 42, 44, 50, 54, 64, 79, 97, 114, 122, 128, 152
Water Witch 169
Watson, William 28, 70, 85, 86, 87, 88, 89, 101, 158, 165, 175
Weil, Benjamin 98, 100, 111, 112, 139, 140, 158, 165, 173
Wells, Charles G. 90
Welles, Gideon 30, 38, 39, 40, 41, 49, 92, 94, 97, 165
Wesson rifles 51, 55
West Florida (*Cephize, Hanover*) 48, 49, 50, 149, 177
West Virginia 145, 146
Whitford, Thomas W. 47, 115, 127
Wild Horse Desert 82
Willard Hotel 34, 35
William 170
USS *William G. Anderson* 91, 92, 94, 95, 113, 114, 120, 141, 155, 168, 173, 176, 177
SS *William G. Hewes* 28, 57, 61, 177
Willson, Meredith 19, 20, 147, 155, 165, 181*n*26
Wilmington, DE 172, 173
Wilmington, NC 13, 14, 171, 174, 178, 180*n*13
Witham, Joseph C. 50–52, 63, 69, 71, 88, 165, 176
Witte Museum 138

Young Men's Christian Association 88

Yturria, Francisco 190*n*15
Yturria, Santiago 17, 18, 165
Yucatan (Channel, Peninsula) 15

www.ingramcontent.com/pod-product-compliance
Lightning Source LLC
Chambersburg PA
CBHW032042300426
44117CB00009B/1160